# WHY DOES FAMINE PERSIST IN AFRICA?

*The Case of South Sudan*

*and Sudan Famine in 1998*

**Luka Biong Deng Kuol**

*A Note from the Publisher*

The publisher wishes to acknowledge and thank Dr Douglas H. Johnson for his invaluable help and support for Africa World Books and its mission of preserving and promoting African cultural and literary traditions and history. Dr Johnson and fellow historians have been instrumental in ensuring that African people remain connected to their past and their identity. Africa World Books is proud to carry on this mission.



Hardcover ISBN: 978-0-6452105-1-4
Paperback ISBN: 978-0-6452105-2-1



Cover design, typesetting and layout : Africa World Books

Africa World Books Pty Ltd

# Dedication

*To the 70,000 innocent lives lost in Sudan*
*by avertable famine in 1998.*

*"African famine is not a visitation of fate. It is largely man-made, and the men who made it are largely Africans"*

*P.J. O'Rourke*

*"Recent famines could have been prevented but were not, because of bad policies"*

*Stephen Devereux*

*"Famine is a political scandal"*

*Alex De Waal*

*"Mass starvations as a crime against humanity"*

*Jenny Edkins*

*"Recent famines could have been prevented but were not, because of bad policies"*

*Stephen Devereux*

# Contents

## Maps



## Figures

**Tables**

# Abbreviations and Acronyms

BBC: British Broadcasting Corporation

CMR: Crude Mortality Rate

DFID: Department for International Development of the UK

EU: European Union

FAD: Food Availability Decline

FAO: Food and Agricultural Organisation

FEWS:Famine Early Warning System

GIEWS: Global Information and Early Warning System

GOS: Government of Sudan

ICRC: International Committee of the Red Cross

LWF: Lutheran World Federation

MSF: Medecines Sans Frontières

MSF (B): Medecines Sans Frontières (Belgium)

NDVI: Normalised Difference Vegetation Index

NGO: Nongovernmental Organisation

NPA: Norwegian People's Aid

ODA: Overseas Development Administration of the UK

OLS: Operation Lifeline Sudan

PDF: Popular Defence Forces

SCF: Save the Children Fund

SPLA: Sudan People's Liberation Army SPLM Sudan People's Liberation Movement

SRRA: Sudan Relief and Rehabilitation Association

SSIA: Southern Sudan Independence Army

SSIM: Southern Sudan Independence Movement.

TMC: Transitional Military Council

UN: United Nations

UNICEF: United Nations Children's Fund

USAID: United States Agency for International Development

WFP: World Food Programme

WVI: World Vision International

# Acknowledgements

This book is based on a research discussion paper entitled that I published in 1999 during my three months' visiting fellowship at the Institute of Development Studies (IDS) at University of Sussex, UK. My fellowship was generously funded by Christian Aid. I am indebted to Christian Aid and particularly Daniel Collison and Sarah Hughes for giving me this rare opportunity for reflection and research. I owe special thanks to Stephen Devereux who has not only sponsored me and diligently supervised my research but also sustained me with much-needed encouragement. I also owe a great deal to Simon Maxwell whose consistent encouragement inspired the conception of this book and my need for reflection after the prolonged emergency in southern Sudan. I would like to thank the IDS for offering me a visiting fellowship and for allowing me access to its staff and facilities, particularly the British Library for Development Studies.

This book is a product of a contribution from some dedicated South Sudanese who were monitoring the livelihoods of their various communities and with whom I jointly share the outcome of this book. I would like to thank Ugo, Arkanjelo, Philip, Geoffrey, Clement,

Joseph, Erib, Nawi, Bior, Kulang, Adet, Mawien, Achor, Tong, Nyang, Deng and Kon for their field work and provision of most of the data I used in this book. I received support, information and advice from many people and in particular I would like to thank the following: Jean, Claude, Jason and Caroline in WFP; Sharp in SCF (UK); Nick and Janet in FEWS;Linda, Paul, George and Nadi in UNICEF, John and D'Silva in USAID; Paul Murphy in CONCERN; Ama and Malcom in Christian Aid; Dan, Peter and Ken in NPA; Kosti, Majak and Mawiir Nyok in SRRA; Green and Julia at the IDS; Gordon Wagner and George Alagiah. I am very grateful to Alison Ayers at the University of Sussex for her sterling help in reading and reviewing the first manuscript. A special appreciation must go to Pat Harper and Kathryn Perry of the IDS for their editorial assistance, which constructively contributed to the value of this book. Thanks to my daughter Anyiel Biong, Marketing and Communication Officer at Queensland African Communities Council in Australia for using her journalistic lens to edit and proofread the first manuscript of this Book.

I would like to dedicate this book to the innocent 70,000 lives lost by a famine that could have been easily prevented. The loss of their lives will continue to remind us of how to prevent futures lives to be lost because of lack of food. The views and any mistakes in this book are entirely my responsibility.

# Preface

In 2017, the United Nations declared the return of famine in north-eastern Nigeria, Somalia, South Sudan and Yemen after disappearance of famine between 2000 and 2011. This return of famine and deteriorating food security started spreading to other African countries, particularly with the surge of COVID-19 that doubled the food insecure population in Africa. This surge in famine led Alex De Waal, a leading scholar on famine, to publish in 2018 a timely book on "Mass Starvation: The History and Future of Famines". This book renewed debate not only about the drivers of famine but how to prevent it in the future.

The launch of this book was followed by a roundtable event organized by Tufts University in Boston, USA under the theme "The Return of Famine". The roundtable discussed various issues including why famine has returned, the challenges of humanitarian action, and the politics and law of starvation. The cases of Yemen and South Sudan were used to elucidate reasons behind the return of famine. The event was well attended by seasoned scholars and researchers on food security and humanitarian intervention such as Alex De Waal,

Dan Maxwell, Patrick Webb, Bill Moomaw, Greg Gottlieb, me and others.

This debate at Tufts University reminded me of my research work with my colleague Paul Howe in the early 2000s on our Doctor of Philosophy dissertations on understanding the 1998 famine in Sudan. Our research work was under the supervision of Dr. Stephen Devereux, a prominent scholar on food security and famine at the Institute of Development Studies (IDS), University of Sussex, United Kingdom. Our research work encouraged Dr. Devereux to organize with him a seminar under the theme of "Why Famines Persist in an Era of Globalization". This seminar culminated in the production in 2002 the special issue of the Journal of the IDS under the theme "The New Famines" (IDS Bulletin, 2002) and publication of a book entitled "The New Famines: Why Famines Persist in an Era of Globalization?" (Devereux, 2006). The main argument of the special issue of the Journal and the book is that the persistence of famines at the start of the twentieth-first century could have been prevented but were not, because of bad policies. In the case of Sub-Saharan Africa and the Horn of Africa in particular, the famine has never departed the region and it has become normal phenomena in light of recurrent rural violent conflicts that are largely caused by governance deficit as manifested in the retreat of democracies and emergence of autocratic states.

The case of the recurrent famines in Sudan and South Sudan provides miniature of rural livelihood vulnerability in Sub-Saharan Africa. Sudan and South Sudan have been experienced recurrent famines since independence in 1956. My first encounter with famine as a child was in the 1960s when I witnessed people migrating in large numbers from rural areas to Abyei town, my home area. By then there was no relief aid and my father, as a paramount chief with other chiefs, used to distribute locally mobilized grain and bread to the needy. This famine became known as "Famine of Bread". During this famine I did not see people dying of hunger.

In 1985, I saw the famine migrants from Western Sudan and Darfur arriving in large numbers to town of Wad Madani in central Sudan where I was a teaching staff at Faculty of Economics and Rural Development, University of Gezira, one of the national public universities. I saw a massive relief from USAID/NGOs that made Sudanese to name this year of famine as year of "Reagan". During this famine, I did not see people dying from hunger. With eruption of the second civil war in the early 1980s, famine occurred in 1988 and then 1993. Although I did not see people dying from the two famines, I saw in 1993 the image in the New York Times of a starving boy collapsed while struggling to reach the nearby feeding centre in southern Sudan with a vulture eyeing at him from nearby as its imminent prey. This image of the struggling starving boy with vulture will continue to remind us that famine is a political scandal and so morally toxic. In 1998, I saw the entire process of famine occurrence in Bahr el Ghazal region of South Sudan and I was not only engaged in monitoring the food security situation but also the level of humanitarian response and impacts. Despite high presence of UN agencies, international NGOs and local NGOs, people died of hunger and it was the first-time seeing people dying from lack of food.

After its independence in 2011, South Sudan has paradoxically been experiencing famine and mass starvation since 2017 and after the eruption of its first civil war in 2013. Malnutrition remains a threat to the survival of children in South Sudan with one in three children is malnourished and 60 percent of population face high level of acute food insecurity. The drivers to famine in the post-independence South Sudan are comparable to the causes of recurrent famines before its independence in 2011 from Sudan with quality of governance as a determining factor. The return of famine or surge of new famines in Africa provide opportunity to renew debate that started at the beginning of the twentieth-first century about the emergence and persistence of the "New Famines". The 1998 famine in Sudan provides a good case to renew such debate about the drivers and level of humanitarian responses and measures to prevent future famines. Although it has been experiencing recurrent famines throughout the 1980s, 1990s and 2000s, South Sudan has not received adequate empirical and analytical research scrutiny.

This book is an attempt to scrutinize analytically the 1998 famine in South Sudan and to assess the relevance of the various famine theories and empirical research findings in its context, with the objective of drawing policy implications for better famine management. The 1998 famine in southern Sudan resulted in crude mortality of at least 100,000 persons and excess mortality of about 70,000 persons. This famine in terms of mortality rate among the resident population is comparable to other recent African famines such as Ethiopia in 1973 and 1984–85, Darfur in 1984–85 and Niger in 1974. The mortality rates among the displaced population were far higher than any other recent African famines, and probably also exceeded those in South Asia.

Despite these high mortality rates among the resident and the displaced population, the situation was not recognised as *famine* by outsiders until July–August, by which time thousands of lives had been lost. Some described the situation in April and May 1998 as one of 'extreme stress' or a 'crisis' but not yet a famine. Despite growing recognition in the 1980s of the need to define famine from the perspective of those who suffer from it, the 1998 famine experience suggests that famine is still consistently defined for its victims by outsiders. This early ethnocentric misconception of famine was responsible for much that went wrong with famine management in in 1998.

The 1998 famine is not a simple phenomenon to be explained holistically by a single cause. Even the new famine jargon, 'war famine', does not explain adequately its cause. Despite the growing recognition in the 1980s that famine is a complicated process which cannot be explained by one or a few exclusive factors in isolation from others, the 1998 famine was narrowly diagnosed by many observers as a man-made famine. This book attempts to analyze the causation of the 1998 as a chain of political, social, environmental and economic factors. The famine emerged from a long history of exploitation and counterinsurgency warfare that was intended to destroy the way of life of the resident population and remove their assets. Prior to the famine in 1998, it was estimated that about 40 per cent of all households in northern Bahr el Ghazal lost all their cattle and about 80 percent of all households had been displaced for at least three times a year as a result of continual counterinsurgency warfare raids during the 1990s.

It is argued in this book that although the historical dimension may not have an apparent bearing on the 1998 famine, it sheds light on the gradual historical erosion of asset endowment that directly affected food entitlement and increased vulnerability to exogenous shocks such as El-Nino. During 1997, the year before the famine in 1998, the resident populations in the Bahr el Ghazal region were exceptionally exposed to physical insecurity, as counterinsurgency warfare and conventional fighting between the Sudan People's Liberation Movement (SPLM) and the Government of Sudan (GOS) intensified during the critical months of cultivation.

Also, the pattern of rainfall during 1997 was exceptionally abnormal in terms of intensity and distribution. This resulted in extreme climatic anomalies known as El-Nino, which affected the growth of crops and wild food plants and produced poor pastures and inadequate water for livestock and the resident population. As the patterns of rainfall and insecurity are the most significant risks to the people's own-food production in the Bahr el Ghazal region, the El-Nino phenomenon, the intensification of fighting between the SPLM and the GOS, and counterinsurgency warfare during 1997 resulted in 'direct food entitlement failure'.

In addition to insecurity and climatic conditions, the book also shows the failure of market strategies of the resident population as one of the primary causes of famine in 1998. It also shows a positive relationship between famine excess deaths and sorghum prices during 1998. The sorghum prices in the epicenter of the famine in the Bahr el Ghazal region doubled and even quadrupled in some counties during 1998, and a 'price ripple' phenomenon was also observed as markets failed to come to the famine victims. It was also observed that the prices of superior food items such as oil seeds gradually fell to the level of sorghum prices in the famine epicenter in 1998, as consumers in search of cheap calories shunned the more expensive food items. Exceptionally high food prices differentials in the famine epicenter of Bahr el Ghazal and food surplus region of Equatoria were observed during 1998 as a result of the spatial disintegration of markets, that created persistent localized food scarcities.

The livestock markets also projected similar market performance failure in grain markets. Inconsistent with earlier findings, the market prices and volume of sale of young herd were shown to have a predictive pattern, while that of core herd gave a descriptive pattern of the famine. This pattern of livestock prices and sale volumes is consistent with the rational sequencing of sales of livestock to smooth consumption during famine situation. Interestingly, the book shows also that the pattern of barter terms of trade can be a powerful predictive indicator of a famine situation, which is an aberration from the earlier findings in the 1980s.

The book recognizes that markets were not the only institutions involved in determining the distribution of food consumption in the Bahr el Ghazal region in 1998 and explores other institutions such as social structures as a social dimension of famine analysis. Implications from the famine for the performance of traditional systems of social safety nets are mixed. The famine revealed that, despite massive and widespread deaths, members of relatively well-off groups were more likely to survive.

This clearly shows that the practice of generalized reciprocity among the Dinka, as an egalitarian society, contracted and that poor groups were progressively excluded until reciprocity became confined within the boundaries of relatively rich households. Some communities even named the 1998 famine as *cok dakruai* (the famine of breaking relationships) as an indication of the failure of traditional social safety nets. On some occasions, cattle were fenced in to deprive famine victims of access to spear them; a traditional practice that allows the poor and famine victims to gain access unilaterally to resources. The traditional practice of eating together *(ruom)* ceased during the 1998 famine as families began to share food only amongst members of households.

Some famine victims were forced to migrate to western Equatoria as their close relatives refused to help them. Despite an apparent decline in the role of traditional social safety nets during the 1998 famine, some customary redistribution mechanisms did manage to play an important role in redistributing resources to the famine victims. For example, the traditional chiefs mobilized all courts to settle only hunger cases *(luok cok)* and the courts became known as 'famine courts'. These courts managed to help famine victims through litigation cases related to marriage *(ruai)*, livestock claims *(keny)* and assistance *(kuony)*.

Also, some vertical redistribution mechanisms, though not widely practiced, managed to pass on resources to the famine victims. Some traditional chiefs collected milking cows from rich families, which were rotated amongst famine victims. Also, the local civil authorities (SPLM) in most counties of the Bahr el Ghazal region imposed a daily meat contribution from all butcheries to be cooked for the famine victims and the famine migrants who had taken refuge around local markets. Also, the traditional chiefs, together with local authorities, ordered all cattle camps to come back earlier than normal from swampy areas *(toic)* and to camp in the areas most affected by famine so as to increase access to milk.

The book goes beyond the analysis of the roles of markets and nonmarket institutions in famine management in 1998 to the role of public action by the SPLM, as the *de facto* government, and the implementing international and national aid agencies in averting the famine. The humanitarian response, as usual, was late, inadequate, reactive, poorly coordinated, poorly targeted, inappropriate and narrowly focused, and failed to avert the famine. The argument that the denial of access by the GOS was the major cause for the delayed humanitarian response is weak and a smokescreen, as the denial of access during 1998 occurred only during the months of February and March and was relatively normal for the rest of the year.

The book shows, also, that the historical pattern of relief deliveries clearly indicates a declining trend, and that the Bahr el Ghazal region was receiving generally smaller quantities (except in 1998) than other regions of southern Sudan despite its apparent downward spiral of increasing vulnerability since 1993. Most of the feeding programs during 1998 tended to ignore the basic accepted international standards of therapeutic feeding that had been adhered to in other countries with similar operational constraints to those in South Sudan. Nonfood interventions – clean water and sanitation, shelter, household assets such as cooking utensils and water containers – as complementary to relief food interventions were not prioritized and resulted in poor hygiene and increased cases of diarrhea and pneumonia, which accounted for most of the recorded deaths. Despite the poorly managed humanitarian response, the food aid deliveries during 1998 had a significant late positive impact on mortality, either through direct consumption or indirectly through stabilization of sorghum and livestock prices.

The SPLM, as a *de facto* government with inherent obligations towards civil society and the civil population in terms of security, provision of social services, humanitarian needs and advocacy, came under enormous criticism for failing to prevent the 1998 famine. Despite the enormously difficult task of balancing the priorities of armed struggle with the immense humanitarian needs of the civil population, the fact that more than 100,000 persons died merely because of lack of food in the SPLM- controlled areas makes the SPLM bound to share blame for the poor management of the famine. It was consistently observed during the 1998 famine that some local authorities showed amazing indifference to thehumanitarian crisis, which was wrongly perceived as the responsibility of the international agencies.

Also, during the entire period of the famine, the relevant authorities of the SPLM at national and regional levels failed to make any symbolic gesture of mobilizing the necessary resources, particularly the excess food in western Equatoria, for the famine victims in Bahr el Ghazal. Even the famine migrants who took refuge in western Equatoria in 1998 had a lukewarm reception from the local authorities. Some feared that they were invading their areas, and this resulted in their complete neglect. Despite the fact that the SPLM leadership was the first to talk about acute food shortage to the media and journalists in October 1997, the relevant SPLM propaganda machinery did not exert adequate efforts to highlight the people's plight and left it to the international agencies alone to spearhead advocacy and awareness-creation about the famine.

The book shows also that the poor management of the 1998 famine was largely related to the quality of information generated by monitoring and early warning systems about the level of vulnerability in southern Sudan, which led to divided opinions among the charity agencies. The Food and Agriculture Organization (FAO) monitoring system, which is food-production-oriented, grossly underestimated the levels of vulnerability in southern Sudan during 1998, and even projected a decline in food needs requirement relative to that in 1997. The assessment of the World Food Program (WFP), based on a food economy approach, also showed not only a considerable decline in vulnerability during 1998 relative to 1997, but also indicated no significant difference in terms of vulnerability between the Bahr el Ghazal and Upper Nile regions.

The endless cycle of assessments, the 'spatial biases', the lack of continuity and institutional memory, together with the burden of current jargon that 'Africans do not starve but they cope', all led a food economy approach to generate information that was insensitive to the changes in people's vulnerability and unhelpful for effective targeting of relief food aid. The Sudan Relief and Rehabilitation Association (SRRA), the humanitarian wing of the SPLM, early warning system, despite its limited resources, managed, paradoxically, to generate information which correctly depicted in 1997 the level of vulnerabilities in southern Sudan, and Bahr el Ghazal in particular, and outperformed other systems. Yet its predictions were not taken seriously. As opinions of the charity agencies were divided about the severity of the 1998 humanitarian crisis, the media, rather than the early warning systems of the implementing international aid agencies, created awareness of the famine and triggered, though late, the necessary international relief response.

This book shows that famine persists because of political choices and it strikes when accountability fails in autocratic and authoritarian political environment. There is a need to define famines and mass starvations within the tools of international criminal law; namely genocide, crimes against humanity and war crimes. There is option of including famine or starvation in the definition of residual category of the Rome Statute of the International Criminal Court (ICC, 2002) as other inhumane acts in the crimes against humanity. In the case of Africa, there is an opportunity in Article 4(h) of the African Union Constitutive Act (AU, 2000) of including starvation or famine as one of the grave circumstances such as war crimes, genocide and crimes against humanity that warrant African Union to intervene in member state.

# CHAPTER ONE

# Introduction

### *Theorizing Famine: Gaps and Limitations*

The famine as a phenomenon is a reality that is widely accepted but its concrete definition has been elusive and difficult to underpin. Devereux (1994) describes famine as like insanity that is hard to define but glaring enough when recognized. It is difficult to theorize famine, plan for its prevention and respond to its occurrence without having its clear definition. There are generally three approaches to the definition of the famine. The first approach is "food availability decline" that came as a result of the recurrent famines in Africa and South Asia in the 1970s that triggered increasing scrutiny of the food supply-side explanation of famine. This food availability explanation was largely informed by the Malthusian or neo-Malthusian view that famine is a question of food shortage caused by the growth of population that outstripped the food production. Besides population growth, this approach attributes famine as a failure of food production caused by natural disasters and shocks such as environmental variability in terms of drought and floods and pests.

The second approach is "food accessibility decline" or "food entitlement failure" that defines famine not as a failure of food production but rather inability to access enough food. This approach introduced the food demand-side analysis of the causes of famine. This approach was informed by Amartya Sen's *Poverty and Famines* (1981) that introduced entitlement theory that restored a much-needed emphasis on an encompassing economic framework for analyzing famine. In particular, Sen (1981:40) defines famine as 'A particularly virulent manifestation of starvation causing widespread death'. Though Sen's work triggered a lot of discussions in the 1980s and into the 1990s, entitlement theory (despite some substantive criticisms) remains, as stated by Swift (1993), the first successful attempt to come up with an inclusive theory of famine and a set of far- reaching policy conclusions. The Sen's work has emphasized the need to examine the particularity of each famine and study specific "persons" or "households" rather than the overall population as well as focusing on relationships (Edkins, 2002).

Ravallion (1996) argues that some of these criticisms are merely the result of misunderstanding of the approach, whereas others are substantive. For example, the criticism that the entitlement approach separates food availability decline (FAD) from the entitlement framework or food inaccessibility is not a substantive one but rather a misunderstanding, as Sen (1981) clearly argues that food availability is only one parameter of entitlement (Ravallion, 1996:7). This point has been made clear by Sen (1981:154):

Even in those cases in which a famine is accompanied by a reduction in the amount of food available per head, the causal mechanism precipitating starvation has to bring in many variables other than the general availability of food. The FAD gives little clue to the causal mechanism of starvation, since it does not go into the relationship of people to food.

The other main criticism – that the entitlement approach is too *static* and that avoiding current hunger may not be the main motive for coping efforts (de Waal, 1989) – is not, according to Ravallion (1996), inconsistent with the entitlement approach: rational economic behavior may lead someone to choose a degree of hunger now in order to avoid starving in the future. Also, given the nonlinearity in the relationship between mortality and consumption, there will be long-term survival gains from stabilizing the consumption of a given person over time (Ravallion, 1996:17). This point was made very clear by Sen (1981:50):

> *Also, people sometimes choose to starve rather than sell their productive assets and this issue can be accommodated in the entitlement approach using a relatively long-run formulation (taking note of future entitlements). There is also some tendency for asset markets to collapse in famine situations, making the reward from asset sales rather puny.*

The criticism that the entitlement approach is less important in explaining famine mortality than health environment (de Waal, 1989) fails to recognize the causal relationship between entitlement failure and health environment (Ravallion, 1996:9). According to Ravallion,

> *The health environment is determined in part by the same variables determining consumption; for example, the exposure to disease of*

> *migrating people during a famine is not exogenous, but (it can be argued) an outcome of the same entitlement failures which led to migration in search of food.*

In explaining the major causes for a death rate in 1985 in Darfur, western Sudan, that was more than three times the normal level, de Waal (1989:19–20) mentioned diarrhea, measles, malaria, typhoid, dysentery, meningitis, pneumonia and social disruption; starvation itself was never cited as a cause of death. But in Arabic there is a clear distinction between *ma'jaa* (famine that kills) and *Waba'a* (epidemic). While both *maja'a* and *Waba'a* imply disaster, *maja'a* is directly linked to starvation and *Waba'a* is associated with outbreaks of disease or health crises. On the basis of the community's perception, the situation studied by de Waal (1989) would not be labelled as *maja'a*; rather it would be called *Waba'a*. Nevertheless, the communities have defined a phenomenon they term *maja'a* – and let us respect their wisdom; thus, it becomes extremely difficult to completely delink destitution from mortality.

Besides this basic community perception about famine, the 'health crisis model' (de Waal, 1989:21) seems to lack hard facts from the Darfur experience to justify its existence, since variables that measure poverty (such as nutritional data for Darfur) clearly indicate a sort of relationship between malnutrition and mortality. Also, despite the fact that de Waal (1989:20) recognizes that 'the omission of starvation as a cause of death is attributed to the fact that health records allow for the mention of only one cause of death, so that the proximate cause (a disease) is normally recorded, rather than an underlying cause, such as starvation', the health crisis model deliberately fails to incorporate 'starvation' as a cause. Though starvation is not often identified as the proximate cause of death during famine, it does appear to have a strong potentiating effect on the incidence and severity of infectious diseases (Ravallion, 1996:9).

One substantive criticism against the entitlement approach is its emphasis on the legal apparatus that defines property rights and personal endowments (Ravallian, 1996:8). Sen (1981:49) stated that 'while entitlement relations concentrate on rights within the legal structure in that society, some transfers involve violation of these rights, such as looting or brigandage. When such extra-entitlement transfers are important, the entitlement approach to famines will be defective'. It will be shown in this book that during the 1998 famine in Sudan people starved to death within a relatively stable legal structure. Despite the prolonged and continuous raids and looting of the properties and assets of the communities in Bahr el Ghazal by GOS militias, with some few exceptions, the communities retained a relatively stable law and order among themselves.

The looting, raids and brigandage activities by outsiders have indeed eroded people's endowments but did not trigger an absence of law and order among the communities of the Bahr el Ghazal region. In 1998 many people died from starvation in areas close to markets with grain and/or near cattle camps as the legal apparatus managed to uphold entitlements and guard ownership rights during famine. Even in a complex political emergency and war situation such as that in Bahr el Ghazal, it is possible to analyze economically famine in the context of entitlement theory.

The third approach is "accountability for the mass starvations" that provides alternative thinking of famine as mass starvations and crime against humanity similar to genocide. This approach moves away from the causes of and response to famine to the fundamental question of how were acts of mass starvation committed and by whom, and how can those responsible be brought to justice (Edkins, 2002: 12). This approach is built on the weaknesses of the two aforementioned approaches that depoliticized famine and reduced it to a technical or managerial problem. Rather than focusing on the victims of famine, this approach shifted the focus to the perpetrators and beneficiaries of famine. So, this approach does not see famine as a technical and managerial problem, but it sees it as a protracted politico-social-economic process of oppression comprising three stages: dearth, famishment and mortality (Edkins, 2002: 14).

The three approaches to understanding famine have their own advantages and disadvantages but they are undoubtedly complementing to each other. The issue of food production in light of recurrent natural disasters largely caused by environmental change and the growing population with increasing unemployed youth in Africa play an important role in understanding famine. Yet, food availability alone is not sufficient to provide coherent understanding of the famine. The food accessibility or entitlements approach brought the much-needed academic insight of theorizing famine in the realm of economics (Edkins, 2002). Besides food supply-side, the food demand-side is equally important in theorizing famine, but both failed to bring the political dimension in conceptualizing famine.

Understanding famine only from the perspective of famine victims is not sufficient as the acts of preparators and beneficiaries of famine are equally important. The three approaches do complement each other and provide the holistic theorization of famine from the lens of three disciplines: agriculture in terms of food production, economics in terms of entitlements and political science in terms of accountability. It is shown in this book how these three approaches are used to understand the 1998 famine in Sudan as a process in a chain of environmental, social, economic and political factors that interact and reinforce each other in producing the mass starvations.

***Objectives of the Book:***

With famine theories mushrooming and after many years of entitlement theory and call for famine accountability, the real challenge is to test how far these theories have benefited famine victims and made the preparators of famine accountable to their acts. As rightly stated by Devereux (1993), too many explanations overlook the complex web of factors that set people up for disaster, and the focus should instead be on the most obvious and immediate symptoms of food crisis. Though it is generally recognized that famine is caused both by food availability decline and by food entitlement decline, there is little evidence that the proliferation in the 1980s and 1990s of theories of famine has been translated into practical policies to prevent or control famine: famines are still recurrent phenomenon and will continue as the current theories seem not to have changed the methods of famine management. The real challenge for the theories of famine and extensive researches on famine is no longer to widen our understanding about famine but rather to translate their findings into policies that will save lives, ameliorate suffering and build confidence in the traditional capacities of the victims of famine as well as making preparators of famine accountable to their deeds.

The recurrent famines in the 1980s in the Sudan, particularly in the northern part, have been adequately researched and have helped immensely to widen our understanding of famine. Alexander de Waal's *Famine that Kills* (1989) extensively analyzed famine in the Darfur region of western Sudan from the perspective of the famine victims and came up with findings which have profound implications for the conception of famine. David Keen's *The Benefits of Famine* (1994) was the first attempt to analyze and document the famine in southwestern Sudan and made a remarkable contribution by analyzing famine in the context of political economy. Cutler (1986) conducted a study on famine in the Red Sea Province of eastern Sudan.

Southern Sudan, though it has experienced recurrent famines in the 1980s and 1990s, did not, however, receive adequate empirical and analytical scrutiny. As de Waal (1993) observed, this is largely a consequence of the hazards of doing field research during wars, and the probability is that war famines will continue to receive insufficient analytical scrutiny. This book is an attempt to scrutinize analytically the 1998 famine in southern Sudan and to reassess the relevance of the various theories and empirical research findings in its context. The book also attempts to assess the usefulness of various famine theories and empirical findings in improving the management of the 1998 famine.

***Data Sources:***

The information on which this book is based came from various main sources. The SRRA in 1995 established an Early Warning Unit with support from Christian Aid, NPA and OLS in order to monitor the food security situation and the livelihood generally of the civil population in areas controlled by the SPLM, particularly the counties in regions of Bahr el Ghazal, Upper Nile and Equatoria (see Map 1). The primary data generated by the monitoring activities of this in 1996, 1997 and 1998 have been used in this book. These data include information on rainfall, market prices, wild foods, population movements, some aspects of coping strategies, and crop performances, as well as secondary data on health, education and water facilities. These data were regularly collected by County Database and Monitoring Officers who were drawn from and selected by the communities concerned. Though the County Database and Monitoring Officers were adequately trained on data collection methods, the food economy approach, participatory monitoring and evaluation, and participatory rural appraisal (PRA), the early data collected in 1995 were of poor quality as the officers' monitoring skills were not adequately strengthened.

*Map 1: Counties of South Sudan*

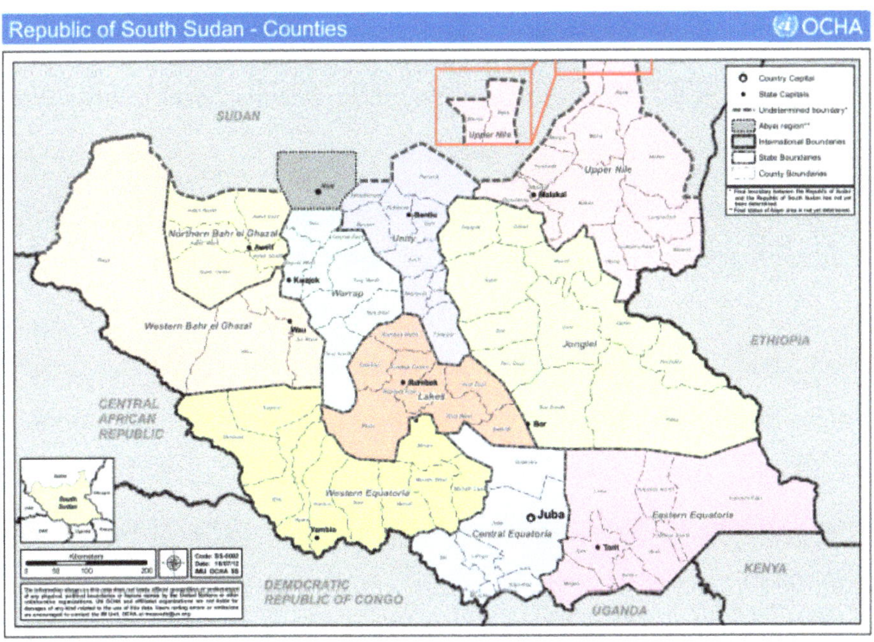

In addition to the data generated by the monitoring activities of the unit, semi-structured questionnaire interviews were carried out by the County Database and Monitoring Officers with the famine victims in the affected *payams* in the counties of the Bahr el Ghazal region. One case study was made at a village called Ajiep by interviewing 943 women. I conducted group discussions with chiefs, elders, women, women whose children had been admitted to feeding centers, adults admitted to the feeding centers and County Database and Monitoring Officers during my continuous visits to various affected areas in the Bahr el Ghazal region. Most of the historical information came from oral sources in addition to secondary sources.

I also used a great deal of data from NGOs, OLS and donors operating in southern Sudan. Food aid data relating to various locations in southern Sudan came from OLS/WFP. FEWS/USAID provided NDVI and rainfall estimates for various locations in southern Sudan. MSF(B) provided data on nutrition andmortality. OLS/UNICEF provided data related to nutrition surveys, deliveries of non-food items, and security and access. Other important reports used in this book include SPLM/SRRA/OLS Task Force reports on vulnerabilities and targeting, annual assessment reports and OLS consolidated appeals.

Also, livelihoods and vulnerability primary data that I collected from May 2000-March 2001 during my Doctor of Philosophy research fieldwork in three villages of Abyei county (Kiir Kou), Gogrial county (Alek) and Cuiebet county (Langdit) are used in this book (see Map 2). Abyei area, being located at the northern end of Bahr el Ghazal, represents communities exposed mainly to exogenous counter-insurgency warfare, while Gogrial area, being located in the central Bahr el Ghazal region, represents communities primarily exposed to endogenous counter-insurgency warfare. The village in Cuiebet area, being located to the southern end of Bahr el Ghazal, represents communities that had been mainly exposed to drought.

*Map 2: Research Areas (red circles) in Abyei, Gogrial and Cuiebet Counties*

*Source: United Nations*

The qualitative and quantitative data were collected using questionnaire-based household surveys and community surveys. Other participatory methods, such as 'participant observation', were used including staying as much as possible within the research communities, which allowed me to obtain information that I could not solicit through other formalistic methods. Besides providing additional information, the 'participant observation' method was also helpful in triangulating the data gained through sample households surveys and community participatory method.

### *Organization of the Book*

The book is structured around the causes of, preparedness for and responses to the 1998 famine in southern Sudan. Chapter Two describes and analyses the current famine in terms of mortality, malnutrition and migration. Chapter 3 deals with the famine's genesis and underlying causes. Chapter 4 analyses its proximate causes in the context of failure in direct food entitlement, exchange entitlement failure, and failure in nonmarket strategies. Chapter 5 discusses the role of public action particularly relief intervention and the responses of local authorities. Chapter 6 assesses the performance of various food security monitoring systems in predicting the current famine and triggering responses. Chapter 7 summarizes the major conclusions and policy implications.

The areas under the administration of the SPLM were divided into five regions; namely Bahr el Ghazal, Equatoria, Upper Nile, Southern Kordofan and Southern Blue Nile. Each administrative region was further divided into smaller administrative units called counties which consisted of a number of *payams.* Though the general area under study was the southern Sudan, the focus is on the Bahr el Ghazal region which was the most affected by the 1998 famine. In the Bahr el Ghazal region some counties and *payams* were more affected than others. As almost all *payams* in Gogrial and Wau counties were affected by the 1998 famine, considerable attention is paid to the data from these counties. The data from other counties in the various regions are used for comparative analysis.

# CHAPTER TWO

## Famine Definition and Measurement

*"There is as yet no famine in southern Sudan, although there is extreme distress."*

*The Times, 30 April 1998*

*"The people of Bahr el Ghazal are facing a crisis, but not yet a famine, Mike Aaronson, SCF (UK)."*

*Financial Times, 4 May 1998*

### *Was it a Famine in 1998?*

The humanitarian crisis in southern Sudan during 1998 was not recognized as a *famine* by outsiders' perception until July/August 1998 when thousands of lives were lost. Despite growing recognition in the 1980s of the need to define famine from the perspective of those who suffer from it, it seems that the 1998 famine was consistently defined for its victims by outsiders. Swift (1989) asserts that the exact meaning of famine should be defined by those who suffer from famine than those who analyze it. This ethnocentricity in defining famine, as mentioned by Devereux (1993), is responsible for much that is wrong with famine definitions and famine management.

The extracts from two widely circulated UK newspapers that head this chapter make a clear distinction between 'crisis' and 'extreme distress' on the one hand and 'famine' on the other. This distinction explicitly sees famine as the last phase of a crisis and synonymous with starvation unto death. This perception of famine is consistent with Amartya Sen's (1981:40) definition of famine as 'a particularly virulent form of (starvation) causing widespread death'. Such definition as has been justifiably challenged by empirical findings which show clearly that famine as understood from the perspective of its victims is a broad concept which includes not only starvation but also the entire process of increasing vulnerability.

Alex de Waal's *Famine That Kills* (1989:76) found that famine in Darfur means 'not merely starvation but also hunger (that is, all manners of suffering), destitution and social breakdown'. Similar findings were obtained in other countries (Laya, 1975; Currey, 1978; Mesfin, 1986). The definition of famine as an event has been extensively criticized and justifiably challenged by various researchers (Rangasami, 1985; Bush, 1985; Swift, 1989; Devereux, 1993; Keen, 1994; de Waal, 1989). Despite lack of commonly agreed definition, famine can be defined as when people face a complete lack of access to food and other basic needs and experience mass starvation, death and destitution (Hufstader, 2020).

The real question is why do the policy makers and practitioners, particularly NGOs and media, still look at famine as an event and in the context of their own perceptions, despite the sound theoretical framework and enormous empirical findings developed in the 1980s? It seems that the perception of famine as starvation is most appealing to the Westerners and their media upon which the voluntary sector entirely depends. Probably the empirical findings and new theoretical framework are not cost-effective for a voluntary sector that is highly competitive and whose own survival often becomes a priority. The voluntary sector emerged as a result of growing dissatisfaction with the poor performance of the public sector and was expected to introduce much- needed efficiency, simplicity and flexibility in resources management, as well as positive new ideas. Given the fragile structure of their funding sources, however, the comparative advantage of NGOs and the voluntary sector will gradually erode until some will eventually become extensions or contractors of the public or private sector.

*Table 1: Local Names for Famine and Vulnerability in South Sudan*

| Community Groups | Famine | Vulnerability |
|---|---|---|
| Lohuto | Amehino | Amehino |
| Acholi | Kec | Kerope |
| Lou | Kec | Ngama ngong |
| Bari | Dang | Padede |
| Moro | Mabu | Mbaraakoba |
| Baka | Bizoro | Gileri |
| Zande | Gberango | Borozingo |
| Balanda | Vowo | Nvesani |
| Dinka/Bor/Yirol | Paweer | Nyob |
| Dinka (the rest) | Cok/Nguiet | Kooc |

*Source: SRRA Monitoring Unit*

### *Community's Perspectives of Famine*

As has been consistently asserted in research such as that of de Waal (1989) and Swift (1989), the starting point for an analysis of famine should be with the understanding of those who suffer from famine. I will therefore try to reflect how various communities perceive famine in their own context. On the basis of group discussions with elders, chiefs, women and SRRA County Database and Monitoring Officers, I have summarized the local names for famine and vulnerability in Table 1. Generally, the idiom for understanding famine is almost the same across various community groups in southern Sudan. The local concept of famine of most communities differs little from their concept of famine, which implies a process of suffering rather than an isolated event. For example, in the *Lohuto* community of Torit county in Eastern Equatoria, famine *(amehino)* is synonymous with vulnerability *(amehino)*.

The Dinka community, which forms the overwhelming majority in southern Sudan and the largest single ethnic group in the Sudan, with its language *Thong Monyjang*, calls hunger *cok,* which is similar to *famine* according to Western definition. *Cok* implies a *low physical level* of food consumption, a *declining trend* of food consumption, and *sudden collapse* of the level of food consumption. Unlike Sen's (1981:41) definition of famine as chiefly a problem of *sudden collapse* of the level of food consumption, the Dinka term for hunger *(cok)* is typically the same as for famine (*cok*). In group discussion with Dinka elders and chiefs at Ajiep in Gogrial county, Chief Ayii Madut defined *cok* generally in the context of historical changes in vulnerability rather than providing a specific definition. In trying to define *cok*, he stated the following:

> *Cok [hunger] varies according to years. For example, in 1949 korum (locust) came during weeding anddestroyed crops and left behind its small offspring and returned back again during harvest which resulted in cokthii (small famine). Other years, drought brings cok and years of floods are relatively better.This year when people moved to Ajiep was made worse than other years by the prolonged war which drained blood (increased vulnerability) from people resulting in acute vulnerability (kooc). In 1994, during the war between SPLA and GOS, Kerubino together with Arab militia came in and displaced people, looted livestock, grain and all assets and left people displaced and vulnerable till 1997. When reconciliation between Kerubino and SPLA was reached early this year [January 1998] it found people exhausted and Arab militia came again in May and June and looted the remaining livestock. This resulted in big hunger (cokdit).*

The chronology of famine vulnerability as a way of defining famine rather than as an isolated event as described by Chief Ayii Madut is consistent with Swift's (1989) assertion of the need for analysis of historical changes in vulnerability.

In other group discussions with elders and chiefs at Ajiep, Chief Alfred Amet described *cok* (hunger) as follows:

> *Cok in Dinka language (thong Monyjang) is when you do not have something to eat … if you do not havegrain to be cooked by your wife then you are termed as facing cok … if you do not have livestock to bring you milk you are also termed as suffering from cok …*

> *if you do not have grain or livestock or even relatives to support you then you will die from cok (nguiet).*

This definition of famine goes even beyond lack of food to social relationships. In Dinka language, the terms *anek cok* (suffering from hunger) and *anguiet cok* (dying from hunger) indicate different phases of suffering; *nguiet* is the last phase of suffering when social support as last resort collapses. The fatal famine in Dinka society becomes glaring only when the dead bodies of the famine victims are not buried but instead are left to be eaten by birds (*nguiet*). Traditionally, Dinka do not bury the corpse of a people whose death is caused by starvation; instead, the dead bodies are moved to nearby forests where probably they are eaten by birds, which explains the term *nguiet*.

Dinka believe that the burial of such corpses will bring back *cok* (hunger) again as it is associated with their strong belief in life after death. Another factor, in addition to such beliefs, is that when the fatal famine (*nguiet*) occurs it becomes practically difficult for family members, themselves physically weak, to bury the dead bodies. In a dispatch from southern Sudan in May 1998, George Alagiah, the BBC's Africa correspondent, showed unburied human bones as an indication of the presence of famine and was criticized by some aid agencies on the grounds that the human bones were actually from the victims of war rather than famine. This criticism reflects the failure to understand the rural communities of some aid agencies, affected as they are by the virus of rural development tourism (Chambers, 1983). Contrary to the extracts from the British newspapers cited above, the communities in the Bahr el Ghazal region were experiencing not only normal suffering from *cok* but a fatal one.

The ways in which the communities in southern Sudan perceive famine are shown by the names they attach to different famines. In Darfur in western Sudan, de Waal (1989) categorized famines according to the hardship they inflicted. The categorization of famines in southern Sudan, however, is conveniently based on the entire cycle of famine.

*Table 2: Local names for the 1998 famine in the Bahr el Ghazal region*

| County | Local Name of Famine | Meaning of the Local Name | Causes of Famine |
|---|---|---|---|
| Yirol | cok dakruai | Breaking of relationships | Drought |
| Rumbek | cok UN | UN famine | Drought |
| Tonj | cok ruon UN | Year of UN | Drought |
| Wau | kec abanban | Displacement and migration | Drought and insecurity |
| Awiel | cok Kerubino/ marahilien | Famine of Kerubino/ Arab Militia | Insecurity and drought |
| Gogrial | cok Kerubino/ marahilien | Famine of Kerubino/ Arab Militia | Insecurity and drought |
| Twic/ Abyei | cok macok gaar | Famine with bell in foot | Inscecurity and drought |

*Source: SRRA Monitoring Unit*

For example, the local names for the 1998 famine in the Bahr el Ghazal region as shown in Table 2 primarily symbolize causes, preparedness, response and effects. While the northern counties (Awiel, Gogrial, Abyei and Twic), which experienced considerable insecurity, use the cause (Kerubino and the militias) to name the 1998 famine, the southern and eastern counties, which were relatively stable, use various aspects of response. Interestingly, in Twic county people gave the name *cok machok gaar* (famine with bell in foot) to indicate that people had anticipated the imminent 1998 famine. This in itself clearly indicates that famine is not necessary a *sudden collapse* as defined by Sen (1981).

In Yirol county the 1998 famine was associated with the collapse in social relationships and was named *cok dak ruai* (breakingof relationships); this shows clearly that famine is caused not only by *food availability decline* and *food entitlement decline* but also by collapse in *social support.* Deng (2010b) shows the erosion of social capital among communities exposed to exogenous counterinsurgency warfare in the 1990s in Bhar el Ghazal region. Inconsistent with Sen (1981), the 1998 famine in Bahr el Ghazal shows that command over food was not the only overwhelming cause; social relationships were equally important. The response of the United Nations agencies and NGOs to the famine has been recognized by the community, which has positively attached the name of the UN to the famine.

It is apparent that the community perception of famine in southern Sudan is different from that of the outsiders. According to the communities in the Bahr el Ghazal region the situation in 1998 was not only one of extreme distress or crisis but a fatal famine.

***Measuring Famine: How Bad was the 1998 Famine?***

Nutritional surveillance is widely used to assess the prevalence of malnutrition among children and to indicate how vulnerable a population is to famine because of nutritional deficit. Though the problems associated with anthropometric surveillance are well documented (Shoham, 1987), as stated by de Waal (1989) it 'retains a powerful grip on the perceptions of famine by international agencies'. The major shortcomings of nutritional surveillance include a narrow conception of famine as 'nutritional deficit' and creation of 'citadel of expertise' which prevents dialogue with the famine victims (de Waal, 1989). According to this argument, nutritional surveillance is also a late indicator of famine and it ignores adults who might be worse affected than children.

*Figure 1: Malnutrition prevalence in Bahr el Ghazal, 1998*

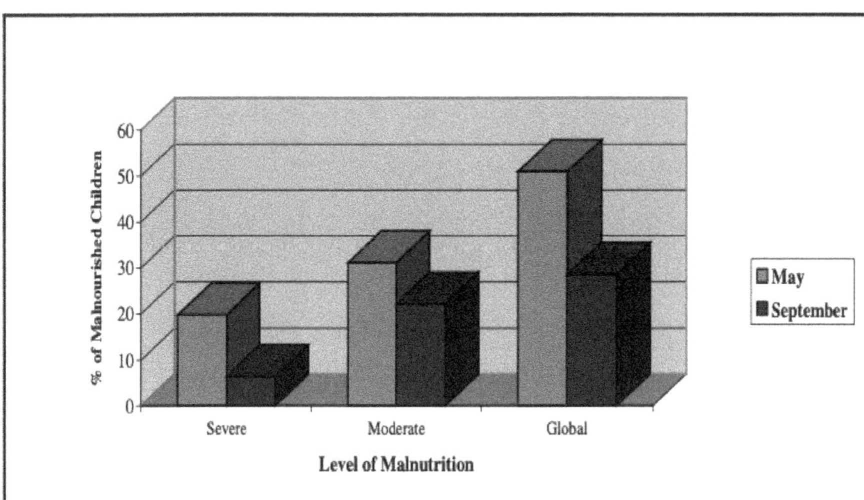


*Source: UNICEF/Southern Sector*

However, Young and Jaspars (1995:26) convincingly argue that 'the widely held view that malnutrition is a late indicator of famine is challenged on the basis of evidence that people often deliberately reduce their food intake as an early response to inadequate food security'. On this basis, I use the results of various nutritional surveys in the Bahr el Ghazal region as early indicators of famine to assess how far they had affected the perceptions of the 1998 famine held by the international agencies operating in southern Sudan.

UNICEF/OLS conducted nutritional assessments in the Bahr el Ghazal region in May–June and again in September 1998 to assess the changing nutrition situation among the children under five years of age. The first survey covered most counties of the Bahr el Ghazal with sample of 4,104 children, that is about 3.3 per cent of the estimated population of children (126,180) under five years of age. Like most assessments carried out in southern Sudan, the survey suffered from 'spatial biases' as it was conducted only around airstrips and WFP food distribution catchment areas and used only one method of measurement despite its full coverage of children.

The survey compromised its quality results by using one measurement; weight for height measurement, instead of using mid upper arm circumference (MUAC) in addition in order to obtain more representative and better-quality results. Though in the context of southern Sudan these problems are understandable, spatial biases in particular greatly underestimated the level of malnutrition in the Bahr el Ghazal region as the majority of the population in southern Sudan live away from airstrips. The results ofthe two nutritional surveys are summarized in Figure 1.

It is clear from Figure 1 that malnutrition in the Bahr el Ghazal reached its highest level in May–June. An MSF (B) nutritional survey in July 1998 in the displaced persons' camp at Ajiep in Gogrial county also revealed extremely high malnutrition rates that have rarely been seen before, with an acute severe malnutrition rate reaching 36.6 per cent (SRRA, 1998). Despite these exceptionally high malnutrition rates, some of international agencies operating in southern Sudan did not change their perceptions of the presence of famine and continued to describe the situation as one of 'extreme distress' or 'crisis'. It was not until September–October 1998 that a considerable improvement in the levels of malnutrition had been observed in the region. An MSF (B) nutritional survey conducted in September 1998 also indicated considerable improvement but nevertheless a high level of malnutrition. This improvement may be attributed both to increased food deliveries and to the high probability that the most severely malnourished children assessed in the May–June survey, given low recovery rates and low admission level to the feeding program, might have died.

### *Who Was Susceptible to Malnutrition in 1998?*

The overall findings of the two UNICEF/OLS nutritional surveys conceal variations among children according to sex, parents' wealth groups, whether residents or displaced, the sex of the head of household and the locations.

### *Sex*

The survey findings show considerable difference when considering the pattern of malnutrition among male and female children separately, as summarized in Table 3. This shows that the malnutrition rate seems to be higher in male children than in female children; it becomes significantly different at the levels of severe and global malnutrition, though there is no significant difference at moderate malnutrition levels.

*Table 3: Malnutrition sex differentials in Bahr el Ghazal, June 1998*

| | Level of Malnutrition (Weight-for-Height Z Scores) | | | | | | | |
|---|---|---|---|---|---|---|---|---|
| | Severe | | Moderate | | Global | | | |
| Sex | < -3 Z Scores | | > -3 < -2 Z Scores | | < -2 Z Scores | | Total | |
| | Number | % | Number | % | Number | % | Number | % |
| Female | 331 | 8.6 | 579 | 15.1 | 910 | 23.7 | 1,892 | 49.2 |
| Male | 431 | 11.2 | 616 | 16.0 | 1,047 | 27.2 | 1,952 | 50.8 |
| Total | 762 | 19.8 | 1,195 | 31.1 | 1,957 | 50.9 | 3,844 | 100 |

*Source: OLS/UNICEF*

As the situationslightly improved in September 1998, the pattern of malnutrition differential between the female and themale population of children started to erode. The results from the two UNICF/OLS nutritional surveys in the Bahr el Ghazal region suggest the presence of malnutrition sex differentials during acute malnutrition which become insignificant as the situation improves. These results seem not to suggest any preferential treatment on the basis of sex during famine. This finding is also supported by Kuol (2021) who found male children were more susceptible to malnutrition than female children during the 1998 famine. Though the Dinka concepts of immortality, procreation and agnatic lineage continuation favor male infants, they do not lead to preferential treatment of male children because female children, according to the Dinka, are a source of wealth.

### *Wealth Groups*

In Dinka community the ownership of livestock is a good indicator of wealth. However, collection of data related to livestock ownership is an extremely arduous task as Dinka rarely reveal the size of their herds directly, preferring to list them by colors or names rather than counting them, as a way of protecting animals from diseases and curses. Instead, a proxy indicator, such as the number of wives for one husband, is used with considerable skill to show the level of livestock ownership. The WFP/OLS conducted a survey at Ajiep, Gogrial county of 661 households with children in feeding program in order to establish the wealth profile of the population with children in feeding program. About 38 per cent of the children of poor families were covered by feeding program, while about 34 per cent of the children of the rich families were covered.

The difference between rich and poor seems not to be significant and clearly shows that there were considerable structural changes in cattle ownership as most cattle have been looted by the GOS popular defense forces (PDF) and its militias. These structural changes in wealth structure have been identified by Deng (2008) who shows that during civil war the non-poor are not necessary less vulnerable than poor households and they might even become more vulnerable than the poor. Also, Kuol (2014) finds a negative relationship between wealth and vulnerability, particularly among communities exposed to endogenous counterinsurgency warfare in Bahr el Ghazal region.

### *Displaced Population*

Almost about 94.4 per cent of the total households covered by the WFP/OLS survey at Ajiep had been displaced; this is consistent with the results of the MSF (B) survey which found that about 93 per cent were displaced. Deng (2010b) finds recurrent displacement of communities in Bahr el Ghazal with overwhelming households got displaced more than three times in the 1990s. Despite a high proportion of displaced population at Ajiep, there was no significant difference between the percentages of children admitted to the feeding program from resident and displaced families. This may be attributed in part to the easy access of the resident population to the feeding program, and in part to the fact that malnutrition overwhelmed the entire community. The increased population movement in the Bahr el Ghazal region during 1998 was triggered by prolonged insecurity, and early centralization of feeding programs and food distribution; it will be elaborated further in the next section.

### *Woman-Headed Households*

About 40 per cent of the total households covered by the WFP/OLS Ajiep survey are woman-headed households. This is high proportion and reflects the effects of war and famine itself. The percentage of children admitted to the feeding program was almost the same for the woman-headed households as for the male-headed households. This finding seems to suggest that in responding to famine, women perform similarly to or even better than men. This is largely related to the fact that wild food collection is traditionally a role of women and children in Dinka society; to lesser extent it reflects the targeting of relief food aid, which favors women-headed households as more vulnerable than male-headed households. Kuol (2021) also shows similar findings that woman-headed households were more resilient than male-headed households, particularly among communities exposed to endogenous counterinsurgency warfare in Bahr el Ghazal region in the 1990s.

### *Locations*

The level of malnutrition during 1998 in the Bahr el Ghazal region varied across counties, *payams* and *bomas* (villages). This variation was the result of many factors related to food availability decline, food entitlement decline, food utilisation, the gradual erosion of the food entitlement base, and insecurity. The UNICEF/OLS nutritional survey of May–June 1998 shows considerable variation across various counties of the Bhar el Ghazal region. Figure 2 shows that malnutrition rates were higher than 30 per cent rate in almost all counties except Awiel West and Yirol counties.

Generally, the pattern of malnutrition seems to be relatively higher in northern Bahr el Ghazal (Wau, Gogrial, Awiel East, Twic) – with the exception of Awiel West county – than in eastern Bahr el Ghazal (Rumbek, Tonj and Yirol). The malnutrition rates in Wau, Gogrial and Awiel East were exceptionally high. The severe malnutrition rate in Wau county, for example, reached 47 per cent which is a record for southern Sudan in contemporary nutrition studies. The difference in the levels of malnutrition across countries is largely attributable to variations in the level of exposure to insecurity, access to markets, and rainfall pattern.

*Figure 2: Prevalence of malnutrition in Bahr el Ghazal, June 1998*

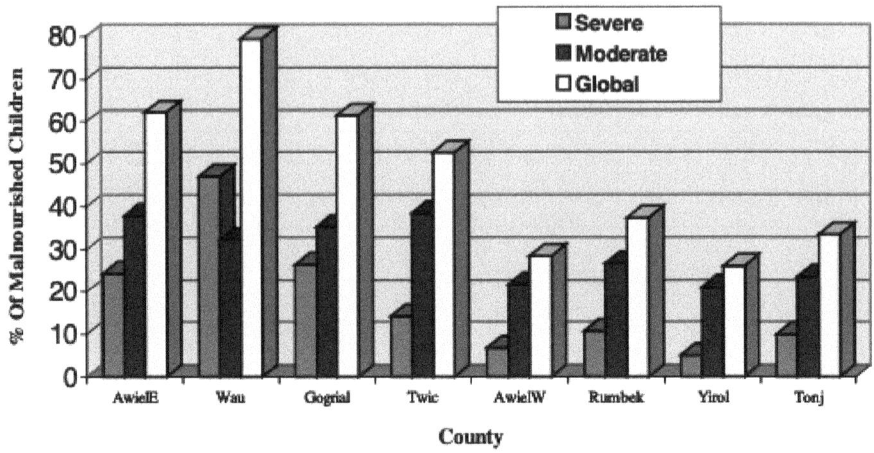


*Source: UNICEF/OLS Southern Sector*

The variations in malnutrition across the counties of the region conceals the malnutrition differences within each county, particularly at *payam* levels. For example, while all *payams* in Gogrial and Wau counties had acute severe malnutrition, only two *payams* (Mangargier and Wathmouk) in Awiel West had higher malnutrition rates (46–62 per cent global malnutrition) than the rest of the local *payams (*30.4 per cent globalmalnutrition). Although malnutrition rates were relatively low in Rumbek and Tonj, the malnutrition situation in some *payams* in Tonj (Thiet and Kuanythii) and Rumbek (Cueibet and Rumbek displaced) was almost similar to that in northern Bahr el Ghazal.

The situation of malnutrition in the Bahr el Ghazal region started improving by September 1998 in most counties as shown in Figure 3. Although remarkable improvement in the situation was observed in the counties of Awiel East and Twic, the situation in Gogrial county did not change much; malnutrition levels had even worsened in Awiel West because of insecurity and late intervention.

*Figure 3: Nutrition status in Bahr el Ghazal, 1998*

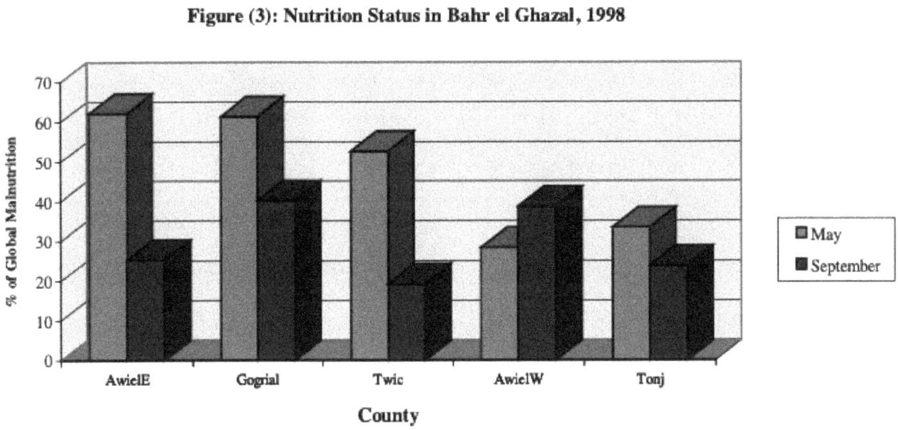


*Source: UNICEF/OLS Southern Sector*

*In current development jargon, Africans do not starve, they 'cope.'*

*John Seaman, 1993*

### *Famine Mortality: The Excess Death Toll*

In a complex political emergency like that in southern Sudan the availability of data related to people's livelihood generally is extremely scarce. Though insecurity has been consistently given as a reason for a failure to collect data, there was no concerted efforts and no commitment from the local authorities and implementing aid agencies to invest in data for effective planning. Though the local authorities (SPLM) in southern Sudan were understandably overwhelmed by other pressing priorities and had only meagre resources, the implementing NGOs – and the OLS in particular since its inception in 1989 – had not only failed to develop their own information systems but even to encourage indigenous and local capacities for data collection. Only in 1995 did the SRRA establish a database and monitoring unit as a genuine effort to set up an information and monitoring system in the accessible areas in the areas under the control of the SPLM.

The OLS relief operation during 1998 was the largest since its inception in 1998. Yet despite this huge operation, limited information existed about the scale of famine in southern Sudan, particularly mortality data. The pattern of neglect of mortality data for African famines has been emphasized by Seaman (1993:27) who observed that 'billions of dollars have been spent in attempting to prevent famine deaths in Africa and very little is known about African famine mortality, and there remains much confusion of view about itsscale and importance'. Though Seaman (1993) attributed this neglect partly to exaggerations by the operational agencies of the risks of mass starvation in Africa, the situation in southern Sudan seems to suggest the contrary, as some operating aid agencies underestimated the magnitude of the crisis in 1998.

The neglect of mortality data is all the more paradoxical since, if famine is defined according to 'outsiders' perceptions of it as starvation that causes massive death, then mortality data are an essential addition to malnutrition data at least to determine whether what happened in southern Sudan in 1998 could be described as famine or not. It is equally essential to know the pattern of mortality as mentioned by Sen (1981) for the light it throws on the nature of the famine.

Though mortality data are scarce in southern Sudan it is essential at least to make rough estimates from available material such as MSF (B) surveys, SRRA mortality records , the demographic survey of January 1999, the results of the 1998 polio immunization campaign, and oral sources through group discussions with chiefs, elders and community opinion leaders.

### *Excess Mortality*

In determining excess mortality, it is essential to have estimates for population affected, expected crude mortality rate (CMR) and actual CMR. The size of the population in southern Sudan was hotly debated by the local authorities, the SRRA and implementing agencies – there were no commonly agreed population estimates. While local authorities tended to put a high figure on the population as a way of attracting more humanitarian assistance, the implementing aid agencies tended to use low population figures in order to match their resources and to a certain degree to reflect the claim of the Government of Sudan that there was no civil population in the areas controlled by the SPLM. Only in 1998 did that improve, when a polio immunization campaign was carried out in March and April in most areas of the southern Sudan; its results became a useful basis for population estimates.

Despite their gross shortcomings, the results of the polio immunization campaign could be used to estimate the population affected by the 1998 famine in the Bahr el Ghazal region. On the basis also of OLS nutrition surveys and SRRA monitoring reports, it was clear that only some areas, in particular the whole of Gogrial and Wau and some *payams* of Awiel East, Rumbek and Tonj counties, experienced considerable numbers of deaths related to famine. Twic county, by contrast, despite prevalent high malnutrition and increased insecurity, did not experience large numbers of excessive deaths as the communities have relatively high levels of endurance and extraordinary ability to cope.

Southern Sudan has had a long history of instability and civil wars since Sudanese independence in 1956; these have caused considerable distortions in the demography of the region, particularly in the patterns of mortality and fertility. During sixteen years from 1983 when the second civil war erupted, southern Sudan experienced major demographic changes. Almost 1.3 million persons were estimated as killed in the war, almost 0.8 million persons were displaced to northern Sudan, about 0.4 million persons took refuge in neighboring countries, almost 0.5 million persons died in the 1988 famine, and about 25 per cent of the resident population were internally displaced in the 1990s. Despite these upheavals in the demographic structure of southern Sudan, I used the limited Sudan 1973 national data census (there has been no comprehensive census since 1955) to estimate roughly the crude mortality rate in the Bahr el Ghazal region.

De Waal (1989), on the basis of Demeny's (1968) analysis of the demography of Sudan, found that 'in Bahr el Ghazal region life expectancy at birth was 34.21 years in 1973, and the crude death rate of 'western southerners" was between 32 and 36 adjusted in 1955–6'. Given the current situation in Bahr el Ghazal, one is bound in calculating the expected CMR in 1998 to take the upper estimate of the 1973 CMR to reflect increased exposure to insecurity, poor health and sanitation services, and displacement.

The estimation of the actual 1998 crude mortality rate is a difficult endeavor because the available data is so limited. MSF(B) compiled quality surveys about malnutrition and mortality in July and September 1998 and January 1999 in the Bahr el Ghazal region. These surveys revealed that at Ajiep in Gogrial county, CMRs in July reached 26 per 10,000 per day in the displaced population and 1.5

in the resident population in Mangergier and Wathmouk *payams* in Awiel East county. The demographic survey covering 943 households/families that was carried out in January 1999 at Ajiep, Gogrial county, found CMR of 351 per 1,000 per year. While SRRA mortality records in Kuajok *payam,* Gogrial county revealed a CMR of about 71 per 1,000 per year for the resident population, the interview with community elders, chiefs and opinion leaders indicated a CMR of around 87 per 1,000 per year for the resident population in Gogrial county.

In order to obtain a relative description of the 1998 famine in Southern Sudan, I used the summary of mortality data for African famines in Seaman (1993) for comparison as summarized in Table 4. It is apparent from Table 4 that the situation in Bahr el Ghazal in 1998 was comparable to other recent African famines. In terms of mortality rates among the resident population, the famine in Bahr el Ghazal in 1998 was similar to the Ethiopian famine of 1973, the Darfur famine of 1984–85 and the Niger famine of 1974; it almost approached in mortality rates that of Ethiopia in 1984–85. The 1998 mortality rates in the Bahr el Ghazal region among the displaced population were far higher than those shown in the records of any other recent African famine, and probably exceeded too those of any in South Asia. It is thus justifiable on the basis of comparative mortality data for various African famines to describe what happened in southern Sudan in 1998 as famine from the perspective of the outsiders from the Western world.

*Table 4: Famine Mortality Data in Africa, 1973–1998*

| **Country** | **Year of Famine** | **Village/Districts/ County** | CMR/ 10,000/ Day |
|---|---|---|---|
| (a) Resident Population | | | |
| Ethiopia | 1973 | Wollo | 1.9 |
| Uganda | 1981 | Karamoja | 5.8 |
| northern Sudan | 1984/5 | Darfur | 1.5 |
| Niger | 1974 | village in Niger | 1.2 |
| Ethiopia | 1984/5 | | 2.9 |
| southern Sudan:<br>SRRA Survey<br>MSF(B) Survey<br>Community Estimate | 1998<br>1998<br>1998<br>1998 | Bahr el Ghazal<br>Kuajok/Gogrial<br>Panthou/Awiel East<br>Gogrial | <br>1.9<br>1.5<br>2.4 |
| (b) Displaced Population | | | |
| Ethiopia | 1984/5 | Wad Kowli | 8.2 |
| northern Sudan | 1985 | Darfur/Umballa | 7.0 |
| southern Sudan:<br>MSF (B) Surveys<br><br><br>Demographic<br>Survey | <br>July 1998<br>Sept./Oct., 1998<br>January 1999<br>July 1998<br>January 1999 | <br>Ajiep/Gogrial<br>Ajiep/ Gogrial<br>Ajiep/Gogrial<br>Panthou/Awiel East<br>Ajiep/Gogrial | <br>26<br>13<br>5.3<br>24.1<br>9.6 |
| (c) Displaced Population (children under 5 years of age) | | | |
| northern Sudan | 1984/5 | Wad Kowli | 30 |
| northern Sudan | 1985 | Darfur/Umballa | 18 |
| Uganda | 1981 | Karamoja | 8.4 |
| Somalia | 1992 | Mogodishu | 16.1 |
| southern Sudan<br>(MSF) | July 1998<br>Sept./Oct. 1998<br>January 1999 | Ajiep/GogrialAjiep/Gogrial<br>Ajiep, Gogrial | 46<br>25<br>9.8 |

*Source: Seaman (1993: 29-31), SRRA, MSF (B).*

With an expected crude mortality rate of 36 and an actual crude mortality rate of 351 in the displaced population and 71 in the resident population, the excess mortality based on the polio immunization campaign's population estimates for the areas affected is shown in Table 5. It is clear from Table 5 that the excess deaths in the displaced and resident population in the Bahr el Ghazal region in 1998 were about 70,000 persons; the death rates in 1998 were more than three times normal. On the basis of both insiders' perceptions and mortality data analysis one can safely say that what happened in southern Sudan in 1998 was not only extreme distress or crisis but also an evident famine.

*Table 5: Excess Deaths Among the Populations of the Bahr el Ghazal region, 1998*

| | | **Deaths** | | |
|---|---|---|---|---|
| **County** | **Population estimates** | **Expected** | **Actual** | **Excess** |
| Gogrial County | | | | |
| Resident population | 324,498 | 11,682 | 23,039 | 11,357 |
| Displaced population | 21,000 | 756 | 7,371 | 6,615 |
| Wau County | | | | |
| Resident population | 132,834 | 4,782 | 9,431 | 4,649 |
| Displaced population | 24,061 | 866 | 8,445 | 7,579 |
| Awiel East | | | | |
| Mangergier *payam* | 38,502 | 1,386 | 2,734 | 1,348 |
| Wathmuok *payam* | 68,082 | 2,451 | 4,834 | 2,383 |
| Displaced population | 32,892 | 1,184 | 11,545 | 10,361 |

| | | | | |
|---|---|---|---|---|
| Tonj County | | | | |
| Thiet *payam* | 57,854 | 2,083 | 4,108 | 2,025 |
| Kuanythii *payam* | 60,885 | 2,192 | 4,323 | 2,131 |
| Displaced population | 35,800 | 1,289 | 12,568 | 11,279 |
| Rumbek County | | | | |
| Cueibet *payam* | 38,874 | 1,399 | 2,760 | 1,361 |
| Displaced population | 27,752 | 999 | 9,741 | 8,742 |
| TOTAL | 863,034 | 31,069 | 100,899 | 69,830 |

*Source: Seaman (1993: 29-31), SRRA, MSF (B)*

### *Mortality Differentials*

The mortality data in Table 5 conceal variations on the basis of sex, season, age and wealth groups. My analysis of mortality differentials is based on the demographic survey that was undertaken in January 1999 for one week at Ajiep in Gogrial county after a significant recovery in the situation. Ajiep had been the epicenter of the 1998 famine in Bahr el Ghazal and received a large degree of media attention. Ajiep had also attracted many people not only from within the *payams* of Gogrial county but also from other counties of northern Bahr el Ghazal, and it became a microcosm of the entire Bahr el Ghazal region . The analysis of the mortality differentials at Ajiep helps to shed light on the scale and magnitude of the famine in the entire region. The demographic survey covered 943 households/families with a total population of about 5,337 persons.

The key informants were mainly women. Informants were basically asked about the aggregate numbers of the family/household who had survived and those who had died during 1998; they were asked to categorize them into children and adults and to further divide the adults into males and females. The timing of the survey was helpful: people were willing to discuss the miseries and agonies of famine as they were certain that they had managed to survive. The fact that the enumerators who carried out the survey were from within the community helped a great deal in encouraging dialogue and relatively good-quality data. The population of Ajiep was estimated by the SRRA to be around 21,000 persons (approximately 3,500 households) while the MSF (B) estimate was about 17,000 persons. Taking the SRRA estimate as the most recent, the survey covered about 26.9 per cent (943 households/families) of households and about 25.4 per cent (5,337 persons) of the total population at Ajiep.

***Sex***

Whilst women accounted for 17.7 per cent of the total deaths at Ajiep, men were about 23 per cent. The mortality rate for men (421 per thousand) was significantly higher than that for women (299 per thousand) during the famine in Bahr el Ghazal in 1998. Kuol (2021) finds the same results of higher mortality among men than women during the 1998 famine in Bahr el Ghazal. The same pattern of sex mortality differential is also observed among children but with no significant difference between male and female mortality rates. Dyson (1993:20) attributed this higher mortality for males during famine to several factors including the higher level of female body fat, a greater propensity of males to migrate, and reduction in conceptions. The situation in southern Sudan seems to suggest that besides these factors, the stigmas attached to the collection of wild foods – the most effective coping mechanism during famine – tend to benefit women more than men. In Dinka society, there are certain wild fruits which, although they have a high calorific value, are eaten exclusively by children and women and not by adult men, merely for sake of pride and dignity.

### *Children*

Children constituted about 59.2 per cent of all deaths during 1998 at Ajiep; their mortality rate was about 347 per thousand, slightly lower than that of adults (359 per thousand). Most recorded mortality data during famines consistently indicate higher deaths among children than adults. The reverse mortality differential between adults and children at Ajiep, though it is not statistically significant, underlines the traditional values of Dinka society and its unique care for children even during famine. According to Lienhard (1961:26), 'Dinka fear to die without male issue, in whom the survival of their names – the only kind of immortality they know – will be assured'. The Dinka belief that children are their greatest treasure is well rooted in their concept of procreation as their fundamental value. In emphasizing the Dinka concept of immortality, Deng (1978:47) stated that:

> *The focus of their concept of immortality is in this world, through procreation and agnatic lineage continuation, which lead to ancestral veneration, almost culminating in worship.*

Traditionally the weaning practice in Dinka society is different from that of other communities, as infants are weaned after three years. De Waal (1989:13) found in Darfur in western Sudan that infant mortality in famine did not rise as much as child mortality because of weaning practices: infants are always weaned after their first birthday. In Dinka society during the entire period of pregnancy until weaning, it is a taboo for married couples to have any sexual contact. This is for the welfare of the child. Dinka believe that if a pregnant or lactating mother has sex, her child will certainly die prematurely. Dinka weaning practices are meant to give adequate time for child-care at the critical time of growth and to reduce exposure to water-borne diseases and protection against infection as well. According to Deng (1978:47), 'While spacing children is practiced through customary rituals of sexual avoidance which are explained in terms of health or aesthetic considerations, birth control by married couples is unknown.'

### *Seasonality*

Mortality during most famines seems to be relatively high during and after rains; it becomes low during harvest (de Waal, 1989; Dyson, 1993). The pattern of seasonal mortality during the famine in Bahr el Ghazal during 1998 reflects the similar pattern of other famines. The SRRA collected monthly mortality data in Kuajok *payam* in Gogrial county for January–September 1998. The population estimate for Kuajok *payam* was about 58,424 persons (based on the results of the polio immunization campaign). With an expected crude mortality rate of about 36 deaths per thousand per year, the monthly mortality and expected monthly mortality (an average of 175 deaths) are presented in Figure 4.

*Figure 4: Monthly Mortality in Gogrial, Southern Sudan, 1998*

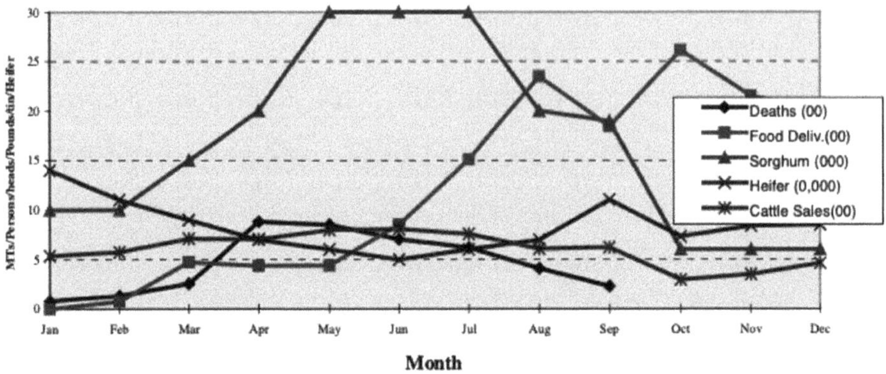


*Source: SRRA and de Waal (1989)*

Normally the rains in Bahr el Ghazal start in April–May and peak in August; the harvest season usually commences in September, threshing starts in December, and the dry season starts in January to April. From Figure 4 it is clear that excess deaths peaked during the rainy season and reached their lowest level at the beginning of harvest. Normally the months of hunger gaps are June and July, but these months did not show the highest excess deaths during the 1998 famine. Though the mortality pattern is associated with the seasons, it is significantly related as well to the pattern of food aid deliveries.

### *Wealth Status*

It has generally been emphasized in the literature of famines that poverty is the root cause of famines and that the relatively rich group of society usually survives during famine. According to Sen (1981:37), 'Famines imply starvation, but not vice versa. And starvation implies poverty, but not vice versa.' De Waal (1989) surprisingly finds no relationship between income and the risk of death in western Sudan.

Though it is true that there is a positive relationship between poverty and famine in relatively stable societies, the 1998 famine in Bahr el Ghazal suggests that this relation also holds true even in societies experiencing prolonged conflicts and war. In my group discussions with various community leaders in the region, they unanimously emphasized that though both poor and rich were affected during the famine as the cattle of both groups had been looted by Arab militias and Kerubino forces, the poor people suffered most. Chief Ayii Madut said:

> *The famine actually affected both groups; the poor and rich. The rich who had some cattle shared them with their relatives, and yet some of their children died and some of them died. Chiefs have also lost some of their children. The real poor have all passed away with all their children.*

It is clear from chief Ayii's statement that although famine affected both rich and poor, the poor suffered more than the rich. This observation is even confirmed by a famine song composed by Mathuc Bol during the famine:

> *The famine that has come with its knife to kill people … until it has blunted the spade whilst digging graves … it is a lie like a fact that the situation of chiefs and the rich is better… And we, the large number of normal people (Monyjang), are squeezed in the middle with no attention … and life hangs very far away … if you try to reach it you are likely to fall into a deep hole.*

Songs in Dinka society play the role of a free press and are generally intended to promote high moral standards or condemn anything which tends to reduce the moral standards; they may also criticize specific bad conduct and express public opinion.

*Migration*

Most famines are characterized by a pattern of unusual population movements to towns and other places where famine victims can get access to food either through relief food and labor exchange or because food prices are relatively lower than in their own areas. The famines in the Sudan were associated with massive population movements: in particular the famine of 1984–85 resulted in thousands of famine victims from western Sudan migrating to the capital Khartoum and permanently settling there. During the much- remembered 1988 famine in southern Sudan, most of the victims from northern Bahr el Ghazal died along the roads leading to northern Sudan in desperate flight to save their lives; as a result of that famine about one million southern Sudanese were displaced in the hostile and almost unbearable desert environment around Khartoum. The pattern of movement of the famine victims is generally towards the center of development and vital economic activities.

During the 1998 famine in the Bahr el Ghazal region a similar pattern of migration occurred with movement towards Equatoria region and the town of Wau (the former capital of the Bahr el Ghazal region) instead of the traditional northwards movement because of increased insecurity. In May–June 1998 around 21,600 persons from various counties of Bahr el Ghazal region were forced by the desperate famine situation to migrate to parts of western Equatoria which was relatively stable and had a good harvest and a normally functioning local economy. These famine migrants were, paradoxically, not adequately attended to by operating aid agencies because food was abundant in markets in western Equatoria. This is a clear case where *food availability* rather than *food accessibility* still dominated the thinking of relief aid agencies in assessing victim's vulnerability and the agencies' interventions.

In June 1998 a further 73,500 persons from various counties of the Bahr el Ghazal region risked their lives by entering the besieged government-held town, Wau. It was estimated that of them more than 5,000 persons (more than 7 per cent) died in Wau town, not because of lack of food but because of poor preparation of food because people were prevented from fetching firewood from nearby forests as the GOS feared they would rejoin the SPLA. People in Wau town were forced to use wastepaper instead of firewood for cooking food, which resulted in cases of indigestion, bloody diarrhea and massive deaths. The high mortality among the famine migrants in Wau county is a clear case of how limited access to fuel and firewood for preparing food is as important as limited access to food in causing famine.

In Bahr el Ghazal region itself, there had been massive population movements which were triggered by many factors including insecurity, denial of access by the GOS to operating agencies, and centralization of relief interventions particularly food distribution and feeding programs. The constant movement of the entire population of the Bahr el Ghazal region for a period of five months (March–July 1998) in a desperate search for food increased mortality as a direct result of physical risks, the risks associated with removal from the physical and social environment of the home, and diseases.

# CHAPTER THREE

## The Underlying Causes of Famine

*"El Nino may have stopped the rain, but it was man who made Sudan's famine."*

*The Times, 30 April 1998*

Since the famines of the 1980s, it has generally been recognized that famine is not a simple phenomenon to be explained holistically by a single cause or framework. The dominant understanding and conceptualization of famine as caused by food availability decline (food supply failure) or entitlements failure (demand failure) has been challenged since the emergence of new famines, as these technical explanations are not sufficient to explain the complex process of famine. Even the so-called 'war famine' cannot be explained simply by war alone as the sole root cause. The evidence from the recent famines consistently suggests that such famines are associated with tragic governance failure and deficit including violent conflict as they are largely either caused deliberately (acts of commission) or are not prevented because of the failure of public actions (acts of omission) (Devereux,

2006). De Waal (2019) calls famine a political scandal, a "catastrophic breakdown or failure in government capacity or willingness to do what [is] known to be necessary to prevent famine. The livelihood shocks like El Nino and drought may cause food supply failure but the response failure of public actions at local, national and international levels is responsible for causing the food shortage to evolve into famine (ibid).

This point is well captured during the 1998 famine by *The Times* that "*El Nino may have stopped the rain, but it was man who made Sudan's famine*". For example, in southern Sudan, though the recalled famines listed in Table 6 by the local communities were mainly triggered by factors related to food supply failure before the 1980s. However, local names of famines since the 1980s have become increasingly associated with governance failure including conflicts and response failure of international community as well as other livelihoods shocks.

For example, though the famine in 1988 in Yirol county was triggered by drought, the name given to it (*Biltil*) emphasized failure in kinship support. This finding is consistent with the observation of Ravallion (1996:4) that though famine is triggered by commonly identified aggregate exogenous shocks such as spells of unusually bad weather and wars, it does not seem to happen by spontaneous combustion. To understand famine and its prevention entails having a clear understanding of the chain of events leading to specific famine rather than attributing it entirely to some exogenous shocks (Ravallian, 1996:5).

*Table 6: Typology of Famines in Southern Sudan, 1937-1998*

| County | Year | Local Names of Famine | Meaning of Name | Major Cause |
|---|---|---|---|---|
| Bahr el Ghazal Region | | | | |
| 1.Yirol County | 1946 | Nyengthiec (R) | Do not give whoever asks for assistance | Locust |
| | 1948 | Mabor Bunbout (C) | Valueless money | Locust |
| | 1956 | Athuc (E) | Sadness/apathy | Drought |
| | 1957 | Nguege§ (E) | Waiting in vain | Drought |
| | 1958 | Gulang (E) | Whatever is eaten does not satisfy. | Pests |
| | 1985 | Nyok (R) | Name of wild food | Drought |
| | 1988 | Biltil (R) | Swear not to assist | Drought |
| | 1998 | Dakruai (R) | Abandon kinship and relationships | Drought and displacement |
| 2. Rumbek County | 1948 | Cok Koryom (C) | Famine of locust | Locust |
| | 1962 | Cok Adong(R) | Famine of first-grade bull being speared by famine victims | Floods and drought |
| | 1967 | Cok Polong (R) | Name of wild food | Drought |
| | 1988 | Cok Apat/ruel (R) | Famine of wild food or heat of sun due to constant search for food from neighbouring areas | Drought |
| | 1998 | Cok UN (R) | Famine of UN | Drought, floods,and displacement |
| 3.Awiel West County | 1948 | Ruon Koryom (C) | Year of grasshopper | Grasshopper |
| | 1966 | Cok Maguak (R) | Famine of groundnuts | Insecurity anddrought |
| | 1988 | Ruon Makurup (E) | Year of massive death | Insecurity anddrought |
| | 1989 | Cok Kerubino (C) | Famine of Kerubino | Insecurity anddrought |

| | | | | |
|---|---|---|---|---|
| 4. Gogrial County | 1948<br>1988<br><br>1998 | Ruon Koryom (C)<br>Ruon Moraja(E)<br>Ruon Kuanyin (C) | Year of grasshopper<br>Year of moping<br><br>Year of Kerubino | Grasshopper<br>Insecurity anddrought<br>Insecurity anddrought |
| 5. Twic County | 1948<br>1988<br><br>1998 | Ruon Koryom (C)<br>Ruon Moraja (E)<br><br>Chok Macok Gaar (R) | Year of grasshopper<br>Year of moping<br><br>Famine with bell foot | Grasshopper<br>Insecurity anddrought<br>Insecurity anddrought |
| 6. Wau County | 1948<br>1988<br><br>1998 | Kec Baanya (&)<br>Kec Paale (R)<br><br>Kec Abanban (R) | Famine of grasshopper<br>Famine of knives<br>Famine of migration and displacement | Pests<br>Insecurity anddrought<br>Insecurity anddrought |
| 7. Tonj | 1948<br>1988 | Cok Koryom (C)<br>Cok Biok (R) | Year of grasshopper<br>Famine of skin | Grasshopper<br>Insecurity anddrought |

*(P) Preparedness*

*(C) Causes of famine*

*(E) Effect of famine*

*(R) Response to famine including coping strategies*

| County | Year | Names of Famine | Meaning of Name | Major Cause |
|---|---|---|---|---|
| | 1992<br>1998 | Cok Abor (C)<br>Cok UN (R) | Famine of floods<br>Famine of UN | Floods<br>Insecurity and drought |
| Equatoria Region: | | | | |
| 1. Torit County | 1945<br><br>1962<br><br>1993<br><br>1997 | 0buor Hotio (E)<br><br>Itular (R)<br><br>No name<br><br>No name | White bone all over<br><br>White grain brought by Northern traders<br>No name<br><br>No name | Locust and drought<br>Locusts<br><br>Drought and insecurity<br>Drought and insecurity |
| 2. Maridi County | 1945 | Bizoro (C) | Locust | Pests |
| 3. Mundri County | 1937 | Tombi (C) | Locust | Pests |
| 4. Tambura and Yam bio Counties | 1945 | Ayere (C)<br>Kolongbo (C) | Locust | Pests |
| Upper Nile Region: | | | | |
| 1. Bor County | 1938<br>1948<br>1961<br>1986<br><br>1992<br>1994 | Awaiyou (R)<br>Koryom (C)<br>Paweer (E)<br>Yak Apat (R)<br><br>Kapoth (E)<br>Janyrueny (R) | Rescued from drowning<br>Locust<br>No name<br>Wild food<br><br>Survived<br>Eating randomly till satisfied | Floods<br>Pests<br>Floods<br>Pests and insecurity<br>Insecurity<br>Drought |

*Source: SRRA Monitoring Unit*

***Genesis of the 1998 Famine: Trajectory of Political and Security Vulnerability***

The chain of events leading to the recurrent famines in Bahr el Ghazal can be traced back to the first contacts of the communities of this region in particular and southern Sudan in general with outsiders. Though the historical dimensions may not now be an essential factor in the causation of famine in Bahr el Ghazal, it sheds light on the historical erosion of endowments and assets-base of the communities that directly affect food entitlements and increase vulnerability to any slight exogenous shocks.

It has generally been documented that the recurrent famines experienced by the people of Bahr el Ghazal in particular and southern Sudan in general are rooted in the political economy and history of the Sudan. David Keen's *Benefits of Famine* (1994) unveils and provides a comprehensive account of the historical perspective on famine in the Sudan and traced its root causes to the mid-1820s. Keen argues that the recurrent famines and vulnerability that decimated the communities of Bahr el Ghazal region were not isolated events but rather emerged from a long history of exploitative processes that threatened to destroy the way of life of these communities and remove their assets. This long history of exploitation and transfer of livelihoods assets can be divided into the following three distinct periods:

***Lawlessness and Slavery, 1820s – 1920***

The first period (1820s to mid-1920s) was described by Keen (1994:20) as the political and economic root of directly human-made famine in Bahr el Ghazal region, as the exploitative processes creating famine remained largely unchecked during Turko-Egyptian rule, the Mahdia rule and British colonial rule. During this period, raiding and slaving from armed camps (*zeribas)* created famine in Bahr el Ghazal on huge scale (Keen 1994:21). According to Gray (1961:61), these raids resulted in loss of grain and livestock and a shortage of labor. Collins (1971:67) emphasized that weaker community groups such as Dengo, Jur (Lou) and Bongo were threatened with extinction. It has been estimated that during this period almost half the population of Bahr el Ghazal escaped slavery only by emigrating to other parts of southern Sudan (Keen, 1994:20).

Turko-Egyptian rule greatly benefited from this process of asset transfer, which partly constituted famine in Bahr el Ghazal. Mohamed Ali's regime was military weak in the 1810s and was desperately seeking to establish financial and political autonomy from the Ottoman sultan. According to Holt and Daly (1988:48) the conquest of Nilotic Sudan offered to provide a docile, loyal slave army and a means of distracting Mohamed Ali's Albanian troops from further in subordination at home. Slaves were not only used as an army, but also came to provide one of the means of paying the Turko-Egyptian standing army (Spaulding, 1982). The goods looted from southern Sudan and slave-trading became major sources of revenue to the Turko-Egyptian state. According to Sanderson and Sanderson (1981:10), by the early 1880s almost two-thirds of the population of Khartoum (around 50,000 persons) were estimated to be slaves.

Asset transfers and cattle raiding also relaxed the severe economic pressures faced in the 1860s by Syrian and Egyptian traders who managed to get to Bahr el Ghazal by river (Holt and Daly, 1988). For example, the Dinka and Nuer were reluctant by the early 1860s to supply traders with major quantities of ivory because of strong competition, but they were weakened after large-scale cattle raiding and subsequently became eager to exchange ivory for stolen cattle.

According to Gray (1961), by 1870 raided cattle had become the universal and indispensable medium of exchange for traders. The petty traders *(jellaba),* who were squeezed out from northern Sudan by high competition from big traders, were propelled into the more dangerous southern slave catchment zone to seek their fortune (Spaulding, 1982). According to Schweinfurth (1873) *jellaba* often came with no morethan a single donkey or bullock and a meagre supply of tradable goods, perhaps including guns, which could be used in raiding (Keen, 1994:25).

The Baggara Arab tribes of Kordofan and Darfur also benefited a great deal both indirectly by hiring themselves to the major traders or by exacting tax for allowing these traders to move slaves across their territory, and directly by doing their own raiding, as a result of which slave owning was widespread among them by the 1870s. According to Schweinfurth (1873:413) the drive to secure slaves from the south was clothed in a thin veil of religious justification: traders were generally known as *fakis* (priests) but only limited efforts by then were made to convert the south to Islam as this would have created problems for the slavers under Muslim law (Keen, 1994:25).

The Turko-Egyptian regime was replaced by the Mahdi in 1881 with full support from slave traders, particularly BaggaraArab tribes. According to Holt and Daly (1988:80–88):

> *Indeed, it had been the threat posed to slave traders and to the Baggara raiding by renewed efforts at suspension had, in large part, prompted the overthrow of the Turko-Egyptian government, with the Baggara playing a critical role among the conglomeration of supporters that the Mahdi called his Ansar. Keen (1994: 27).*

According to Holt (1958), the Mahdi invaded Bahr el Ghazal in 1884, with support from a variety of groups with interests in the slave trade, and the Baggara Arab tribes took the chance to acquire substantial booty (Keen, 1994:27). When the Mahdi government was overturned by the forces of Britain and Egypt in 1898, there was a renewed commitment by the Anglo-Egyptian Government to suppress slavery, at least in theory (Keen, 1994). In early 1900s, British colonial rule was faced with opposition from Dinka and other southern groups because of its attempt to reduce administrative expenditure and to harness southern resources with forced labor and heavy livestock taxes (Collins, 1971; Alier, 1990; Keen, 1994).

The southern opposition was quelled by large-scale of destruction and devastation of the Dinka areas and confiscation of Dinka cattle; this repression allowed the government to soften its commitment to the Dinka to suppress slavery; it therefore allowed domestic slavery in Kordofan to appease the Baggara Arab tribes. The softened position of the Anglo-Egyptian government over slavery encouraged Messiriya Humr Arab tribes to attack Twic Dinka of Bahr el Ghazal in 1906 and Rizeigat Arab tribes to attack Malwal Dinka of Bahr el Ghazal in 1908. British officials argued that such raids were to be tolerated since the Dinka were resisting the Anglo-Egyptian government (Henderson, 1939; Keen, 1994).

### *Native Administration, 1920s – 1950s*

The second period of the exploitation of the communities of Bahr el Ghazal region, from the early 1920s to the late 1950s under Anglo-Egyptian rule (Keen, 1994:31), saw concerted efforts by tribal and central leaders to construct some degree of protection against directly human-made famine. The then southern Sudan was partially integrated into the Sudanese state and the priority of Anglo-Egyptian rule was to provide protection to the southern Sudanese against exploitation by northern Sudanese as well as protecting the weaker southern peoples against the militarily stronger ones, particularly the Nuer (Johnson, 1989). This significant shift in the policy of the Anglo-Egyptian administration towards the southern Sudanese in general and the Dinka in particular was mainly triggered by the wholesale rebellion of the Dinka of Bahr el Ghazal in 1922.

During this period the Anglo-Egyptian administration learned from its experience of quelling rebellious peoples in southern Sudan with punitive raids in the early 1900s; it adopted instead a collaborative approach by involving the 'traditional leaders' so as to secure the obedience of their followers to British rule. According to Keen (1994:32) such a system of indirect rule was held to be preferable to the creation of an indigenous educated class to swell the British bureaucracy. This system of indirect rule, known as Native Administration, not only used its judicial and executive powers to build a loyal following but also came to provide the southern Sudanese with a genuine political voice and with some degree of protection against famine (Keen, 1994:33).

In Bahr el Ghazal, Upper Nile, Darfur and Kordofan the Native Administration of Dinka, Nuer and Baggara Arab tribes, together with local authorities and security forces managed to establish a system that carefully regulated grazing and minimized tribal disputes by means of annual tribal conferences. The Native Administration managed in 1924 to resolve the long-standing border dispute between Malwal Dinka of Bahr el Ghazal and Rizeigat Arab tribes of western Sudan (Keen, 1994).

### *Counterinsurgency Warfare, 1950s – 1990s*

The third phase of the history of the exploitation of the communities of Bahr el Gahazal was the post-independence period till the late

1980s during which the system of protection against famine paradoxically began to weaken (Keen, 1994:36). Despite the departure of the British and the eruption of the first civil war, the system of Native Administration continued to provide a measure of protection at least at local level till the mid-1960s.

The 'southern' resistance against central government started, with Equatoria as its epicentre, in 1955, even before the formal independence of the Sudan in 1956. According to Sanderson and Sanderson (1981) the Dinka started identifying themselves with southern rebels during the first civil war, probably as a result of the government's failure to address famine in Bahr el Ghazal in 1959 and three years of devastating floods in the Bor Dinka area in the early 1960s. Even when the first civil war spread to Bahr el Ghazal from Equatoria, some traditional leaders in northern Bahr el Ghazal, such as the chiefs of the Ngok Dinka, played a delicate balancing game in the hope of providing protection to the civil population. By the mid-1960s the increasingly close identification of the Ngok Dinka with the rebels tended to erode their rights to state protection; Messiriya raids on Ngok Dinka villages became commonplace, and little action to prevent these raids was taken by the police and the army, who became instead involved themselves (Deng, 1986; Keen, 1994).

According to Johnson (1989b:482) these raids, combined with declining veterinary services during the civil war, drastically reduced Nilotic cattle population; this made local people vulnerable to natural disasters, and resulted in recurrent human-made famines in the 1960s. According to Keen (1994:41), these recurrent human-made famines were accompanied by increasing abuse of those who migrated to the north and who were denied protection by the state. In 1965, for example, seventy-two southern Sudanese who had sought protection at Babanousa police station in western Sudan were burned to death by a crowd of local women and children in the presence of armed police (Saeed, 1982).

Despite large-scale cattle raiding and abuses of the southerners by both Baggara Arab tribes and the army, the central government did not encourage Baggara Arab tribes raiding and the Native Administration was still providing mechanisms for conflict resolution until 1969, when a military regime took power. The Native Administration in the north was abolished in 1971 and a new local government drawn from 'progressive' and 'modern' forces was established (Karam, 1980). During the 1970s the local government system failed to build good working relationships with traditional political leaders in southern Darfur and Kordofan and subsequently reduced the effectiveness of cross-border disputes settlement (Mawson, 1990:140). This marginalisation of the traditional political leaders, together with the drought that affected western Sudan, particularly the areas of Misseriya and Rizeigat in 1985, and resulted in famine, triggered again the raiding of Dinka areas.

The poor harvest and failed pastures of 1984–85 forced Rizeigat and Misseriya Arab tribes to sell their remaining cattle to merchants in western Sudan for the livestock markets in the major cities such as Omdurman. Impoverished Rizeigat Arab tribes also travelled among the Malwal Dinka selling cattle, donkeys and horses in order to buy grain; and other Rizeigat and Misseriya Arab tribes, however, acquired cattle by raiding into northern Bahr el Ghazal (Mawson, 1990:140). The cattle raids took place throughout 1983–1985, but in the latter part of 1985 the Dinka experienced a dramatic intensification of such raiding by Rizeigat and Misseriya Arab tribes. The raiding parties, sometimes numbering hundreds of individuals on horseback, attacked Dinka villages in the north of Awiel, Gok Macar and around Abyei with considerable savagery and abducted children and women.

Although stealing cattle continued to be the central purpose of the raids, many attacks were conducted witha degree of violence that suggests that destroying the Dinka communities and confiscation of their land were also aims (Mawson, 1990:142). These raids resulted in Dinka abandoning their territory, particularly areas far north; Dinka villages and cattle camps were destroyed, Dinka herds were ravaged, and not less than 30 per cent of the population fled to the towns and cities of northern Sudan. Others took what remained of their herds to the southern Jur river, and not less than 5 per cent died as a result of the raids or as casualties of famine.

### *Murahaleen Phenomenon, 1980s*

The second civil war in the Sudan was mainly triggered by the cumulative grievances experienced in the early 1980s by the Sudanese people in general and by the people of southern Sudan and marginalized areas of southern Kordofan and southern Blue Nile in particular. These grievances include political marginalization, economic deprivation, abrogation of the 1972 Addis Ababa Peace Agreement, border disputes, disputes over Jonglei canal and access to oil reserves, and gross abuses of basic human rights. Unlike the first civil war, the resistance to the central government started in Upper Nile and in the region of Bahr el Ghazal. The people of northern Bahr el Ghazal in particular started organizing their resistance in 1981 – before the formation of the SPLA in 1983 in response to their local grievances, and in particular the failure of central government to provide the necessary protection.

This early start is not surprising since the rural people of Malual, Abiem, Twic and Ngok Dinka in northern Bahr el Ghazal and Ruweng Dinka in northern Upper Nile – the central borderlands between north and southern Sudan – have been among those most seriously affected by the policies of central government and the activities of its proxy forces (Murahaleen). When the SPLA was formed in 1983 with clear national slogans, the people of northern Bahr el Ghazal, Abyei Ngok Dinka and Ruweng Dinka were the first to join it, their overriding motive being to gain arms and training in order to protect their lands from Rizeigat and Misseriya. This attempt proved to be in vain: the SPLA effectively reached northern Bahr el Ghazal in early 1987 but its priority was its national objective, and the area was left increasingly vulnerable to the raids of Murahaleen as most of the youth had joined the SPLA, taking with them all their locally acquired light weapons.

The genesis of the recurrent vulnerability in the Bahr el Ghazal region has been described by Mawson (1990:138):

> *Successive Sudanese governments have used proxy forces, so-called militias, as integral part of their war with the rebel SPLA. The Rizeigat and Misseriya of South Darfur and South Kordofan created armed bands, known as Murahaleen, in order to raid cattle from the Dinka to their south. Massive raids have depopulated swathes of territory south of Bahr el-Arab, killing tens of thousands of people and leading to the destruction and displacement of unknown numbers of others. Famine in western Sudan fueled the early raids, but*

> *the scale of the devastation wrought from 1985 onwards was the result of government complicity and assistance. More recently, since the coming to power of the current military government in Khartoum in June 1989, the relationship between the army and the Murahaleen has beenformalized through the creation of Popular Defense Forces.*

The phenomenon of the Murahaleen emerged as successive governments, following the overthrow of the Nimeri regime by popular uprising in 1985, made desperate attempts to contain the military successes of the SPLA. The Transitional Military Council (TMC), which replaced the Nimeri regime, included some members who had close personal, business and political links with merchants in western Sudan and considered the western Sudanese cattle raiders to be a suitable proxy force to fight a cheap counter-insurgency campaign against the SPLA (Mawson, 1990:145). A series of meetings were held in western Sudan, involving at least one senior member of the TMC, militia leaders and key merchants, which sanctioned Murahaleen raids on Dinka. Similar meetings were held at the same time with the leaders of the Bul Nuer pro-government Anyanya Two, and it was agreed that the Murahaleen would not raid the Bul Nuer and in return the Anyanya Two would supply arms to Arab militia (Mawson, 1990:145).

When a coalition government was formed by the Umma party and the Democratic Unionist party after the April 1986 elections, the Umma Party which derived much of its support from rural western Sudan and much of its finance from wealthy western Sudanese merchants, some of whom were involved in the livestock trade fueled by raiding Dinka lands, was very keen to support the Murahaleen (Mawson, 1990:145). Umma supporters in the armed forces assisted the Murahaleen as a way of building up a militia loyal to the Umma party. According to Mawson (1990:145) most of the devastating raids on Bahr el Ghazal occurred during 1986–1987, and coincided with the breakdown of peace talks between the Umma party and the SPLA in August 1986.

Immediately one year after the formation of the coalition, a massacre of over 1,000 displaced Dinka occurred at Ad-Daien in western Sudan. The report into the massacre that was produced in July 1987 by human rights activists unequivocally declared that the government was 'at the root' of the massacre and accused it of having 'squarely introduced the Rizeigat ethnic group into its war with the SPLA' (Mahmud and Baldo, 1987: 19). In response to the report, the Umma party gave contradictory remarks. While Sadiq al-Mahdi, the leader of the Umma, said in August that popular efforts were necessary for the protection of the area, in September Fadalla Burma, a former member of the TMC and Minister of State for Defence, denied any government involvement. Only four days later Umar Nur al-Daiem, then Minister of Agriculture, announced that the government 'was arming and would continue to arm all those willing to fightthe rebels' (Mawson, 1990: 146).

Knowing that the government was intending to formalize the existence of the Murahaleen and was not taking serious steps towards reaching peace, in February 1989 the armed forces issued an ultimatum to the government asking it to take serious actions towards peace and to end its policies which threatened the cohesion of the armed forces. As the army was on the verge of overthrowing the civilian government, the prime minister, announced that the government intended 'to work for the dissolution of armed groups and to absorb them into civil defence under the leadership of the armed forces'. The Umma party was planning to incorporate into the Popular Defence Forces between 10,000 and 15,000 men and gave a clear indication that it would give priority to the Murahaleen.

The military coup in June 1989, which brought to power a fundamentalist-dominated government, interrupted the creation of the Popular Defense Forces. The new government was swift to indicate its continuing support for the general policy of using militias (Mawson, 1990:146). This was not surprising as the leader of the military government, former president Bashir, was well known to Murahaleen from his 1988–1989 military position in western Sudan and Bentiu.

Renewed SPLA military activities in the Nuba mountains in 1989 eroded Misseriya access to pastures in Dinka areas and threatened government control over the mountains. This provided the right moment for the government to resurrect its plans for Popular Defense Forces, and in November 1989 it promulgated a Popular Defense Act (Mawson, 1990:146). The government eventually managed to co-opt the Murahaleen to the Popular Defense Forces, and it used them effectively during the 1990s as one of its important counterinsurgency strategies.

### *Counterinsurgency Warfare, 1990s*

The main feature of this period was the adoption by the GOS of insidious modern counterinsurgency strategies with the apparent intention of controlling effectively a potentially hostile population in the SPLA- controlled areas. The SPLA had been describing its relationship with the people using Mao Tse Tung's famous description of the guerrilla as a fish swimming in the water of the people, and the GOS decided to use counterinsurgency strategies that would drain away water to enble it to catch the fish with ease.

According to de Waal (1993:36) the most systematic exponent of counterinsurgency theories has been the French military. One of the first theoreticians was its General Lyautey who described a guerrilla as 'a plant' which 'grows only in certain ground ... the most efficient method is to render the ground unsuitable for him'.In relation to the Algerian war, Lyautey described this strategy as follows:

> *Anything that could facilitate the existence of the guerrillas in any way, or which could conceivably be used by them ... must be systematically destroyed or brought in. All inhabitants and livestock must be evacuated from the [guerrillas'] refuge area. When they leave, the intervention troops must not onlyhave destroyed the [guerrilla] bands, but must leave behind them an area empty of all resources and absolutely uninhabitable. (de Waal, 1993:36).*

According to de Waal (1993:36), counterinsurgency warfare in a poor area is tantamount to creating famine through population displacement, control of trade especially in foodstuffs, and control of movement of people. In addition to these components of counterinsurgency, particularly in a complex political emergency, denial of access to the needy population in the rebel-held areas and direct destruction of properties or looting of assets are equally important.

During the 1990s, the GOS substantially increased its military expenditure as shown in Figure 5 as a clear indication of its commitment to wage intensive counterinsurgency warfare in southern Sudan. Whilst the deficit financing extensively used by the government resulted in inflation never experienced in the history of the Sudan, military expenditure as a proportion of the annual revenues reached about 35 per cent during the 1990s, the highest level recorded since 1978.

The pattern of devastation and destruction in Bahr el Ghazal during the 1990s resembled that in the era of Turko-Egyptian rule and the Mahdi. Instead of relying on the Murahaleen and Anyanya Two, the GOS effectively used a divide-and-rule policy and managed to penetrate the SPLA, which resulted in a split in 1991 and the formation of the South Sudan Independent Army (SSIA) as another feature of Anyanya Two. Later another faction, called SPLA- United, under the command of Kerubino Bol and Lam Akol, separated from the SSIA.

All these small political and military groups did not have significant implications for the balance of power in Khartoum, as they were simply war on the cheap and a way of opposing the SPLA without undue expenditure of northern Sudanese lives and government money (Mawson, 1990). The main military and political agenda of the Islamic government in the Sudan during the 1990s was to weaken the SPLA by destroying the Dinka communities, the main supporters of the SPLA, through counterinsurgency measures to be carried out by Murahaleen and smaller southern factions.

*Figure 5: Sudan Defence Expenditure, Revenue and Deficit, 1978–1998*

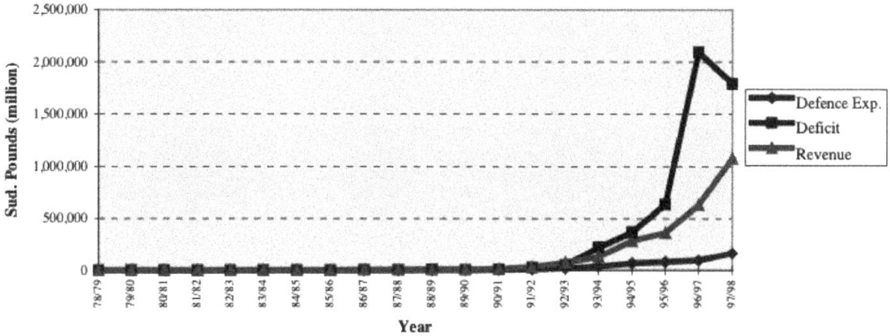


*Source: Economic Intelligence Unit*

The SSIA, which was predominately supported by Nuer, was incited by the government to raise tribal slogans and to wage vigorous tribal war against the Dinka community in Upper Nile. In the last months of 1991 and the beginning of 1992, forces of the SSIA attacked the Bor Dinka in Upper Nile; the attacks resulted in horrific devastation never before experienced in the history of tribal conflict in southern Sudan. It has been estimated by some journalists that thousands of people, mainly children and women, were massacred in a horrific manner comparable to Al-Dien massacre.

An average family lost at least two members and some entire families perished. Besides this massive loss of human lives, all the livestock (sometimes estimated to be around 60,000 head of cattle) in the Bor area were looted or slaughtered. People who survived the massacre (estimated to be around 200,000 persons) were displaced into Bahr el Ghazal, Equatoria region or the neighbouring countries of Kenya and Uganda. Ruweng, Ngok and Padang Dinka in the Upper Nile region experienced similar attacks by the SSIA forces which resulted in loss of life, looting of livestock, and massive displacement of communities.

In 1993 in Bahr el Ghazal, the militia forces of Murahaleen, Nuer and Kerubino Bol started a series of vigorous campaigns and continuous attacks on the northern Bahr el Ghazal region with full military and logistical support from GOS military garrisons in Abyei and Gogrial towns. While the Murahaleen attacked Dinka areas during the dry season, the Nuer and Dinka forces were there all year round. With weak and unorganized SPLA forces in northern Bahr el Ghazal (except Awiel and Wau), by 1997 almost the entire population of Abyei, Twic and Gogrial counties, with estimated 600,000 persons, was displaced internally more than three times yearly and some moved with their cattle southwards to safe areas in Tonj and Rumbek counties; all houses were burnt, livestock and grains were looted and crops in the field were destroyed.

According to SRRA estimates, almost 60 per cent of the livestock population in northern Bahr el Ghazal was lost during the 1990s as a result of counterinsurgency activities and more than 40 per cent of families lost all their livestock. It was rare to see goats or sheep or even chickens in Abyei, Twic and Gograial counties as there has been a massive depopulation of small livestock. The abduction of children and women for forced labor and slavery became commonplace in northern Bhar el Ghazal; it was practiced by the Murahaleen and paradoxically by the Dinka and Nuer forces as well on their own people.

While Murahaleen forces used the abducted children and women for forced labor and slavery, the Dinka and Nuer forces used them for forced labor such as carrying their booty, and forced marriage. It is estimated that during the 1990s more than 10,000 children and women might have been subjected to forced labor or slavery in northern Bahr el Ghazal. The militia forces of Murahaleen and Kerubino developed a lucrative culture of looting and raiding in the area, which lured some SPLA soldiers to join them and tempted some defectors from the SPLA to start looting grain and small livestock from the civil population.

### *Changing Rural Livelihoods and Economy in the 1990s*

A clear understanding of the effects of war on the livelihoods and food security of the communities of Bahr el Ghazal, particularly Dinka as the largest ethnic group, entails a brief description of their tradition and culture. According to the 1956 census, the Dinka were the largest ethnic group in southern Sudan and constituted about 12 per cent of Sudan's total population. The area inhabited by Dinka was estimated by the 1983 census to be about 13 per cent of the total area of the Sudan.

According to the 1983 census, northern Bahr el Ghazal was one of the most densely settled Dinka areas, with the second-highest population density (28.7 per square mile) after Lakes (El-Bohayrat) (30.2 persons per square mile) in southern Sudan. The Dinka live overwhelmingly in rural societies with an extreme physical environment ranging from a wet season (May–October) to extensive flooding and a marked dry season during the remainder of the year involving drought and desiccation (Mawson, 1990:139). The area is virtually flat, a mixture of open grassland,swamps (*toic*) and savannah forest.

The culture of the Dinka, like other Nilotic groups, is centred around basic values, with procreation as the foundation of and yardstick for stratification (Deng, 1973:85). According to Deng (1973:86), procreation is only a starting point for a complex set of values such as affection, respect, rectitude, and the power of persuasiveness which rank higher than material value. In reinforcing this observation Keen (1994:19) remarks that Dinka have sometimes valued the maintenance of their culture and economic independence more highly than they valued their own short-term consumption; they appear to put a higher value on their way of life than on life itself.

At the core of this complex set of values is what Dinka call *cieng,* a concept of ideal human relations which is reinforced by the ideals of human dignity expressed in the Dinka word *dheeng* (Deng, 1973:86). The strong commitment of Dinka to preserve their tradition and culture as a way of confirming the existence of their ancestors, and contributing to the culture of their progeny, led some observers to describe them as conservative, resistant to change and proud. Major Titherington (1949) who worked among Dinka under the Anglo-Egyptian condominium observed the following:

> *One of the determinants of the rapid and slow spread of Christianity in the South has been provided bythe contrast between seminomadic cattle-breeding Nilotic tribes (Shilluk, Nuer and Dinka) and the settled agriculturists. The life of the former is bound up with a cow economy, this animal being a veritable god. They are intensely conservative and very proud of their civilization. They have acted as a bastion against the penetration of Islam by having proved impervious to its seduction. (Deng, 1973:87).*

This observation is also shared by Audrey Butt who made the following observations about the Nilotes in 1952:

> *They consider their country the best in the world and everyone inferior to themselves. For this reason they … scorn European and Arab culture … Their attitude toward any authority that would coerce them is one of touchiness, pride, and reckless hatred of submission, and is ready to defend himself and his property from the inroads of others. They are self-reliant, brave fighters, turbulent and aggressive, and are extremely conservative in their aversion from innovation and interference. (Deng, 1973:87).*

According to Deng (1973:90) the Nilotes' resistance to change, their cultural ethnocentrism and their isolation have been exaggerated enormously: they have been exposed to external influences for centuries and some of the cultural elements they have adopted have become integral part of their culture. With modern education and increased cross-cultural interaction, Nilotes have demonstrated a high degree of adaptability to change such as money, war, and the State that was never predicted by outsiders (Deng, 1973:90, Hutchinson, 1996).

***Rural Livelihoods and Economy before War in 1983***

The concept of livelihood is central in understanding rural vulnerability and susceptibility to food insecurity and famine. Despite its recognition in development studies, the definition of livelihood has been elusive with no consensus. Ellis (2000:10) recognizes livelihood as a process and defines it in terms of assets, activities including income, and access to these assets. In the Dinka language the term livelihood is synonymous with "*peer*" that literally means "a living". Based on the definition provided by Ellis (2000) and the literal Dinka meaning of livelihood, Kuol (2021:31) defines livelihood as *"A livelihood consists of the assets, the livelihood activities and the access to these, that together constitute a means of a living (peer) of the individual or household".*

The livelihood analysis provides the right 'lens" through which to monitor food security, to plan disaster mitigation, emergency response and long-term development. Such analysis will require appropriate and relevant information about how people and communities live and to inform any intervention that is appropriately designed to strengthen the existing local livelihood strategies rather than undermining them. Based on various livelihood information gathered during the war, the United States Agency for International Development (USAID), the Famine Early Warning Systems Network (FEWS NET) and Save the Children UK (SCUK), with assistance from the South Sudan Centre for Census, Statistics and Evaluation (SSCCSE) prepared livelihood zones map for South Sudan (see Map 3) (SSCCSE, 2006).

*Map 3: South Sudan – Livelihood Zones*

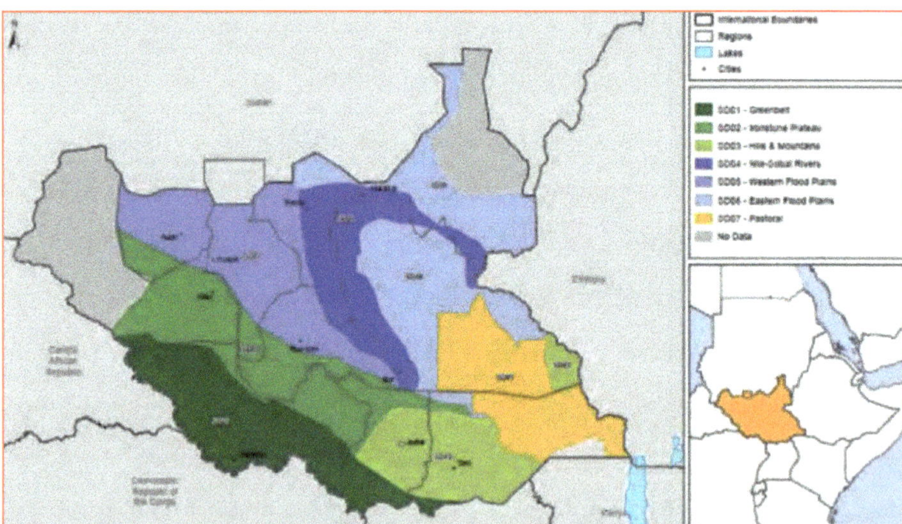


Source: South Sudan Centre for Statistics and Evaluation and Save the Children UK, *Southern Sudan Livelihood Profiles: A Guide for Humanitarian and Development Planning*, 2006.

The Livelihood Zone Map shows the division of southern Sudan into relatively homogeneous zones, defined according to a livelihoods framework. These livelihood zones are defined as areas within which people share broadly the same pattern of livelihood such as the same production system - agriculture or pastoralism - and the same patterns of trade and exchange. Each zone has its unique profile that describes the major characteristics of each zone, including a brief differentiation of different wealth groups as well as the major hazards and the relative capacity of different types of households in different places to withstand these hazards are also identified (SSCCSE, 2006:9).

The Dinka communities of Bahr el Ghazal fall within the livelihood zone called "Western Flood Plains". In this zone, livestock, crops, wild foods and fish are the main food sources. However, the livelihood activities in northwestern counties of Aweil, Gogrial and Twic are slightly different from those in the southern counties of Rumbek, Tonj and Yirol (SSCCSE, 2006:29). For example, while seasonal migration of households to northern Sudan for labour and petty trade is significant in the northwestern counties, the southern counties are characterized by larger numbers of livestock and significant exchange and trading activities. The poor households increase their reliance on fish, wild foods and, to some extent, labour, petty trade and tobacco sales during difficult years (SSCCSE, 2006).

Before the eruption of civil war in 1983, the Dinka economy was based on transhumant animal husbandry, agriculture, fishing and trade and was less dependent on wild food. Labour migration in particular used to play an important role particularly in northern Bahr el Ghazal. The monetisation of Dinka economy in the 1960s and the 1970s encouraged a new pattern of labour migration, particularly to southern Kordofan and southern Darfur. This labour migration fitted flexibly into the cultivation pattern of the Dinka: they finished with their fields first and could take advantage of the later rains in Darfur and Kordofan. Besides its direct economic value, labour migration reduced the sale of cattle to buy essential commodities in the markets. There were also opportunities for young Dinka girls and boys to obtain employment as domestic servants in most major towns in northern Sudan. According to Ryle, the Dinka and especially the Nuer came to provide a significant proportion of the construction workers in Khartoum. Wage labour became a major means of earning money and thus acquiring livestock and marrying (Ryle, 1989:13).

The trading between south and north through Arab traders (*jellaba),* though resented by southerners for the apparent excessive exploitation it involved, greatly helped in making essential goods available to the various parts of southern Sudan. In times of famine, the *jellaba,* driven by profit maximisation, would take all possible risks to rush grain to the affected areas. The fact that the 1962 famine in Torit (see Table 6) was locally called *itular* (white grain brought by northern traders) is clear evidence that north–south trading had some positive role in addressing food shortages. Another example comes from Abyei where acute shortage of food was experienced in 1966: the year became known locally as *runrakieb* (year of bread) as people were rescued mainly by purchasing bread on the market.

### The Wartime Rural Livelihoods and Economy

The World Food Programme in conjunction with SCF (UK) used the food economy approach to assess the adaptive livelihood strategies local people used during war, as shown in Figure 6. According to FEWS

(1997:5), the civil conflict curtailed trade, and households could no longer rely on markets for their food. With their herds destroyed by raiding, local residents had increased their reliance on fishing, wild foods, and crops. The drastic change that occurred in people's livelihood strategies is illustrated in Figure 6, which shows the rough magnitude of the strategic choices made by residents in one county in northern Bahr el Ghazal region. Though Figure 6 is only a rough gauge, it shows a general trend of the effects of war on people's livelihoods and access to food.

However, the food economy methodology has underestimated the role of markets and concealed the variation in adaptation of livelihood strategies adopted by various communities of Bahr el Ghazal during prolonged violent conflict. This methodology was on and off with limited monitoring and predictive abilities, issues that are discussed more in later chapters. Also, the communities of Bahr el Ghazal were exposed to different degrees of livelihood shocks during the prolonged civil war and had subsequently adapted differently their livelihood strategies.

Based on the local monitoring of the livelihoods in Bahr el Ghazal, the changing livelihoods during prolonged violent conflict is depicted as shown in Figure 6a. Unlike the assessment of food economy methodology of the adjustment in livelihoods during war, the local perspectives suggested overall contraction of livelihood activities with exception of farming and gathering of wild foods, while trading and exchange did not disappear.

Despite generalization of the changing livelihoods in Figures 6 and 6a, there are variation among communities in Bahr el Ghazal in the way they adjusted their livelihoods during wartime. While the civil

*Figure 6: Changing Livelihoods in Bahr el Ghazal, Outsiders Perspective*

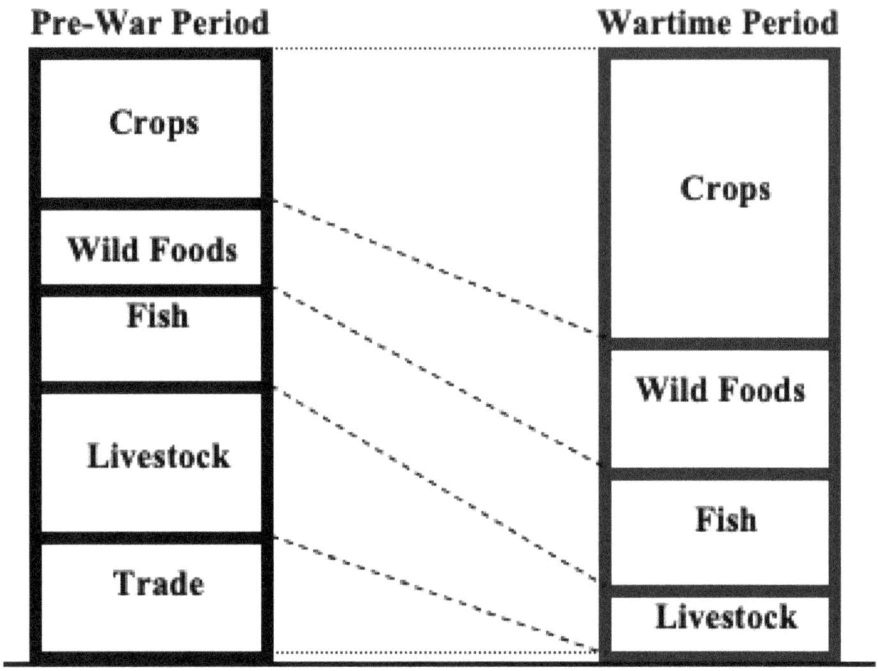


*Source: WFP/SCF/FEWS/USAID*

war between the GoS and SPLM affected generally all communities in South Sudan, the way the war was conducted in terms of insurgency and counterinsurgency warfare affected communities differently, particularly in Bahr el Ghazal region (Deng, 2010b). In other words, while the conventional warfare between the SPLA and Sudan Armed Forces (SAF) created generic livelihood shock, the counterinsurgency warfare created idiosyncratic risk (specific), as communities and households became exposed to different and specific type of counterinsurgency warfare.

*Figure 6a: Changing Livelihoods in Bahr el Ghazal, Local Perspective*

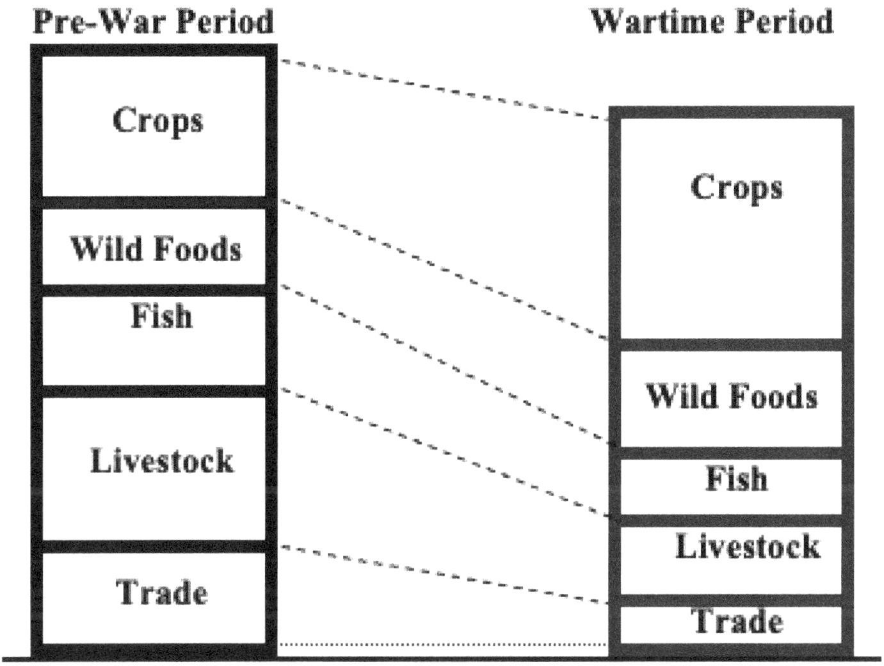


*Source: SRRA Monitoring Unit*

For example, the households in Abyei county who were exposed to exogenous counterinsurgency warfare (Arab militias) were able to increase or maintain livelihood activities such as farming, exchange, fishing, kinship and gathering (see Figure 6b). In particular, the households in Abyei invested in social capital and kinship as one of the effective livelihood strategies to confront the Arab militia counterinsurgency warfare (Deng, 2010a). On the other hand, the households in Gogrial county who were exposed to endogenous counterinsurgency warfare (Dinka militia) became increasing reliant on gathering, exchange and fishing, while their main livelihood activities such as livestock rearing, and farming contracted considerable during civil war in the 1990s (see Figure 6c).

*Figure 6b: Changing Livelihoods in Abyei*

*Figure 6c: Changing Livelihoods in Gogrial*

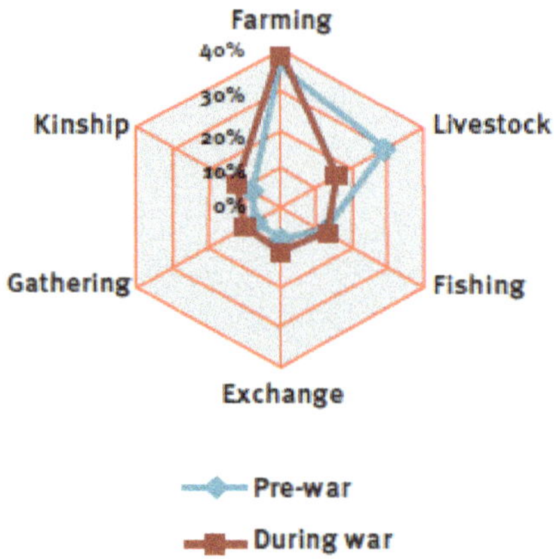


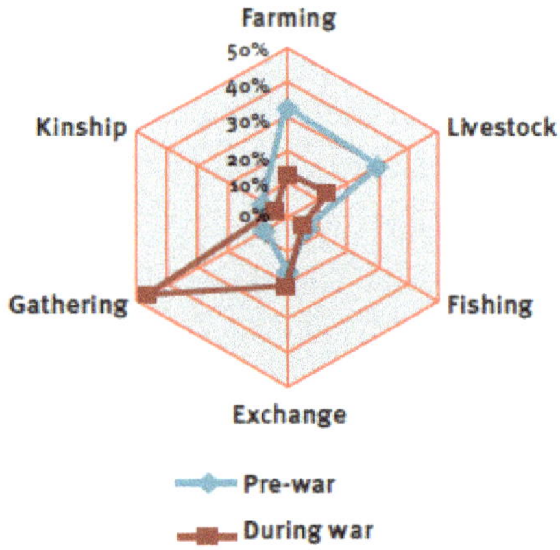


*Source: Deng (2013)*

To elaborate more on the general trend of the strategic livelihood choices made by households in Bahr el Ghazal region, each livelihood activity adopted during civil war is examined separately.

### *Crop Production*

Before the civil war in 1983, the households in Bahr el Ghazal became too dependent on the markets for accessing grain, particularly after considerable trade integration took place between north and south after relative peace during the Addis Ababa Peace Agreement (1972-1983) that ended the first civil war (1955-1972). The Arab traders *(jellaba),* together with other southern traders, used to bring grains from northern Sudan at lower prices. The monetisation of Dinka economy and increased opportunities for wage labour during the relative peace of the 1972 Peace Agreement made the Dinka dependent on bought grain and greatly reduced the general reliance on local food production. However, there were some exceptions: some few farmers, particularly in Abyei and the Awiel area in northern Bahr el Ghazal, increased their acreage under cultivation considerably in response to increased demand for grain by the growing urban population in the major towns of Bahr el Ghazal region.

During the war, as a result of limited trading between north and south, limited labour migration, the drastic depletion of livestock through counterinsurgency warfare raids, and the lack of wage labour and employment opportunities, local residents of Bahr el Ghazal became increasingly reliant on their own-food production (direct entitlement). The area cultivated increased considerably, from almost one feddan (acre) before the current civil war to more than 1.5 feddans for an average household in most counties of Bahr el Ghazal. With increased counterinsurgency warfare in northern Bahr el Ghazal, particularly in the Abyei area, people resorted to sowing and cultivating their crops by moonlight so as to avoid raids during the day. It is remarkable that in most counties of Bahr el Ghazal, the resident population adopted the ox-plough for cultivation – this used to be taboo before the war because of the special respect given to livestock. Unlike before the war, crop production became a source for buying cattle and even for marriage. With intensification of Dinka counterinsurgency warfare in Gogrial country, the households were pushed to pure farming by necessity (Deng, 2010b).

### *Wild Foods Gathering*

Before the 1983 civil war, the role of wild foods was declining in importance because of the monetisation of the Dinka economy, wage labour, and modernisation. During the 1950s and the early 1960s, education was largely woven around people's life and culture with a well-balanced reconciliation between modernisation and tradition. The traditional life cycle of Dinka is a continuous process of acquiring, experiencing, possessing and sharing traditional knowledge and values. Traditionally, wild foods play an important role in Dinka life, not only during famine but also in normal times. The Dinka interaction with their environment, particularly their physical environment, starts at an early stage of childhood. Small boys spend most of their time looking after cattle in pastures and forests, during which they get most of their snacks from the environment. Girls accompany their mothers as they collect wild foods and firewood in nearby forests.

The Dinka's relationship with their environment was greatly affected in the 1970s and the 1980s as a result of intensive cross-cultural interaction, the drastic monetisation of the local economies, and the modern education which disguised local traditions and cultures and tended to dissociate children from them. The British colonial policies had kept tribes isolated and tried to preserve traditional cultures, but the successive post-independence national governments in the Sudan had consistently adopted policies of ethnic cleansing and assimilation which eroded the role of traditional African cultures.

Paradoxically the war had resurrected and renewed the traditional relationship between the Dinka and their environment. Because of the limited options available for survival, the importance of wild foods during war has been recognised and the need to preserve local knowledge of them has become a priority. During the 1998 famine in Bahr el Ghazal, wild foods contributed more than any other food sources, including relief food, in saving the lives of large numbers of famine victims because of its unique characteristic of being easily available and affordable by all. The importance of wild foods in Dinka life was made conspicuous in contemporary songs. Atiam Thon, a Dinka poet living in Gogrial county, lamented how the abandoning of Dinka tradition, particularly the traditional reliance on wild food and increasing reliance on town life, has made the Dinka increasingly vulnerable to famine:

> *You our people,*
> *You have abandoned the collection of weeds. Let me show you these weeds.*
> *Dig (agony) in rocky land,*
> *Add also apam … and also beleak … And the tree called aneet;*
> *Thou is put in water and then eaten and tastes bitter and sweet as well;That is what is called survival.*
> *Then cuei is also soaked … and kei is uprooted,*
> *Ajuet is pounded and akuatha also,*
> *And also aruaja are uprooted … whatever warms the mouth All these have been abandoned by Monyjang [Dinka];*
> *They turned their life to the towns. Now you see with your eyes,*
> *And hear with your ears,*
> *The land has come to an end.*

Also, from Table 6 it is apparent that the naming of famines after wild foods was common after the eruption of the 1983 civil war; particularly among the famines thus named were the 1985 famine in Yirol (*Nyok*), the 1988 famine in Rumbek (*Apat*) and the 1986 famine in Bor (*Apat*). This naming shows the important role played by wild foods in the 1983 civil war as the most attainable coping mechanism.

Some wild foods that are available and collected by the Dinka during normal and bad times in Bahr el Ghazal are listed in Table 7.

Comparison of the various types of wild foods with sorghum/millet, which has about 326 kilocalories per 100g, makes clear the nutritional value associated with these wild foods. These wild foods are available in various seasons, and particularly during the rainy season when the stocks of harvested sorghum are lowest (May–August). Interestingly the community perception of these types of wild food does not conform to their nutritional values. For example, *ajuet*, which has about 580 kilocalories per 100g is perceived by communities as distress food. This difference between the community perception of wild foods and their nutritional value is extremely important in early warning systems. The community perception of various wild foods also varies from area to area and from group to group. In certain areas one type of wild food is perceived as normal; in other areas a similar type of wild food is considered to be distress food or is not eaten at all.

***Table 7: Some Types of Wild Foods Collected in Bahr el Ghazal, 1998***

| Local name (Dinka) | Community perception of year of collection | Description and/or scientific name | 5ilocal-ories per 100g | Months of collection |
|---|---|---|---|---|
| Seeds/kernels | | | | |
| Akuedha | Normal | Mixed grass seed | 391 | August–Sep. |
| Amijuong | Distress | Mixed grass seed | 370 | February–April |
| Gor | Distress | Nymphaea sp. | 380 | March–April |

| Akondok | Normal | Boscia senegalensis | 150 | April |
|---|---|---|---|---|
| Cuei | Distress | Tamarindus indica | 380 | February–April |
| Thou | Normal | Balanites aegyptiaa | 567 | December–February |
| Ajuet | Distress | Caparis sp. | 581 | April–May |
| Akon | Distress | Parkia bigloboso | 499 | March–April |
| Tubers/roots | | | | |
| Ngaana | Distress | Discorea sp. | 300 | July–August |
| Touk | Normal | Borrassus aethiopicm | 213 | April–July |
| Fruit/berries | | | | |
| Dhiot (fresh) | Normal | Nauclea latifolia | 59 | November–December |
| Dhiot (cake) | Normal | Nauclea latifolia | 303 | November–December |
| Cum (fresh) | Normal | Diospyros mespilifom | 125 | November–January |
| Cuei (dry) | Normal | Tamarindus indica | 250 | February–April |
| Lang (dry) | Normal | Ziziphus sp. | 300 | November–January |
| Ngap | Distress | Ficus sycomorous | 56 | July |
| Oil | | | | |
| Raak | Normal | Vitellaria paradoxa and Seeds from shea tree and | 895 | May–June |

*Source: SRRA Monitoring Unit and WFP*

Despite the advantages associated with wild foods, considerable costs, risks and side effects were also associated with their consumption as people started eating new wild foods during the famine. The frequency and intensity of consumption of wild foods and the methods used to process and prepare them determine the level of toxic components, which may have both immediate and long-term effects on people's health. For example, in eastern Equatoria which experienced famine in 1998, the communities at Lopit village who were faced with a severe food shortage became increasingly dependent on one type of wild food called *amalwa* (a famine wild food). Normally *amalwa* takes about six to seven hours to be cooked before it becomes suitable for consumption, but during 1998 people were forced to shorten the period of cooking which resulted in the poisoning and subsequent deaths of three people.

The intensity of usage and poor processing of normal wild foods such as wild yams resulted in the deaths of over twenty-one persons in Imehejek village and five in Lohutok village in Torit county from high levels of toxins; the deaths were at first blamed on cholera. In Lalanga village in Torit county, 141 residents were affected in April 1998 by poisoning related to poor processing and intensity of consumption of wild yams. This resulted in 119 patients being treated in May 1998 at the health centre; eleven patients died and about twenty-one patients were placed under close medical supervision in the health unit.

### *Livestock Rearing*

Before the 1983 civil war, livestock was the mainstay of the Dinka economy. During the era of strong Native Administration under

Anglo–Egyptian rule and the relative peace after the Addis Ababa Peace Agreement of 1972, the Dinka managed to restock considerably because of improved veterinary services. Improved employment opportunities with the regional government in southern Sudan and wage labour opportunities in northern Sudan reduced the need to sell livestock and instead increased livestock populations. The public servants in the regional government who were educated in the 1950s and the 1960s had special admiration and affection for cattle and invested a large portion of their savings in the acquisition of livestock. Though the life of the Dinka was not bound up with a cattle economy, nevertheless livestock constituted the core of their identity and social status.

During the 1983 civil war, livestock became a source of Dinka misery and increased vulnerability as they became targeted by counterinsurgency warfare. According to Keen (1994:19) it was precisely the resources of the Dinka that made them vulnerable to exploitative processes that threatened to destroy their way of life and remove their assets. Dinka became increasingly exposed to famines not because of their poverty but rather because of their livestock and their land. It is estimated that in northern Bahr el Ghazal at least 40 per cent of all households lost all their cattle as a result of continual raids since 1993. Although veterinary services improved, cattle rustling and raiding and the 1997 drought, along with restricted movement of cattle and distress slaughtering during the 1998 famine, all resulted in a drastic decline in the population of livestock.

Some cattle owners employed a wide range of strategies to mitigate the effects of escalating counterinsurgency warfare, off–taking, cattle rustling and raids. Some spread the increased risk by scattering cattle into various cattle camps or entrusting them to various individuals and keeping their herds small. Some cattle owners preferred to invest in social relationships by marrying into various families, thus reducingtheir herds to a manageable number. Others abandoned agricultural activities entirely and became pure pastoralists with an effective early information system to alert them to any potential raids.

Given the characteristics of cattle that made them direct targets of the counterinsurgency warfare, some non-poor households reverted to pure pastoralism livelihood (Deng, 2021:128). This group is an extremely high-risk-taking group and depends entirely on local markets to acquire grain. Other groups decided to migrate southwards to Tonj and Rumbek counties which were relatively peaceful. Deng (2010) finds that the non-poor households in Bahr el Ghazal became more susceptible to the raids of counterinsurgency warfare that made them more vulnerable than poor households.

### *Trade and Exchange*

There is no doubt that during the 1960s and the 1970s there was considerable expansion in trading between southern and northern Sudan. This was accompanied by an expansion in the public sector with the establishment of a regional government in southern Sudan which created a huge demand for modern goods which could only be obtained from northern Sudan. Private and public sector schemes, particularly agricultural and construction in northern Sudan, offered massive employment opportunities to southern Sudanese war veterans and returnees from the neighbouring countries. They also found the southern Sudanese labourers inexpensive and loyal.

These factors encouraged a proliferation of northern traders, particularly less efficient ones, in southern Sudan. The trading service industry developed an oligopolistic structure as northern traders established strong networks to control local markets, and the indigenous southern entrepreneurial initiatives suffered a great deal in such highly competitive environment. Though the southern regional authorities started to support some indigenous entrepreneurial initiatives, these were buried at early stage as they became damaged by excessive favouritism and became corrupt and inefficient.

During the 1980s in particular, when the civil war reached most parts of southern Sudan, free trade and movements to and from the areas of the fighting became limited, but there was a gradual growth of local markets in the areas under the SPLA. During the 1990s there was a proliferation of main markets with satellite markets in most parts of the areas under control of the SPLA. These main markets encouraged a gradual interaction between the traders in the SPLA and GOSs areas and began to convince the various fighting parties to allow free movement of traders. For example, in Awiel East county there was one main market called Warawar; this was the largest market in Bahr el Ghazal with northern traders bringing most essential goods for exchange with cattle and with the SPLA committed to provide security and to ensure free trading.

This market used to supply most markets in Bahr el Ghazal. The participants of Warawar market, particularly Dinka and Arab traders, moved beyond trading to peace initiatives and formed a peace committee to resolve low-level conflict. For example, in 1996 the market was attacked by the Arab Popular Defense Forces (PDF) which burned all the shops, looted goods and livestock, killed people and abducted twenty-nine children for slavery and forced labour. The Arab traders who were in the market during the attack took refuge with the Dinka and were provided with protection by the SPLA from some grieving Dinka families whose children were abducted or had family members killed by the PDF.

The market peace committee decided to send its Arab members to bring back the abducted children and they managed to bring all the children back except one. The trading activities between the government-held towns particularly Wau, Gogrial and Abyei and the areas under SPLA control were encouraged by both parties. These market activities helped a great deal during the famine, particularly those at Warawar and the GOS held town of Abyei, as people managed to buy grains.

There was also trading activity between Bahr el Ghazal and Uganda via Equatoria region with Dinka traders crossing a hundred miles to and from the northern Uganda border town of Arua. Dinka from Rumbek and Yirol in particular used to move cattle, mainly bulls, to Uganda and come back carrying on their heads second–hand clothes and medicine. Besides these trading activities there were also opportunities for wage labour within the region, particularly with Lou (Jur) in Wau county and Bongo communities in Tonj county. This account shows that trade and exchange did not vanish during the 1983 civil war but its contribution to livelihoods shrunk considerable in Bahr el Ghazal, but it persisted instead and even increased in some cases (Kuol, 2021:147).

# CHAPTER FOUR

## The Proximate Causes of the 1998 Famine

### *The Exogenous Shocks Leading to Failure of Food Entitlement and Famine*

The underlying causes of famine, particularly the trajectory of political vulnerability that changed and eroded means of livelihoods, as discussed in Chapter 3 were not sufficient by themselves to trigger the 1998 famine. However, these underlying causes of famine had made the livelihoods of the people of Bahr el Ghazal so vulnerable and susceptible to livelihood shocks such as drought and insecurity. The people of the Bahr el Ghazal region earn most of their livelihood, as discussed earlier, from crop production, animal husbandry, fishing, and wild foods. This makes own-food production or 'direct food entitlement' the mainstay of the people's food entitlement. Thus, the relative risk associated with 'direct food entitlement' constitutes one of the most important determinants of vulnerability to foodinsecurity in Bahr el Ghazal.

As 'direct food entitlement' in Bahr el Ghazal depends entirely on the level and pattern of climatic and security conditions, rainfall and insecurity are the most significant risk to people's food entitlement. Sen (1981:115) in his analysis of drought and famine in the Sahel argues that 'while there are factors other than the drought in the causation of the famine, it would be stupid to pretend that the drought was not seriously disruptive'. The rainfall and insecurity constituted the most common exogenous shocks to food entitlement in Bahr el Ghazal and became essential primary factors in famine causation.

On the basis of the household survey, the communities of Bahr el Ghazal identified the Dinka militias, the Arab militias and drought as the main risk events that confronted them in the 1990s (see Table 8). The conventional warfare between the government army and the rebels did not feature at the household level as one of the most important sources of risk that they faced during the 1990s. The households in Gogrial county in the centre of Bahr el Ghazal region, besides attaching unambiguous importance to endogenous counter-insurgency warfare (Dinka militias), they also assigned considerable importance (28%) to exogenous counterinsurgency (Arab militias). This clearly suggests that the households in Gogrial county were more exposed to both exogenous and endogenous counter-insurgency warfare as well as drought.

***Table 8: The Sources of Livelihood Risk in Bahr el Ghazal Region in the 1990s***

| Main Risk Events | Abyei | Gogrial | Cuiebet |
|---|---|---|---|
| Dinka Militias | 38 (18%) | 141 (69%) | 0 |
| Arab Militias | 170 (80.6%) | 57 (28%) | 0 |
| Drought | 3 (1.4%) | 7 (3%) | 99 (100%) |
| Total | 211 (100%) | 205 (100%) | 99 (100%) |

*Source: Deng (2008)*

The households in Abyei county in northern part of the region, were mainly exposed to exogenous counterinsurgency warfare (Arab militias) and to a lesser degree to Dinka militia and drought. The simultaneous exposure to both types of counterinsurgency warfare in the Gogrial county, and to a lesser degree in Abyei county, is associated with the distinctive characteristics and nature of endogenous counterinsurgency warfare (Dinka militias). The households in Cuiebet county, in the southern part of the region, were primarily exposed to drought with minimal exposure to counterinsurgency warfare.

***Insecurity Shock and Food Production Failure in 1997***

The year 1997 was an exceptionally bad year for the entire region of Bahr el Ghazal in terms of community exposure to insecurity risks. During the year, there was intensification of counterinsurgency warfare and fighting between the SPLA and the GOS. The region saw in 1997 a considerably greater incidence of fighting, bombings and other incidents (landmines, ambushes, evacuations or violation of ground rules) than did 1998 (see Figure 7 and Table 9). The pattern of insecurity became intensified during critical months of cultivation (April–July) (see Figure 7 and Table 9). Table 9 details how the incidents of counterinsurgency warfare were exacerbated by conventional war between SPLA and GOS during the critical months of cultivation (April– July). This meant that most of the population in the Bahr el Ghazal region failed to cultivate effectively during 1997. Towards the end of 1998 and beginning of 1999 there were an increasing number of incidents of insecurity, particularly fighting, triggered primarily by counterinsurgency warfare (see Figure 7).

According to the SRRA annual assessment report (SRRA, 1997:17):

> *During 1997 physical insecurity in Southern Sudan continued to be a significant cause of food insecurity as it has eroded households' entitlement base through serious economic disruption in agriculturally productive zones, decline in food production, food stocks and livestock looted.*

*Figure 7: Insecurity Incidents in Southern Sudan, 1997-1999*

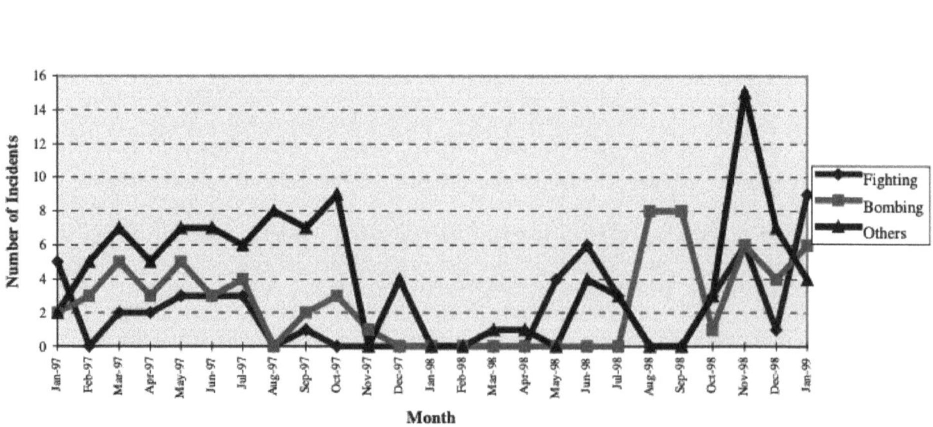

*Table 9: Insecurity Incidents in Bahr el Ghazal, 1997-1998*

| | |
|---|---|
| January 1997 | Kerubino militia forces raided and devastated Akoc in Twic county.<br>Kerubino forces attacked Panthou in Awiel East county. |
| February 1997 | PDF attacked and devastated Udici payam in Wau county |
| March 1997 | PDF raided Ameth area in Twic and Awiel East counties. |
| April 1997 | PDF raided and devastated Abyei, Twic, Awiel, Gogrial and Wau counties. |
| May 1997 | Agaigai area in Gogrial county attacked and looted by SSIA/Nuer militias.<br>Rumbek GOS garrison town captured by SPLA.<br>Heavy fighting around GOS garrison in Gogrial between SPLA and GOS and captured temporarily by SPLA and recaptured by GOS three days later. |
| June 1997 | Kerubino militia forces attacked Ayien in Gogrial county.<br>GOS garrison town of Yirol captured by SPLA. GOS garrison town of Tonj captured by SPLA.<br>Heavy fighting between SPLA and GOS around Abyei garrison. |
| July 1997 | Akak area in Twic county attacked by Kerubino militia forces.<br>Malualkon area in Awiel East attacked by PDF militia who burned Warawar market. |
| September 1997 | Fighting between SPLA and GOS forces, PDF and Kerubino forces in Kuajina payam in Wau county. |
| October 1997 | Train movement to Wau town created devastation of villages along railway in Awiel East and West counties by PDF militia forces.<br>PDF, Kerubino militia forces and Nuer militia attacked most areas in northern Bahr el Ghazal. |
| December 1997 | GOS troops devastated Udici payam in Wau county. |
| January 1998 | Heavy fighting in Wau, Awiel, Abyei and Gogrial towns between SPLA and GOS which resulted in the displacement of more than 150,000 persons to SPLA-controlled areas. |

*Source: SRRA and OLS*

Though various types of insecurity had existed in southern Sudan, the dominant one in Bahr el Ghazal in 1997 was counterinsurgency warfare as shown in Table 9. The SRRA annual report clearly indicated that the militia forces of the GOS had devastated the entire counties of Gogrial, Wau, Abyei and Twic and displaced the entire population during critical time of cultivation. In Awiel East, the most highly populated *payams* (Mangargier and Wathmouk) were also devastated, resulting in the displacement of about 100,000 persons. In Awiel West the *payams* along railways (Malual East and Mariem) were affected by a series of attacks associated with the movements of trains from Babanusa and Wau: PDF, accompanying the trains on horseback, looted livestock and household assets and destroyed agricultural fields. Wau county, the food basket of the region, was also a target of PDF activities, particularly the high-potential agricultural *payams* of Udici and Kuajina.

Like the counterinsurgency warfare, the conventional warfare between the SPLA and GOS intensified during 1997 particularly during April and May, the critical months for cultivation in Western Equatoria and Bahr el Ghazal. The SPLA captured the major towns of the Bahr el Ghazal region – Tonj, Rumbek, Wunrok and Yirol – during May–June and captured temporarily the towns of Gogrial and Awiel; it controlled almost the entire region with the exception of two GOS garrisons in Wau, Raja and Abyei. The SPLA military successes resulted in massive displacement of the civil population in and around these towns, with a civil population estimated to be around 160,000 persons displaced in 1997.

The massive military activities in the region and the huge displacement of civilians exhausted the good harvest stock of 1996, particularly in Tonj, Yirol, Rumbek and Wau counties; it also affected cultivation during critical months of May–June as the civil population voluntarily participated in and physically supported SPLA military activities. In Western Equatoria the SPLA managed to capture the major GOS garrisons in Yei, Kajo-Keji, and Amadi during March–April and the entire region came under SPLA control. In response to this considerable military defeat, the GOS resorted to aerial bombing as shown in Figure 7 and intensified its counterinsurgency warfare, exogenous (Arab militias) and endogenous (Dinka militias), in the region in order to create panic and fear among the civil population.

***Exogenous Counterinsurgency Warfare: The Arab Militias in the 1990s***

Generally, the nature of Arab militia counterinsurgency is that it was quasi-generic (less specific with a semi-random pattern), seasonal (as it mainly occurs during dry season) and with sudden and swift effects for a short period of time. The geographic and social spread of exogenous counterinsurgency warfare (Arab militias) in the 1980s had generally targeted the communities in the extreme northern Bahr el Ghazal areas (Abyei) that border the Arab nomads' homeland in western Sudan (Southern Kordofan). With the devastation and massive displacement of the rural communities in these areas in the 1980s, the activities of the Arab militias expanded and extended southward in the 1990s into new areas in Gogrial. In fact, the massive displacement and protracted insecurity in the extreme northern areas of Abyei resulted in a drastic change in vegetation cover which was gradually replaced by thorny shrubs that make the area less suitable for grazing. This change in vegetation and the withdrawal of Dinka cattle to safe areas in the southern and central areas of Bahr el Ghazal provided the necessary incentive for Arab militias to extend their activities southwards into the new areas in the 1990s.

Besides its increased geographical spread, exogenous counterinsurgency warfare (Arab militias) is correlated to both drought and, most importantly, to endogenous counterinsurgency (Dinka militias) warfare, particularly in the 1990s. The most distinctive feature of exogenous counter-insurgency warfare is that it was carried out by militias (Arab or Nuer) who were not from within the targeted communities. The main difference between the communities exposed to exogenous counterinsurgency and those exposed to endogenous counterinsurgency is that the rural communities who are adjacent (Abyei) to Arab nomads' homeland have been able to learn from their past experience with the raids from Arab militias in the 1980s. On the other hand, the communities in central Bahr el Ghazal (Gogrial) had limited experience in dealing with Arab militia attacks in the 1990s.

Unlike drought, there is more of an imbalance between the perceived threat of counterinsurgency warfare and its actual impact, because of its high specificity, unpredictability, and its potentially devastating consequences, particularly among communities with limited past experience (e.g. Gogrial). The threat of counterinsurgency warfare may be very real, but by the same token, it may not be. Owing to the potentially immediate consequences of counterinsurgency warfare, rural households were likely to perceive it as having a higher probability of materialising, and subsequently, such perceptions affected the choice of livelihood strategies. There is sometimes an overestimation of the welfare loss (Hendrickson et al, 1996) associated with counterinsurgency warfare, particularly with exogenous counterinsurgency (Arab militias), as other factors, such as the communal collective action to protect their land (social capital) and past experiences, are likely to discount such perceived welfare loss.

Exogenous counterinsurgency warfare (Arab militias) has some characteristics that are more or less similar to that of drought, such as asymmetric information and the normal threat after the occurrence of risk events (post-period threat). Information about the livelihood strategies adopted by households to confront exogenous counterinsurgency warfare was not easily available with Arab militias. Despite the fact that exogenous counterinsurgency has a rapid onset, its seasonal occurrence during the dry season reduced the threat of raids during the rainy season.

### *Endogenous Counterinsurgency: The Dinka Militias in the 1990s*

The distinctive characteristics associated with endogenous counterinsurgency warfare make it the most important and dangerous source of risk faced for the first time by the rural communities in Bahr el Ghazal region in the 1990s. The activities of the Dinka militia in the 1990s had a profound negative impact on the livelihoods of the Dinka communities in northern Bahr el Ghazal and that contributed to the famine in 1998. The devastation caused by Dinka militia on their communities during the 1990s is summarised by one key informant during the community survey in the Gogrial area who said:

> *'Crisis caused by God such as drought (riak Nhialec) is better than crises caused by human beings (riak raan), but the crisis caused by your own person (riak raan dou) is the worst of all.'*

The most unique and distinctive characteristics of endogenous counterinsurgency warfare (Dinka militias) include specificity, symmetric information, year-round duration, high correlation with drought and exogenous counterinsurgency, limited past experience, and post-period threat. These distinctive characteristics made endogenous counterinsurgency warfare exceptionally more threatening to livelihoods than other risk events such as drought and exogenous counterinsurgency warfare. Unlike exogenous counterinsurgency warfare and drought, endogenous counterinsurgency warfare was more specific as it targeted households more than communities. The members of the Dinka militia were from within their Dinka communities in northern and central Bahr el Ghazal and, most importantly, from some of the dissatisfied SPLA Dinka soldiers, who had the knowledge and detailed information about livelihood strategies adopted by their communities. The duration of the endogenous counterinsurgency warfare in the 1990s was year-round, unlike the seasonal or occasional occurrence of exogenous counterinsurgency warfare and drought.

The Dinka militia used to coordinate their counterinsurgency activities and raids in Bahr el Ghazal in the 1990s with the Arab militias during the dry season and with Nuer militias all year round by providing the local knowledge and information. This suggests that although endogenous counterinsurgency warfare was not directly related to drought, its apparent correlation with exogenous counterinsurgency (Arab militias) made it indirectly associated with drought in the 1990s. Unlike drought and exogenous counterinsurgency warfare, the rural communities in Bahr el Ghazal had limited experience with the endogenous counterinsurgency warfare that erupted in the 1990s.

These characteristics of specificity, unpredictability, and year-round presence made rural communities in Bahr el Ghazal to attach a relatively higher welfare loss to endogenous counterinsurgency warfare than to any other risk events during the 1990s. Also, the year-round presence of endogenous counterinsurgency warfare made the threat of its occurrence continuous and constant, unlike the occurrences of drought and exogenous counterinsurgency that were followed by normal periods of calm. Generally, the characteristics of endogenous counterinsurgency were unique and less comparable to the characteristics of other risk events such as drought and exogenous counterinsurgency warfare.

### El-Nino Phenomenon and Food Supply Failure in 1997

The rains in southern Sudan normally start in March–April and increase progressively until June when a short dry spell occurs; more rains begin in July, and they reach a peak in August when rainfall starts declining until October–November. This pattern of normal rainfall usually sustains crop and wild food production and provides adequate pasture and water for livestock and fish. In the context of this normal rainfall pattern, normal drought usually reduces the amount of rainfall, but the rains remain evenly distributed to the extent that crops, wild foods and pastures do not suffer moisture stress.

Drought is generally an intrinsic feature of the rural environments in Sudan, particularly in Bahr el Ghazal, and has become one of the few risk events to which households are well adapted. The characteristic of a drought of being slower onset, as its threat materialising slowly, usually allows rural households to adjust their perception of the threat it poses to their livelihoods and to plan accordingly. This slow onset occurrence of drought makes possible a balance between the way its threat is perceived and its actual impact and subsequently allows households to proactively adopt appropriate livelihood strategies.

Besides the nature of the occurrence of drought, its geographical and social spread is generic and covers a wide range of areas and communities. However, the generic nature of drought has been questioned in recent years as climatic conditions have changed drastically and resulted in a quasi-generic pattern in rainfall. The phenomena of El-Nino and La-Nina created climatic anomalies across Africa during the 1990s (FEWS, 1999). In Bahr el Ghazal region, the pattern of rainfall in the 1990s varied drastically, not across various counties, but even within counties and communities. The monthly variation in the Normalised Deviation Vegetation Index (NDVI) during the 1990s shows a general downward trend, reaching as low as 40 percent in northern Bahr el Ghazal, particularly during critical cultivation months (May-October).

Although the rainfall volume pattern deteriorated generally in Bahr el Ghazal during the 1990s, the areas in northern Bahr el Ghazal (Abyei and Gogrial) experienced more of a downward trend than did areas in southern Bahr el Ghazal (Cuiebet). Unlike the situation in northern Bahr el Ghazal in the 1980s when drought was no more than a secondary factor in causing livelihood vulnerability (Keen, 1994:84), it became one of the main factors in the 1990s. This suggests that the intensity of drought was relatively more severe in Bahr el Ghazal region during the 1990s, as compared to the rainfall in the 1980s.

Despite the fact that the volume of rainfall in Bahr el Ghazal deteriorated in the 1990s, there were periods of normal rainfall in 1995 and 1996. Importantly, people in Bahr el Ghazal have amplified their perceptions over the years about the threat of drought according to past experiences. For example, some communities in Bahr el Ghazal region used traditional and local indicators, such as the movement and nesting of some birds, the flowering of some wild plants, and the appearance of some stars, as ways of predicting the pattern of rainfall (Deng, 1999). Though these traditional indicators of rainfall pattern may not precisely predict when drought will strike, they generally help the rural communities in forming their perceptions about the threat of drought.

One of the important characteristics of drought is its interaction with other risk events such as counterinsurgency warfare. The rainfall pattern in northern Bahr el Ghazal was undoubtedly associated with the occurrence, duration, geographic spread, intensity, and frequency of exogenous counterinsurgency warfare (Arab militias). Arab nomads rely heavily on pastures and water sources in northern Bahr el Ghazal during the dry season (December-April).

Besides the fact that drought makes Arab nomads more desperate to access water and the pastures in Bahr el Ghazal region, it allowed the easy mobility of Arab militia, who used horses for their movement. The rural community's perception of the threat of drought in northern Bahr el Ghazal was greatly influenced by the fact that the occurrence, duration, and intensity of exogenous counterinsurgency warfare were known to increase when drought occurs. This close association between drought and exogenous counterinsurgency warfare makes it difficult to dissociate the actual occurrence and perceived threat of exogenous counterinsurgency warfare from the effects of drought and their subsequent impact on the choice of livelihood strategies adopted by households.

The pattern of rainfall all over southern Sudan in 1997, the year before the 1998 famine, was exceptionally abnormal in terms of intensity and distribution. It resulted in extreme climatic anomalies which affected crops and wild food growth and produced poor pastures and inadequate water for livestock and fish. Although the rains started normally in April but with above-average rainfall, below-average rainfalls occurred in May–June and August–September which are critical periods for crop pollination, fertilisation and fruit (grain) formation. According to the SRRA (1997:15) the first planting season almost failed as a result of the abnormal dry spell in May–June in most areas except Yambio and Tambura which had above-average yields.

The second planting season, which is the main cultivation season as it affects more than 60 per cent of the area to be put under crop, was disrupted by a long dry spell in August–September and resulted in below-average crops yields. In October–November, unexpectedly, there was above-average rainfall which did not help the stunted long-maturing sorghum. This pattern of rainfall was observed in most counties of southern Sudan through field observations, the SRRA rainfall records from more than twenty-seven locations in various counties of southern Sudan and the satellite (unmasked METEOSAT and NDVI) imaging data.

The SRRA (1997:5) stated that 'there is every reason to believe that the pattern of rainfall in 1997 in southern Sudan could greatly be attributed to the El-Nino phenomenon'. The El Nino phenomenon exists when the Pacific Ocean is unusually warm, whilst the La-Nina phenomenon develops when the Pacific Ocean is unusually cold. During 1997 there was an abnormal rise in the temperature of the Pacific Ocean; coupled with unusually high temperatures in the Indian Ocean, this resulted in a huge body of warm water vapour, the size of the African continent, which hovered above the clouds of the south Pacific Ocean and disrupted any weather pattern around it. When this phenomenon occurs, even where the rainfall pattern might be normal, poor temporal and spatial distributions will be common. The 1997 El-Nino brought the worst weather changes in a hundred years; it resulted in extreme worldwide climatic anomalies such as drought, floods, and abnormally hot and cold temperatures. Most countries of the Greater Horn of Africa suffered a great deal from El-Nino in terms of crop failure, destruction of infrastructure such as roads, and displacement of large numbers of people.

Rainfall records show that in Bahr el Ghazal the pattern of rainfall in 1997 was one of extreme climatic anomality. When the rainfall pattern in Wau county during 1997 is compared with that of 1996 which was a normal year in Bahr el Ghazal, the climatic anomalies become apparent (see Figure 8). The level of rainfall in 1997 was below the normal level, particularly during the critical months, May-June and August-September, for crop pollination, fertilisation and fruit (grain) formation.

When the satellite imaging data for 1997 for Wau county are compared with average data, the satellite imaging data as shown in Figure 8a indicate a similar trend to that of Figure 8 with a consistent pattern of declining rainfall below the historical average. However, Figure 8a fails to show the climatic anomalies that are shown in Figure 8.

*Figure (8): Rainfall Pattern in Wau County, Bahr el Ghazal, 1996/97*

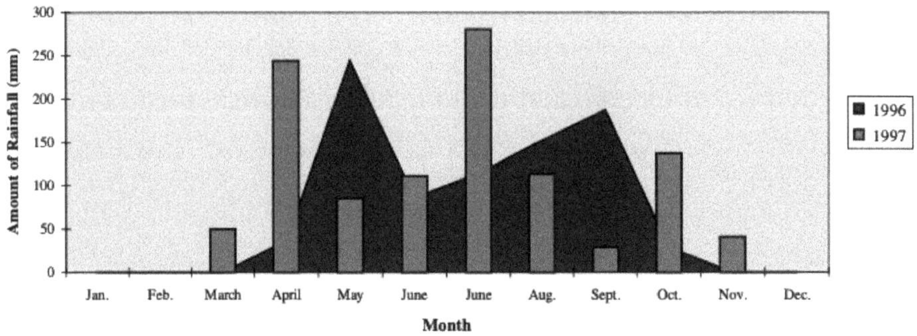


*Source: SRRA Monitoring Unit*

*Figure 8a: Pattern of Rainfall (NDVI) in Wau County, 1997-99*

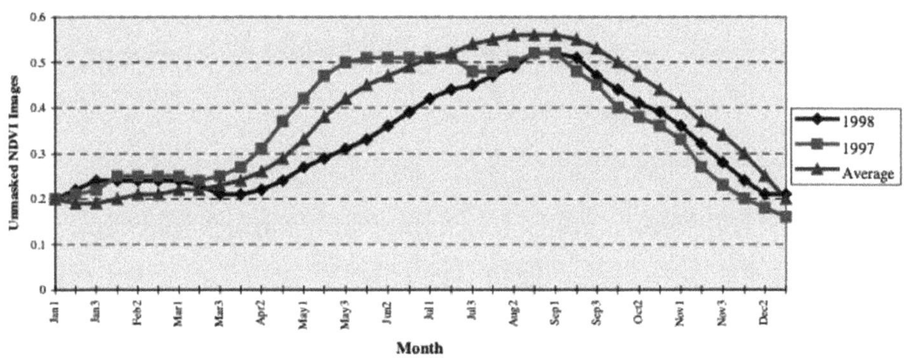


*Source: FEWS/USAID*

The satellite imagery reports on the overall vegetation, and this discrepancy shows that it is necessary to complement it with ground rainfall data in order to reflect the real rainfall pattern on the ground, and variations within the season that impact on the crop production. This clearly suggests a pattern of declining rainfall since 1995, and that 1997 was only exceptional in terms of rainfall distribution and not in the overall quantity (which was a typical pattern during an

El-Nino phenomenon). However, when the variation in the vegetation index during 1995–97 is compared across various counties of Bahr el Ghazal region, there is a general downward trend, particularly in northern Bahr elGhazal, reaching more than 40 per cent, particularly during critical months of cultivation (April–July) as shown in Figure 9.

*Figure 9: Percentage Range of NDVI Variation (1995-97) in Bahr el Ghazal*

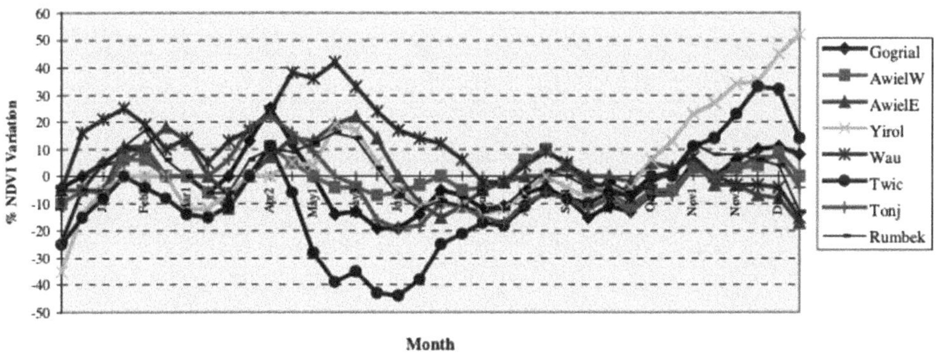


*Source: FEWS/USAID*

The climatic anomalies during 1997 that resulted from the El-Nino phenomenon had far-reaching effects. The 'direct food entitlement' of the average household was considerably eroded, particularly in Bahr el Ghazal and parts of eastern Equatoria. According to the SRRA (1997:66–67) out of a total of fifty-one *payams* in all the counties of Bahr el Ghazal, forty were assessed as facing acute food deficit during 1998. Yields from the major crops declined by more than 80 per cent of the normal yield according to estimates, and some *payams* failed to harvest any crop.

In addition to the failure in crop production, during 1998 vegetation cover and pastures dried up early, not only affecting livestock products but also threatening their survival. Large numbers of livestock died because of poor pastures and poor access to water during 1998. People too faced acute shortages of water as water sources (shallow wells, water boreholes, swamps and open wells) dried up. In Yirol county, people fought over water, as a result of which six persons were killed and thirty-three were seriously wounded. In Rumbek county, men were forced to spend nights queuing for water around open wells and women spent most hours of the day fetching water from far away. The climatic anomalies during 1997 also caused a significant reduction in the yields of wild foods which forced people to resort to new types and to famine wild foods during 1998.

***Food Demand Failure: Market Intervention***

In addition to insecurity and climatic conditions, the primary causes of the famine, the food demand failure and inability of people of Bahr el Ghazal region to access food played a critical role in understanding the 1998 famine. Key failures that shed light on the evolution of the famine process were in relation to the purchase of grain and the sale of livestock. Despite the fact that exchange entitlement theory is a relatively comprehensive framework for analysing famine causation, it does not help in identifying the factors that caused the shift in the conditions of exchange which trigger entitlement failure. As famine often arises from contraction of purchasing power in affected region, market becomes an important institution to prevent famine through allocation of food resources to the needy (Dreze and Sen, 1989).

Hence, a thorough understanding of famine entails understanding the atypical performance of markets and institutions as they determine the factors that bear on the likelihood that an exogenous shock will turn into a mass entitlement failure and hence famine (Ravallion, 1996:20–21). Though most famine studies in Africa, South Asia and Europe have identified a large increase in the price of food as an important proximate cause of food entitlement collapse and hence famine, the precise ways in which entitlement changes impact on mortality have not been adequately explored.

According to Ravallion (1987: 1), 'to understand starvation deaths, one must understand the relationship between individual food consumption and survival chances'. Though famine studies suggest that survival chances are concave (positively related) in consumption, it does not imply that survival chances will be concave in food prices as food demand functions are likely to be convex (negatively related) in price (Ravallion, 1996:13). According to Ravallion (1996:14), it is only when survival chances are increasingly and sufficiently concave functions of income, that price variability over time will increase expected famine mortality and will still be an empirical question. Econometric investigations of the relationship between mortality and food grain prices over periods encompassing two severe famines in South Asia indicate that high and unstable prices contributed substantially to the excess mortality (Ravallion, 1987:41–42).

Casual inspection of Figure 10 which assesses the relationship between excess famine mortality and food prices by using data from Kujok *payam* in Gogrial county, suggests that high simsim and sorghum prices are positively related to excess deaths. In determining the direction of the relationship between mortality and grain prices, Ravallion (1987:39) found from South Asian famine experience that high grain prices were an important cause of famine, with high and positive price elasticity of mortality and price instability responsible for about one third of famine mortality.

The policy implication of such an evident and strong relationship between price instability and famine mortality is the relevance of food aid to stabilise prices and hence survival chances in subsistence and isolated economies like those that exist in Bahr el Ghazal where most available income is spent entirely on food. Besides food aid intervention, investment in markets even during civil war becomes an important prevention mechanism of famine and mass starvation.

*Figure 10: Food Prices and Excess Famine Mortality in Gogrial, Bahr el Ghazal, 1998*

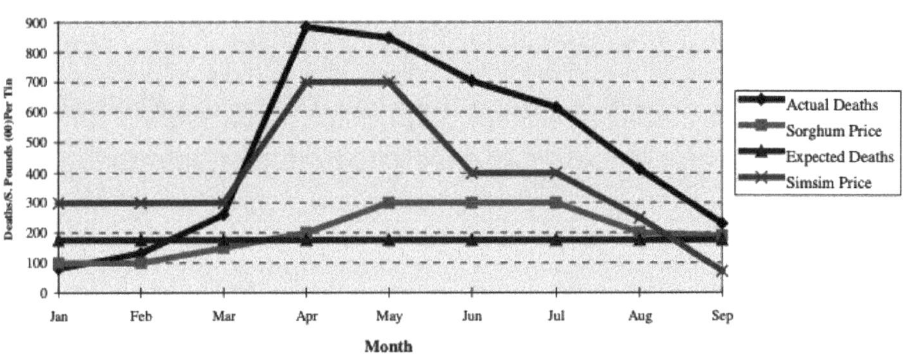


*Source: SSRA Monitoring Unit*

### *Grain Markets*

The behaviour of grain markets usually reflects household strategies in dealing with food shortages. On the basis of his analysis of the pattern of food prices in Ethiopia, Cutler (1984:56) observed that high food prices are typical of famine zones, but food markets may at first behave relatively normally on the edge of these zones. Sen

(1981:94–95), however, observed a normal pattern of food prices during the Wollo famine in Ethiopia and attributed this to limited purchasing power as a result of crop failure. Seaman and Holt (1980) observed from the behaviour of food prices during famines in Ethiopia and Bangladesh that high food prices are typical of famine conditions. Devereux (1993:90) argues that 'the reason why prices double or quadruple at times of scarcity is simply that food is a basic necessity, so that its demand is highly inelastic around the subsistence level'.

The behaviour of food prices during 1998 in northern Bahr el Ghazal, the epicentre of the famine zone, appears to correspond to the pattern observed by Cutler (1984). Figure 11 shows clearly that sorghum prices were higher in 1998 than in 1996 which was a relatively normal year. The pattern of sorghum prices indicates that the process of famine in Bahr el Ghazal effectively started during 1997 with exceptional increases in sorghum prices in relation to the prices in 1996. The behaviour of sorghum prices in Gogrial county, the worst-hit area, corresponds to Sens (1981:94–95) observation of a normal pattern of food prices during famine due to limited purchasing power as a result of crop failure.

The communities in Gogrial county suffered a lot from the two major shocks that affected Bahr el Ghazal, cattle raiding and displacement, as Gogrial county was the epicentre of counterinsurgency warfare and hard-hit by drought. When food shortages reached their worst level during 1998, people in Gogrial started migrating to other nearby counties, particularly Wau county, in a desperate search for food. With the important entitlement base of cattle ownership eroded and complete crop failure during 1997, the purchasing power of the

*Figure 11: Sorghum Prices in Northern Bahr el Ghazal, 1996-98*

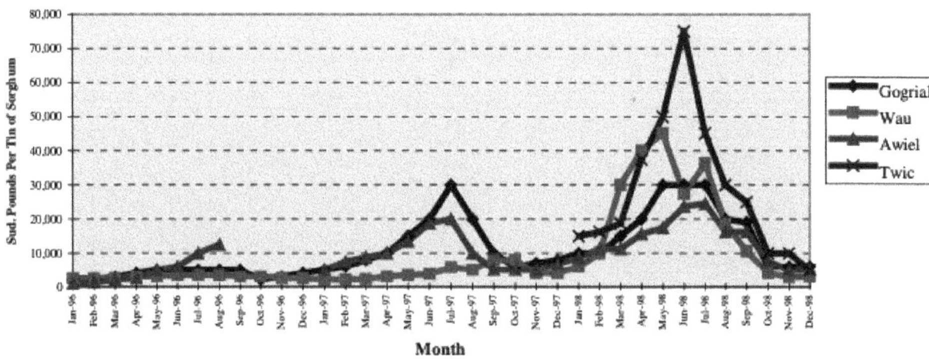


*Source: SRRA Monitoring Unit*

communities in Gogrial county became limited and failed to exert upward pressure on food prices through excess effective demand.

The exceptionally high sorghum price in Wau county during 1998 was basically caused by two factors: Wau county became an attractive centre for famine victims from other counties because of its relatively good harvest during 1996 and 1997, and, moreover, it usually provides labour opportunities for the Dinka from other counties. The situation in Wau county was further exacerbated by a huge influx of displaced people (an estimated 160,000 persons) from Wau town when it was attacked by the SPLA in January 1998.

The price behaviour in Wau county is consistent with the 'price ripple hypothesis': prices got pushed up because the famine victims in the famine epicentre were forced to migrate to Wau county as markets failed to come to them (Devereux, 1993:97). The behaviour of grain prices in Wau county corresponds to the observation of Seaman and Holt (1980) that high food prices are typical of famine conditions.

The relatively stable behaviour of sorghum prices in Awiel county was mainly due to the good performance of Warawar market which managed through its northern Arab traders to bring some grain with camels, donkeys and oxen from northern Sudan. The exceptionally high sorghum price in Twic county during May and June was mainly a result of PDF attacks in those two months which devastated the county and closed the trading route to Abyei market, the main supplier of grain.

When assessing the pattern of sorghum price behaviour in the counties at the edge of the famine epicentre zone, we observe that the pattern of sorghum prices tends to become relatively stable as we move away from the famine epicentre zone as shown in Figure 12. Rumbek county is the nearest county to Gogrial county, the epicentre of the famine zone, followed by Yirol, Maridi, Tambura and Yei; Rumbek experienced relatively higher sorghum prices and these progressively became lower until they reached their lowest level in Yei county.

During the 1998 famine the prices of superior food items, particularly oil seeds such as groundnuts and simsim, gradually fell to the level of the price of sorghum, as shown in Figure 11a. As from June 1998 the price differential between sorghum and simsim diminished until September 1998 when it was reversed. According to Cutler (1984: 51), this unique relationship between the prices of 'inferior' food staples and those of 'superior' food staples during famine is probably attributed to exceptionally high demand for cheaper food grains while the more expensive grains are shunned by consumers in search of cheap calories.

*Figure 11a: Sorghum, Simsim and Groundnut Prices in Gogrial, Bahr el Ghazal, 1996-98*

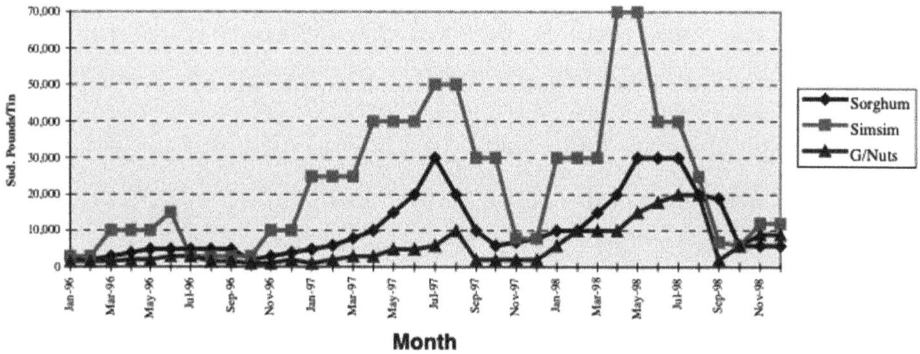


*Source: SRRA Monitoring Unit*

### *Distress Migration*

The behaviour of sorghum prices during the 1998 famine in the epicentre of the famine zone (see Figure 11 and Figure 13) and in the areas at the edge of the famine zone (see Figure 12) provide not only a reasonably precise map of famine conditions but also indicate the likely direction of distress migration of famine victims. During 1998, famine victims from the Bahr el Ghazal region (estimated by the SRRA to be around 27,000) started migrating in May and June to various counties in western Equatoria in search of employment and easy access to food. Some moved with their few remaining livestock to sell in food-surplus counties in western Equatoria. Some famine migrants moved with their families with virtually nothing to sell except their labour.

Most of these famine migrants were those who had no livestock, peasants who dependent entirely on agriculture and fishermen relying primarily on fishing and agriculture. Most of the famine migrants came from the *payams* of Bahr el Ghazal that were most affected by drought, particularly Tonj, Rumbek and Yirol. Some famine migrants who came from Wau to Tambura, however, were rich and industrious farmers who had become victims as a result of off-taking activities such as the looting of their produce. Another wave of distress migration occurred in northern Bahr el Ghazal across various counties and *payams* as the possibility of movement towards northern Sudan had been affected by increased PDF activities in May and June 1998.

As most famine migrants came to Western Equatoria towards the end of the first planting season and the beginning of the second planting season, the male migrants managed to work on the residents' farms and women managed to do domestic work such as pounding in exchange for food. After the planting season was over, most famine migrants were forced to move to towns in Western Equatoria where they fetched firewood. The unusual movement of such a large population of Dinka with families to Western Equatoria for the first time triggered a feeling of uneasiness among the host population, who were not aware of the famine in Bahr el Ghazal.

The famine migrants were seen by some residents and host communities as people coming to settle on their land; such feelings limited the migrants' opportunities for access to work and support. The language barrier between the famine migrants and the host communities did not help effective communication and sometimes resulted in hostilities and the denial of services to famine migrants. Some local authority officials from the host communities in western Equatoria failed to recognise officially the famine migrants as people with genuine problems.

*Figure 12: Sorghum Prices Outside the Famine Epicentre, 1996-98*

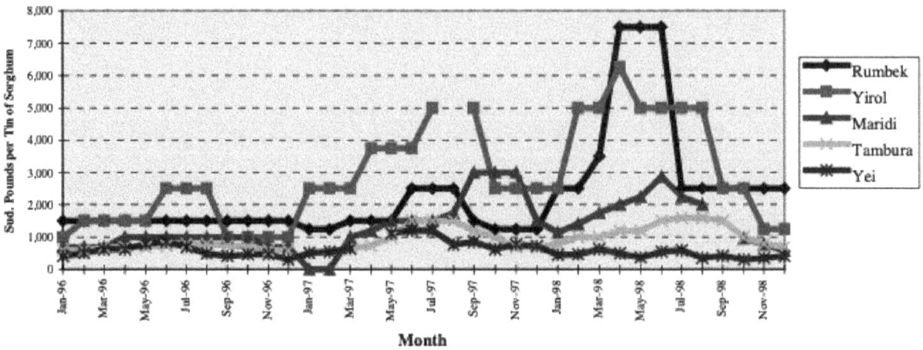


*Source: SRRA Monitoring Unit*

### *Spatial Price Differentials*

There were high spatial food prices differentials during the 1998 famine, as is clear from Figure 12 which raises a basic economic question about market integration amongst the regions of southern Sudan. Devereux (1993:95) argues that the extent to which regional food shortages are translated into local food prices will depend not on whether markets are integrated or fragmented but on their degree of integration. Figure 12 shows that the Tambura, Yei, Maridi counties of Western Equatoria had relatively abundant foodstuffs in their markets during the famine in Bahr el Ghazal region; the exceptionally high food prices there failed, however, to attract food supplies from Western Equatoria.

Ideally a spatial competitive equilibrium could easily be arrived at through trade between Western Equatoria and Bahr el Ghazal, which would then experience similar prices to those in Western Equatoria but raised to cover the transport costs incurred by moving food supplies between the two regions. The situation in southern Sudan clearly suggests the existence of significant impediments to trade between

Western Equatoria and Bahr el Ghazal which greatly contributed to the spatial disintegration of markets, as a result of which localised food scarcity persists. On the top of these impediments, the transport infrastructure that existed between Bahr el Ghazal and Western Equatoria was seasonal and exceptionally costly and slow, particularly during the rainy season.

It is widely believed that the incidence and severity of famine may be directly related to the level of development of transport networks, particularly roads and railways (Devereux, 1993:95). But even if the necessary transport infrastructure had existed, a spatial competitive equilibrium would have not been achieved because the indigenous entrepreneurial and trader class has not been allowed to develop and southern Sudan became too dependent on Arab traders *(jellaba)*. The few petty traders who were operating in the SPLM-controlled areas had not been adequately provided with a conducive atmosphere because of excessive, unorganised and unstandardised taxes imposed by various authorities at different levels.

The prices of foods such as pulses (simsim and groundnuts) may give a better indication of the behaviour of food prices during famine because of the distorting effect of the distribution of relief foods which were usually cereals as shown in Figure 13. The pattern of simsim prices is similar to that of sorghum prices except for the presence of unusual food prices turbulence during 1998. Figure 13 shows that the price of simsim increased more than fivefold during 1998. Gogrial county had the highest increase in prices, followed by Wau county and Awiel county.

The food security situation in Gogrial started worsening in 1997 when food prices increased remarkablyfor an even longer period, and sustained up to and beyond harvest time than they would in 1998. The isolation of the impact of relief food on the behaviour of normal food prices makes the price of simsim more representative than sorghum prices. This suggests that in a situation where there is food aid distribution, it is appropriate to use in any early warning system the market prices of the food items not included in relief food.

*Figure 13: Simsim Market Prices in Northern Bahr el Ghazal, 1996-1998*

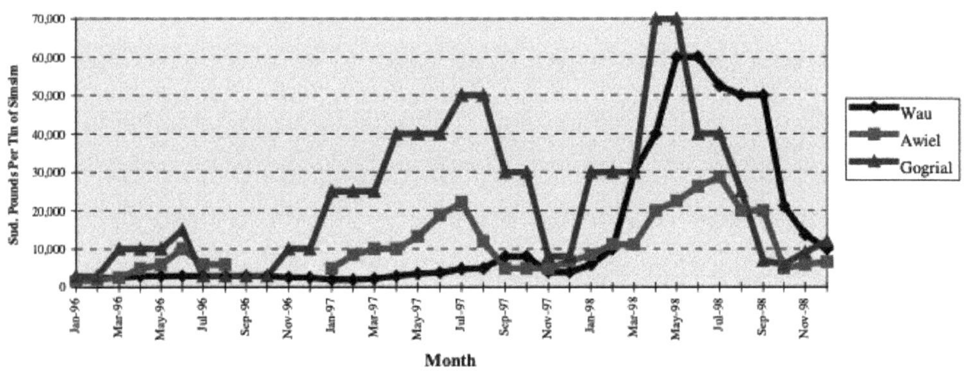


*Source: SRRA Monitoring Unit*

***Livestock Markets***

In Dinka society the sale of livestock in particular involves an important set of market transactions which is critical in the famine process. The performance of the livestock market helps greatly in understanding how exogenous shocks such as drought and insecurity will turn into mass entitlement failure and hence famine. Beside the social role that livestock play in Dinka society, they are an important marketable asset which protects consumption. The use of livestock in particular in pastoral economies for consumption smoothing is well documented (Ravallion, 1996:25). According to Ravallion (1996:26), 'the highly covariate nature of the shock during a famine means that large numbers of people must simultaneously sell their livestock to buy grains, with a consequent (often) sharp fall in livestock prices relative to food grains, and other goods'.

Cutler (1984:49) elaborates that during crop failure people tend to sell off goats first, as relatively unimportant assets, while cattle are kept as long as there is water and pasture to support them and oxen are sold off as a last resort as they are needed for ploughing and are therefore vital to crop production. According to Cutler (1984:55), while the market prices of livestock may not be a reliable indicator of famine conditions though probably a useful indicator of actual distress, information on the volume of livestock sales figures may well be useful for famine forecasting.

It has been observed that low grain production as a result of drought and insecurity usually forces pastoralists to distressfully exchange their livestock for grain at very low terms of trade, affecting not only the size of herd but also the core of the herd which acts as a base for future production; such sales subsequently increase the vulnerability of pastoralists' livelihood (Swift, 1989; Keen, 1994). Devereux (1993:91) also argues that the 'distress sales' are very serious for the poor, since they entail the conversion of a potential stream of future income into a single cash payment which, when consumed in the form of food, is lost forever and exposes the poor to increasing vulnerability.

During periods of increased food insecurity, the agro-pastoralist Dinka households used livestock to smooth their consumption during long period of hardship. They started with the sale of goats and small oxen/bulls (one to three years of age) and when the situation worsened and the prices of the young of the herds declined, they resorted to the sale of the core of the herd particularly heifers, cows and big oxen and bulls (more than four years old) which have special social value. It was only when there was no market for their livestock that they resorted to distress slaughter of their livestock for consumption. In normal circumstances, Dinka rarely slaughter livestock for direct consumption except for special occasions such as the presence of guests, rituals or funerals.

It is clear from the sequencing of livestock sales that the prices of young animals are useful for famine forecasting, as are data on the volume of such sales. The prices of the core of the herd, particularly cows, pregnant cows, heifers and socially-valued big oxen and bulls, are a useful indicator for actual information on distress; the volume of such sales is equally useful for forecasting famine and a good indicator for actual distress as well.

### *Livestock Market Prices*

It is clear from Figure 14 that while prices of core herd animals, particularly ox/bull4 (four years of age), ox/bull5 (five years and more), pregnant cows, cows and heifers did not exceptionally decline except during actual distress in 1998, the prices of young animals such as ox/bull1, ox/bull2 and ox/bull3 experienced a declining trend from 1997, reaching their lowest level in 1998.

The prices of livestock started falling during the early months of 1998 as unusually large numbers were offered for sale, both because of pressure to smooth consumption and because access to good pastures was limited. Livestock prices declined further till they reached their lowest level in July 1998 because of the worsening food security situation and pasture conditions, exacerbated by panic selling of livestock in anticipation of falling prices. Similar patterns of livestock prices had been projected by means of similar data from Awiel, Yirol and Rumbek counties.

*Figure 14: Livestock Prices in Gogrial, Bahr el Gahazal, 1996-98*

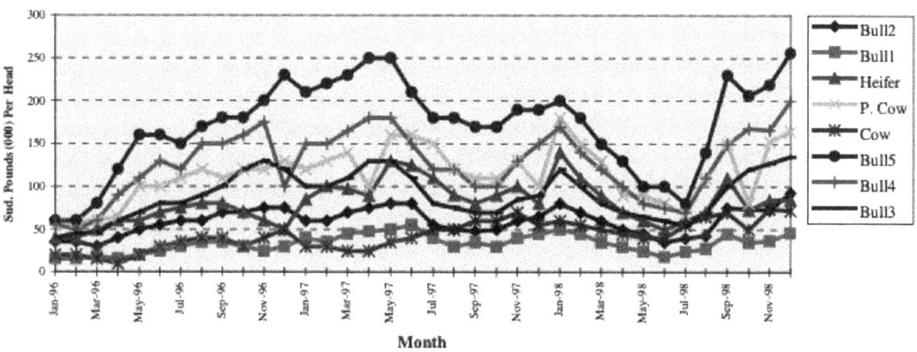


*Source: SRRA Monitoring Unit*

The behaviour of livestock market prices as shown in Figure 14 clearly indicates unusual price decline in 1998; importantly Figure 14 suggests that the prices of young animals have a predictive pattern, while the prices of the core herd give a descriptive pattern of the actual crisis. This observation is inconsistent with that of Cutler (1984) who observed that livestock market prices have no predictive behaviour useful for a famine early warning system. The apparent implication of the behaviour of livestock market prices is that an early warning system in agro-pastoralist economies should use young herd prices as reliable early indicators of famine.

*Figure 15: Volume of Livestock Sales in Gogrial, Bahr el Ghazal, 1996-98*

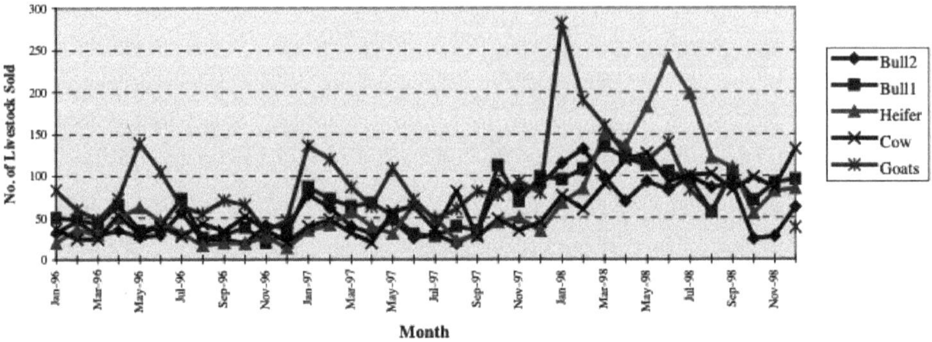


*Source: SRRA Monitoring Unit*

***Volume of Livestock Sales***

Analysis of the volume of livestock sales is one of the ways of understanding the process through which a household sequences the sale of livestock to smooth consumption. The aggregate volume of livestock salesis is an important indicator for famine forecasting. Figure 15a shows the pattern of livestock sales volumes in various counties of Bahr el Ghazal. The volume of cattle sales in the famine zone of Gogrial county showed an increasing trend, with the highest volume of sales during 1998. The pattern of volumes of cattle sales on the edges of the famine zone showed a similar trend, particularly in the nearest county, Rumbek, and a normal trend in Yirol county which is relatively far from the epicentre of the famine zone.

*Figure 15a: Volume of Cattle Sales in Bahr el Gahzal, 1996-98*

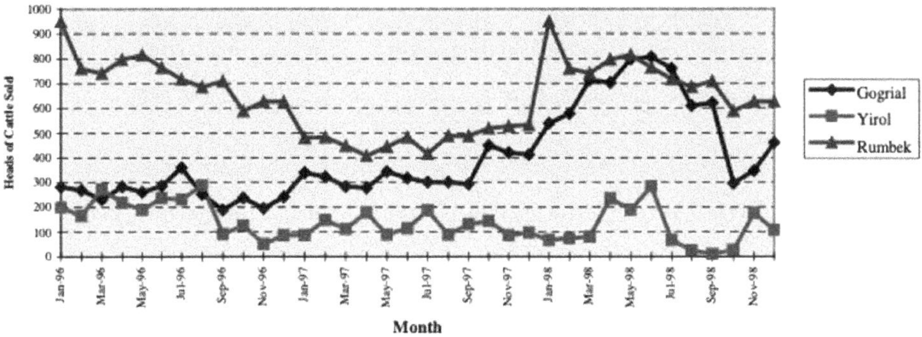


*Source: SRRA Monitoring Unit*

Though the aggregate livestock sales figures are a useful indicator for forecasting famine, they conceal the dynamic and mechanism of the sequencing of sales of livestock for smoothing consumption while minimising the risk of losing the productive core of the herd. During 1996 in a normal situation, small animals such as goats and young bulls or oxen were sold to smooth consumption during minor exogenous shocks and core herd were retained. During major shocks like those of 1998, the number of small animals sold increased before the distress situation and declined during the distress situation, which was accompanied by a substantial increase in the number of core herd sold, as shown in Figure 15.

The pattern of livestock sales volumes in Gogrial clearly shed light on the behaviour of livestock market prices shown in Figure 14. Figure 15 seems to suggest that the volumes of livestock sales of small animals are useful and early indicators for a famine situation while the figures for the core herd are probably a useful indicator for a distress situation. For example, from Figure 15 it is apparent that sales of small animals such as goats, ox/bull1 and ox/bull2 progressively increased until January 1998 when they suddenly started declining. On the other hand, while the sale volumes of heifers and cows, the most productive and important animals, were almost normal during 1996 and 1997, they increased remarkably during 1998. This pattern of livestock sale volumes is consistent with the rational sequencing of sales of livestock to smooth consumption during a famine situation.

### *Barter Terms of Trade*

As a result of rise of sorghum prices during 1998 and exceptional decline in the market prices of livestock, the barter prices of livestock in terms of sorghum deteriorated considerably during 1998, as shown in Figure 16. The loss of animal stock because of drought and raiding, and coupled with worsening terms of trade of animals for grain, contributed to starvation as price movements reinforced the decline in the quantity of livestock. Interestingly, the pattern of terms of trade as shown in Figure 16 shows that the situation started deteriorating during 1997, reaching its worst level in 1998. This clearly suggests that terms of trade are powerful predictive indicators of a famine situation. Such behaviour of pastoralist terms of trade contradicts the observation of Cutler (1984).

During the 1998 famine the informal market which was based on social relationships was functioning effectively. For example, the bartering of livestock for grain started first among relatives as people prefer to retain their livestock within the sphere of lineage. Only when all possible transactions were unavailable from relatives and friends did people resort to markets. This practice had greatly disadvantaged poor families with weak social networks. Terms of trade have the powerful analytical features of linking asset base (endowment) to

*Figure 16: Heifer barter terms of trade in Bahr el Ghazal, 1996-98*

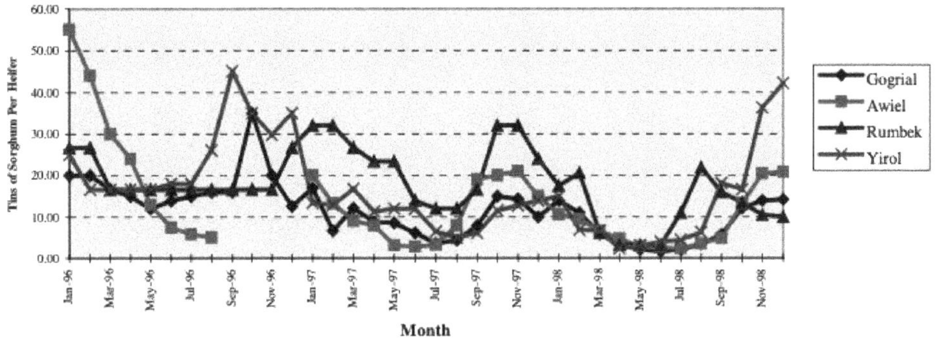


*Source: SRRA Monitoring Unit*

food entitlement (the relationships of people to food) and this makes them a reliable indicator for predicting both famine and a distress situation.

In Gogrial county, for example, whilst a heifer after harvest in September 1996 was priced at almost thirty-five tins (a tin is about 20kg) of sorghum, its price in September 1998 had fallen to almost five tins of sorghum. It is interesting that the barter terms of trade became almost the same during 1998 for both the epicentre of the famine zone (Gogrial and Awiel) and the edges of the famine zone (Yirol and Rumbek).

### *Livestock Slaughtering*

The slaughtering of livestock for consumption was the last resort of the agro-pastoralist Dinka society during famine after exhausting all possible survival options, and in particular after the apparent failure of grain markets when the price of a heifer plummeted to almost 1.5 tins (about 30kg) of sorghum during April–August 1998.

Thus, in addition to the widespread death of livestock because of poor pastures and diseases, a large number were slaughtered for consumption. The slaughtering of livestock is a complex process as it involves factors related not only to the survival of members of the household but also survival chances of livestock herds and social obligations to other relatives.

In Dinka society there is a standard traditional distribution of the meat of all parts of any livestock slaughtered to all members of the extended family; this is because livestock are owned by the family and probably the community at large, whilst private ownership is limited to livestock products and other social obligations. Even the sale of livestock involves a similar social distribution mechanism, but the mechanism is more apparent in meat distribution. Usually, the part of the meat that remains with the primary owner of the slaughtered animal will be so little as to discourage slaughter.

The social stigma attached to the slaughter of animals and the high social cost involved seem to be effective traditional mechanisms of preserving livestock in Dinka society, at least in normal years. During the famine when prices of livestock reached the lowest levels, most households decided to slaughter their remaining livestock at butcheries in the nearby local markets which attracted many famine migrants. Figure 17 shows the number of livestock slaughtered in the butcheries in local markets in Yirol and Gogrial. It is clear that the number of livestock slaughtered increased substantially during 1998.

*Figure 17: Livestock Slaughtered for Consumption in Bahr el Ghazal, 1996-98*

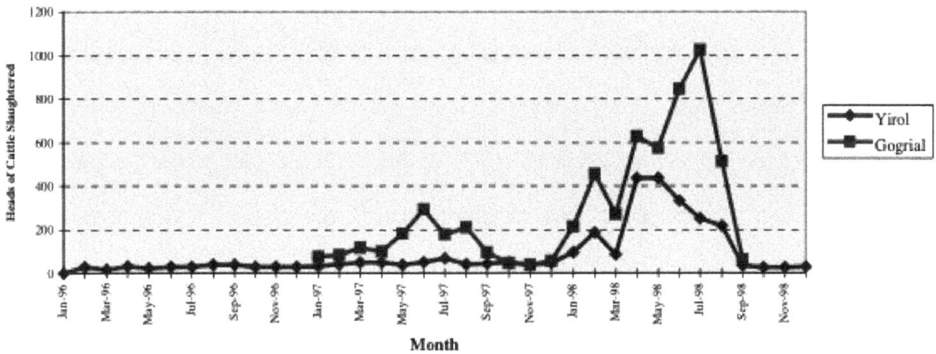


*Source: SRRA Monitoring Unit*

### *Food Demand Failure: Nonmarket Livelihood Coping Strategies*

Despite the fact that it has been recognised that markets are not the only institutions involved in determiningthe distribution of food consumption, there are still some doubts about whether the other institutions and social structures that provide nonmarket sources of food would perform effectively and efficiently during famine. It has generally been argued that in addition to market performance failure during famine, the parallel collapse of social structures that sustain important nonmarket sources of food is one of the causes of famine (Dirks, 1980).

It has been extensively researched and documented that the right to make claims on others, like the obligation to transfer a good or service, is well rooted in the social and moral fabric of therural community as a collective means for mutual insurance against risks and exogenous shocks (Scott, 1976; Platteau, 1991). The real question is whether the nonmarket strategies and traditional social structures doperform effectively during famine.

During the 1970s and 1980s most researchers emphasised that with the expansion of market exchange, population growth and the rise of modern state, claims and transfers are atavistic vestiges of a 'merrie' moral economy of time past (Adams, 1993:41). Some researchers (Swift, 1993; Platteau, 1991) emphasised that local coping strategies have become increasingly unviable as a result of the joint impact of market penetration, population growth and the rise of a modern state system. Sen (1981:126–7) for example argues that while commercialisation in the Sahel may have opened up new economic activities, it has also tended to increase vulnerability with a long-term trend of partial breakdown of the traditional methods of insurance.

Deng (1972) emphasises that the traditional Dinka nonmarket survival strategies have been eroded by their increasing reliance on markets. Adams also argues that nonmarket transfers are irrelevant vestiges of awaning moral economy, and are of little significance relative to the market-oriented strategies widely employed to overcome food insecurity (Adams, 1993:47). According to Ravallion (1996:26–7) it is not surprising that famines can put considerable stress on normally social-risk-pooling arrangements as they cannot cope with the covariate shocks which usually trigger causation of famine.

Dirks (1980) proposed a model which identifies three phases of social and economic behaviour as food insecurity intensifies. The model suggests that while the erosion of social ties begins during the second phase (resistance) and is further eroded as deprivation reaches the third phase (exhaustion), the first phase (alarm) shows an intensification of nonmarket exchange. Adams (1993) observes a similar pattern and similar phases of gradual erosion of socialties in Mali.

### *Decline of Customary and Traditional Collective Coping Strategies*

The experience of the 1998 famine in Bahr el Ghazal has mixed implications for the performance of traditional systems of social security in Dinka society. Though it is a fact that the extension of markets, the prolonged civil war, and modern state power have eroded the customary collective coping in Dinka society, their level and degree of impact require close scrutiny.

### *The Extension of the Market and Erosion of Social Safety Nets*

The market and trade integration between northern and southern Sudan and the monetisation of Dinka economy have made Dinka increasingly dependent on markets, which has greatly affected their ways of life, including their social safety nets. Money increasingly became the dominant medium of exchange, gradually supplanting cattle around which all Dinka social and economic activities and communal ownership had been centred.

The introduction of money brought about an individualistic attitude and a tendency to privatise communal ownership. Social and economic activities started shifting gradually towards money and away from cattle as the traditional epicentre for social safety nets. Dinka resisted the encroachment of money into their lives, as is clearly reflected in their reluctance to enter into the ivory trade or portering work in the nineteenth century and their reluctance to seek work outside their home areas, sometimes even to the point of choosing death as an alternative (Keen, 1994).

The sale of livestock was vigorously resisted as well as the use of oxen in ploughing, even during the early 1980s. According to Keen (1994:47), wage labour was seen by Dinka as shameful and was associated with the forced labour of the recent past and with neglect of obligations to kin. A Dinka urban labourer lamenting the evils of money sang the following song (Deng, 1972:162):

> *The family has lost its value.*
> *Blood ties have been severed in the pockets ...*
> *In the towns people dance to the drums in their pockets. If one has nothing, one goes with nothing.*

Despite the apparent impact of the extension of the market onto their ways of life, Dinka did not submit entirely to the rules of the market, and they still retain some of their distinctive social characteristics and values. During the post-independence period and before the 1983 civil war, the majority of Dinka were leading their normal livelihood in their traditional rural areas; educated Dinka were being gradually absorbed into urban life but maintained close links to their rural areas.

The rate of illiteracy among Dinka before and during the 1983 civil war was and is still among the highest in southern Sudan. This is not surprising as Dinka resisted education and started recognising its benefits only during the 1980s when war erupted again. The second civil war had actually forced most Dinka who were in towns to take refuge in northern Sudan, whilst the majority of rural people decided to remain behind in southern Sudan.

With limited trading activities between northern and southern Sudan and reduced wage labour opportunities, the rural people, despite the apparent evils of war, started consolidating their traditional livelihood; livestock started to regain its traditional importance and role. Even some of the educated Dinka, former wage labourers and town dwellers who decided to remain in rural areas instead of taking refuge in northern Sudan, adapted swiftly to the rural livelihood.

### *Traditional Authority and Civil War*

Although Dinka have shown a clear tendency to consolidate their traditions during the civil war, the culture of war had also produced undesirable changes in Dinka way of life. The proliferation of small rifles in Dinka society and particularly in the hands of youth has brought a considerable change in the relationships between age groups and has greatly shifted the centre of traditional authority away from older age groups. The strong traditional aspiration of youths to become elders and to enjoy the fruits of older age as figures of respect, wisdom and knowledge has gradually been fading out with the emerging militaristic culture (Kuol, 2017).

Traditional Dinka songs during civil war started to project self-esteem and dignity in the personality of the soldier rather than the ideals of human dignity expressed in the Dinka word *dheeng* (human dignity). It is true that traditionally the youth in Nilotic communities have the traditional role of protecting their community from any external danger; they were, however, within the sphere of traditional authority. Today, while most youth manage amicably to reconcile their roles as both a soldier and a member of the society, some misuse their possession of rifles and undermine the traditional structures.

The role of elders as a centre of authority has gradually been diminished and supplanted by the new military authority; this has affected the traditional social mechanisms. During the 1983 civil war, because of increasing incidence of cattle raids by Nuer militia and

Missserya Arab militia, the communities in Bahr el Ghazal – particularly in counties neighbouring Nuer areas – organised the youth into groups known as Ghel/Tiit-Weng to guard cattle and armed them with firearms rather than spears to match the weapons used by the Nuer and Arab raiders (SPLM/SRRA/OLS Task Force, 1998).

Even these groups have been bestowed with the responsibility of protecting the cattle, they are likely to be unruly and uncontrolled; some of them will easily be tempted to use their firearms to assert themselves as a new authority and are likely to undermine the traditional structures and probably encourage tribal conflicts. During the 1998 famine some of these groups were responsible for some incidents of internal food looting. Some of the Dinka youth were cheaply recruited by the GoS into militias that waged counterinsurgency warfare that devasted the lives and livelihoods of communities of Bahr el Ghazal in the 1990s.

The Dinka way of life and ideal human relations (*cieng*), which is traditionally reinforced by the ideals of human dignity (*dheeng*), are increasingly in danger because of the culture of firearms. The continuous and massive population displacements have also weakened social ties and the traditional social safety nets which rely heavily on repeated interaction amongst people who come to know and trust each other.

### *The Extension of Modern State Power*

Dinka are among the least touched by the forces and benefits of modernity. Deng (1998) argues that Dinka marginalisation in the modern world is both the result of their cultural outlook and the preservation policies of British colonial administration, which were meant 'to build up a series of self-contained racial or tribal units with structure and organization based....upon the indigenous customs, traditional usage and beliefs'. According to Deng (1998), part of the motivation for this preservation policy was fear of nationalism as people were introduced to education and modernity, particularly as the Nilotics – especially Nuer and Dinka– had fiercely resisted British rule for two decades. The 1924 rebellion against the colonial rulers was led by young officers of Nilotics background in the Egyptian army. This encouraged the colonial administration to close off southern Sudan and permitted only the Christian missionaries to pass into southern territory in order to exercise a pacifying influence among the natives (Deng, 1998).

The moral and spiritual principles of Dinka are traditionally used to guide and control the exercise of political and legal authority which is fundamental to Dinka moral and civic order. Dinka law is not a dictate of the ruler with coercive sanctions; it is rather an expression of the collective will of the community which is generally respected, observed and sanctioned largely through persuasion or, if need be, spiritual sanctions (Deng, 1998). Major Titherington, who served as a colonial administrator among the Dinka in the late 1920s, observed that:

> *The higher moral sense which is striking in the [Dinka]. Deliberate murder – as distinct from killing in fair fight – is extremely rare; pure theft – as opposed to the lifting cattle by force or stealth after a dispute about their rightful ownership – is unknown; a man's word is his bond, and on rare occasions when a man is asked to swear, his oath is accepted as a matter of course. (Deng, 1999:9).*

Also, Sir Gawain Bell, who served as District commissioner among the Ngok Dinka in the 1950s, commented that *'I cannot remember that we ever had any serious crime in the part of the district. Among the Baggara [Arabs]...there was a good deal of serious crime: murder and so forth; and the same applied to Hamar in the North...The Ngok Dinka were a particularly law-abiding people'* (Deng, 1999:9).

Until the advent of colonial rule, there were no police or prisons; the effectiveness of leaders depended largely on the moral force of their character, which was, in turn, dependent on the degree of adherence to the values subsumed in the overriding principles that guided Dinka society (Deng, 1998:10). The introduction of the coercive use of the police and imprisonment were extremely resented by the Dinka as inimical to their notions of human dignity (*dheeng*) and became a popular subject of protest and lamentation songs (Deng, 1998:10).

Even during the 1983 civil war the administration of the civil population was entirely military until 1994 when the SPLA called its first national convention which unanimously decided to separate civil administration from the military. This gave birth to a civil society and recognition of its role in rehabilitation and grassroots peace-building efforts in the areas under the control of the SPLA. The transition from military administration to civil administration was an uphill and arduous task, despite concerted efforts by the SPLM leadership to speed up the process.

After the SPLM national convention in 1994, the role of traditional leaders and customary law was well recognised and they became well placed in the judiciary and civil administration. Though most chiefs recognised the important changes brought by the SPLM national convention, some were still skeptical about the actual devolution of power to them as they saw the military administration in one way or another as still dominant.

### *Traditional Redistribution Mechanisms and Safety Nets*

Dinka society is more egalitarian than most and has social systems that actively work to maintain equality (SCF, 1998). As in other agro-pastoralist societies, the social safety nets and traditional risk pooling arrangements of the Dinka range from customary economic exchanges such as generalised, balance and negative reciprocity to customary redistribution systems such as horizontal and vertical redistribution (Swift, 1993:6). There is limit to the extent to which the traditional redistribution mechanisms can perform effectively during famines.

The experience of the 1998 famine in Bahr el Ghazal shows that despite massive and widespread deaths (estimated to be around 100,000 persons), members of the relatively well-off groups were more likely to survive. This clearly shows that generalised reciprocity in egalitarian society does not hold during famine. As rightly argued by Torry (1987), systems of reciprocity have limits to what they can achieve particularly when resources run out. Swift (1993:6) argues that with declining resources during intensified stress, sharing is no longer a solution and the practice of generalised reciprocity contracts so that groups of people are progressively excluded until it becomes confined within the boundaries of the household. The 1998 famine showed a progressive contraction in the practice of generalised reciprocity in Dinka society, and some communities named this famine *cok dakruai* (the famine of breaking relationships).

During the 1998 famine, the dwindling of resources as a result of cattle raids and drought affected the Dinka generalised reciprocity system. At community level, livestock are perceived by Dinka as communally owned, particularly during crisis, and a famine victim is entitled to gain access to livestock by spearing any type of livestock (a sign of desperation) which will be slaughtered automatically and paid back during a normal time. During my visits to areas most affected by the 1998 famine, I personally observed on certain occasions that cattle were fenced in to deprive famine victims of access to spear them. I attended a case being settled by one of the traditional courts where some sub-chiefs were found guilty of failing to distribute relief food to their subjects and were fined. Some communities were asking for the chiefs who abandoned them during famine to be replaced.

At the household level, Dinka have a tradition of eating together (*ruom*), particularly among adults (women and men separately) and children in neighbouring families.This habit of eating together ceased during the 1998 famine as families started to share food only among members of the household. Within the household it is a tradition that women's role is to manage food while that of men is to procure resources. During the famine, however, men started encroaching into the role of food management, which resulted in increased cases of divorce and conflict. There are many recorded cases of men abandoning their children and wives; some barred their children and wives in their huts to face death. In my discussions with famine migrants in Western Equatoria, some told me how some of their close relatives refused to help them with cattle.

In explaining what happened to the Dinka way of life during the famine, chief Ayii Madut said that their way of life did not change: what happened was that resources eroded drastically as a result of cattle raids and crop failures, which forced people to look inward and save their own lives. Chief Ayii Madut compared the 1998 famine with that of 1988, when people did not die in the same numbers as people managed to help each other with livestock:

> *We have not abandoned our cieng [our way of life]. Those who were rich and supposed to help the poor had been affected by war as their cattle were raided, and it is not that we have changed our way of life. As resources became scarce people started to look to themselves. For example, the rich man who was supposed to help and had five or six wives with their children, when the cattle were raided and only five cows were left he would be concerned with the family and would not be able to help others. It is not that people have changed their way of life, it is only that life became extremely hard as cattle were raided and with no proper cultivation during these years. How would you then support others when you are also starving, even chiefs who were supposed to help. Thus, it is not that we have changed our way of life, it is only that life became hard as a result of Kuanyin (Kerubino) activities and also God brought drought for two consecutive years and rains came late when we did not have seeds. It is not that we have changed, it is only the resources which have been eroded as we used to have children, wives, cattle, goats and grains from our field.*

Despite an apparent decline in the role of moral economy during famine, some customary redistribution mechanisms did manage to play an important role in redistributing resources during the 1998 famine. These customary redistribution mechanisms included the following:

### *Marriage*

The most important mechanism in Dinka society for managing risk and exogenous shocks is through investment in social relationships, in most cases through marriage *(ruai/thiik)* which is not allowed within lineage or friendships *(maath)*. It is interesting that the word 'marriage' *(ruai)* in Dinka is synonymous with the word 'relationship' (*ruai*) as Dinka see marriage in a wider context of social relationships. Marriage is an endless process which involves a series of social claims, obligations and transfers of livestock and which tends to build and consolidate social relationships.

The initial brideweath *(hok ruai)* is a collective and legally enforced standardised contribution of livestock from the groom's father's family and his mother's family andfriends as well. The bride's family also has a social obligation to pay from their own cows *(arueth)* to the groom's family to confirm mutual relationships and consolidate the social status of their daughter. The process of swapping cows *(arueth)* is also seen as a process of cross-breeding as the bridewealth livestock are carefully selected. The family of the groom does not usually urge immediate payment of *arueth* which are loosely paid over longer period.

The family of the bride has also an obligation to pay to the groom some cows called *hok dom* from the brideweath of one of their unmarried girls, in most cases the younger sister of the bride. This marriage cycle goes on: when the daughter of the groom gets married the two families will be entitled to a standardised share from the bridewealth, and likewise the two families make contributions to the marriage of the son. When a woman fails to perform her duty properly, she will be temporarily sent to her family; the problem is usually resolved amicably and with a payment of a cow known as *Weng awac* to the man's family. It is apparent that marriage involves strong social and economic relationships and binds people from different lineages with an effective system of claims and transfers of livestock, establishing an extremely interconnected society.

In such an interdependent and tightly woven society, it becomes questionable whether one can view famine or mass starvation as a simple sum of many individuals' independent hungers (Ravallion, 1996). This structure of the Dinka society does much to explain the prevalence of mass mortality during famine. In a situation of stress or famine people resort to settling their claims and obligations, particularly *arueth, hok dom,*and *hok ruai*. During the 1998 famine, the traditional chiefs mobilised all courts to settle only hunger cases *(luok cok)* and these courts became known as 'famine courts'. Most of the cases settled were claims and obligations related to marriage, and the courts managed effectively to redistribute resources, particularly livestock, to some famine victims (Deng, 2010a).

### *Animals Loan*

Dinka do not follow up their loans and claims seriously during normal times. It is only during crisis orfamine that they vigorously pursue their debts and claims. Some of these claims are deliberately used to diversify sources of survival and to stock or save for smoothing consumption during times of severe food shortage.

During the 1983 civil war, when livestock became the object of looting and raiding by the GOS's militias including Dinka milita forces, Dinka cattle owners sought to hedge themselves against such attacks by reducing their herd to a manageable size by entrusting *(kuei)* some of their livestock to their closest relatives. In most cases the trustee would only be entitled to animal products such as milk. This practice, known in Dinka as *kuei/amac*, does not involve any contractual relationship and usually creates extensive litigation in courts as the trustee in most cases dishonours the agreement by either disposing of the animal or concealing its progeny.

Given the insecurity situation in Bahr el Ghazal in the 1990s, people opted for this practice of *kuei* as the cost of losing all the livestock was higher than the cost of default by the trustee. This practice helped a lot in reducing the exposure of cattle to the risk of raiding by PDF, Dinka militias and Nuer raiders. During the 1998 famine, people resorted to call back (*keny*) their *kuei/amac* animals to smooth their consumption. The famine courts managed to settle most of the cases related to default in *kuei/amac* in favour of famine victims.

Another animal loan practice in Dinka society is *amuk/amec* which is defined in the *Bahr el Ghazal Customary Law Act 1984* as 'Any property delivered by a debtor (*raan-koony*) to a creditor (*raan-kony*) as a form of security or guarantee for the repayment of a debt (*keny*) or discharge (*cuot*) of existing obligation (*keny*).' This practice (*amuk*) usually occurs when a person would like to slaughter an animal either for guests, marriage, funerals or any other occasion; if he does not have young oxen or small livestock such as goats or sheep, he will be obliged to borrow from a friend or relative or any person willing with a bond (*amuk*), which in most cases is either a heifer or cow.

It is apparent from this transaction that the creditor obtains legal possession with an obligation to exercise reasonable care for the safety of the bond (*amuk*), while ownership is still vested in the debtor unless he fails completely to repay the debt at the fixed time. The difference between *kuei* and *amuk* is that the duty of care imposed on the trustee of property is not based on contractual agreement as in the case of the creditor but rather on his acceptance that the property remains under his domain (Makec, 1986). *Amuk* is a practice which clearly reflects the Dinka traditional practice that promotes the preservation of the population of reproductive animals such as heifers and cows.

This practice of *amuk* was extensively practised in Bahr el Ghazal, particularly in the 1990s when most small animals such as goats and sheep (which are normally left free with minimal supervision) were drastically depopulated by continuous raids by Dinka and Nuer militias. In northern Bahr el Ghazal, in particular, it was rare in the 1990s to see goats and sheep around as most of the small animals had been looted; this increased demand for young oxen as the most likely substitutes for slaughtering for any social occasions. In most cases *amuk* also involves extensive litigation, particularly when the time of repayment is not fixed and the security (bond/cow) starts producing or when the creditor is dishonest or unfaithful and disposes of the security (bond) without notifying the debtor. During the 1998 famine, the hunger courts settled the cases related to *amuk* and managed greatly to redistribute livestock, particularly to the marginalised groups in the community.

### Horizontal Redistribution

Generally horizontal redistribution takes place between individuals, households or small groups of nearly equal standing within the framework of various levels of community social structures and takes various forms of reciprocity (generalised and balanced) (Swift, 1993:6). As in other egalitarian societies, generalised reciprocity is still widely practised, particularly during normal times, in Dinka society in the forms of help *(kuony)*, hospitality and generosity *(dheeng)*. Despite the fact that generalised reciprocity does not involve immediate return in Dinka society, people expect indirect long-term social return in terms of respect and good name.

Although the classic statement by Evans-Pritchard (1951) of the absolute presence of generalised reciprocity among Nuer pastoralists in southern Sudan may not be relevant now, some forms of generalised reciprocity are still practised in a limited way during starvation and famine. Deng (1998:10–11) argues that where famine threatens Dinka, the famine victims are entitled to seize the property of a relative and, if necessary, of anybody, so as to relieve hunger, on the implied understanding that appropriate compensation will eventually be provided when conditions become normal. The same principle applies where illness threatens death and requires an animal sacrifice to ancestral spirits to bring relief (Deng, 1998). Like other pastoralists, Dinka generally fear public criticism and everything that affects their dignity, and songs usually act as a free press to deter aberration from the traditional values, norms and way of life *(cieng)*, particularly hospitality and generosity.

During the 1998 famine, generalised reciprocity was practised, particularly among communities that were relatively less affected and received famine migrants whom they politely call guests *(jaal)*. Though famine migrants were accommodated and provided with food by the host family, they offered their labour to perform certain duties that might be sufficient to cover the costs of services rendered to them. Within the enlarged lineage the assistance *(kuony)* is an obligation with no any immediate attached return and its refusal usually leads to litigation in courts. Outside the enlarged lineage, chiefs have an obligation to provide assistance *(kuony)* to their subjects during crisis without expecting any material return.

Deng (1998:11) emphasises that the chief as the head of the tribe is ultimately responsible for providing relief against famine or illness within his means. During the 1998 famine, more cases than usual were recorded of children being abandoned in the houses of chiefs so that they would be obliged to take care of them. Chief Ayii Madut in Gogrial county had to take care of more than sixty abandoned children during the famine. As the severity of the famine subsided, some parents came to take their children back. When the chief asked some of them to pay for the service they had received, they answered him, 'What, do you expect to be paid when you have now a good name which consolidates your position as chief?'. During the 1998 famine there were more court cases related to assistance *(kuony)* and courts settled these cases in favour of famine victims. This is one of the most effective customary redistribution mechanism in Dinka society which people resort to during times of difficulty.

Another form of horizontal redistribution, which is widely practised in Dinka society in both normal years and bad years, is balanced reciprocity, which involves an expectation of immediate or short-term returns. The common practice is assistance *(kuony)* which is extended beyond the enlarged lineage to all famine victims but it involves a commitment and negotiated repayment after the famine. A starving man has a right to ask for assistance (in most cases a milking cow) from a rich person, and such assistance is normally finalised in the court to guarantee the repayment. As the risks associated with such a transaction are extremely high as the survival chances of the starving person are low with a high probability of default, the repayment of assistance is sometimes designed in a way that extends the liability to the relatives.

In some desperate situations, the famine victim resorts to the direct spearing of an animal (in most cases a bull or ox) belonging to a rich person: the speared animal will be automatically slaughtered and given to the famine victim with a clear agreement that repayment must be made after the famine. This practice of unilateral gaining access to assistance by spearing animals was common during the 1998 famine and particularly in the famine epicentre zone, while the practice of asking amicably for assistance was mostly prevalent at the edges of famine zone.

### *Vertical Redistribution*

Vertical redistribution takes place usually within hierarchic economic and political systems, where elites or rulers extract resources through a system of taxes, levies or other forms of contribution from less needy people to be redistributed to the neediest people during time of stress (Swift, 1993:6–7). The vertical redistribution mechanism was not widely practised during the 1998 famine in Bahr el Ghazal. The traditional community leaders, particularly some chiefs, played an important role in convincing some cattle owners to make available some milking cows which were rotated among the starving families and which certainly saved some lives.

Some voluntary women's groups in a village called Akon in Gogrial county set up a feeding centre from the contributions of their members for the malnourished and abandoned children of the famine victims. The local SPLM civil administration in most counties of Bahr el Ghazal imposed a daily meat contribution from all butcheries to be cooked for the famine victims and famine migrants who took refuge around local markets. Also, some SPLM local authorities together with traditional leaders ordered all cattle camps to come back earlier than normal from swampy areas (*toic)* and to camp in the areas most affected by hunger so as to increase access to milk.

# CHAPTER FIVE

## Failure of Public Action

The book by Dreze and Sen (1989) on "Hunger and Public Action" provides an outstanding scholarly contribution to the literature on antihunger policy and intervention through public provision of resources. The book prescribes not only things to do but also a way to think about what we should do to prevent famine (Ravallion, 1992:1). Despite such scholarly antihunger prescriptions, the public action continues to fail to prevent famine but also not to respond effectively when it occurs.

Famine is a tragedy that can easily be prevented; it is recurrent simply because of a lack of public action with effective public policies and public intervention to prevent it and contain it. Despite the failure of markets and nonmarket strategies to contain the 1998 famine in Bahr el Ghazal, joint public action by SPLM as the *de facto* government, the implementing aid agenciesand the international community could and should have averted the famine. Some 100,000 lives would thereby have been saved.

The fact that so many lives have been lost simply because of lack of food and in the era of globalization (Deng, 2006) makes it necessary to extend our analysis beyond household food entitlement failure to the role of public action in failing to remedy this entitlement failure and contraction of food purchasing power. The increasing emphasis on war makes for a simplistic analysis of the process of famine, and war sometimes becomes a scapegoat for the failures of other actors.

It is true that GOS contributed substantially to the causation of the 1998 famine through counterinsurgency warfare and denial of humanitarian access, but it is also true that other actors such as SPLM, UN agencies, international donors and international NGOs could have prevented the 1998 famine. The deliberate activities of the GOS such as counterinsurgency warfare and the denial of access to aid agencies were exogenous shocks to people's food entitlement just as El-Nino was – with the difference that the activities of government with their effects could have been prevented or minimised by public action of other actors.

### *Humanitarian Response*

The humanitarian response, particularly of the international community, to famine has been increasingly the effective last resort. But, as argued by Devereux (1993:190), despite its growing importance the humanitarian response often arrives too late, is inappropriate and too narrowly focused:

> *... famine relief programmes have invariably been criticized for arriving too late (being activated only once the terminal stages of crisis are visible), being inappropriate (imported food aid rather than locally purchased food or cash relief, emphasizing food more than medical*

*supplies), and too narrowly focused (treating famine as a crisis independent of long-term processes).*

The recurrent vulnerability to famines in southern Sudan is largely associated with the increasing historical interest of 'outsiders' including northern Sudan, Egypt, Turkey and the Western world in exploiting local resources. The colonial powers, particularly Britain, undoubtedly contributed immensely to the present political and economic vulnerability of south Sudan by insufficiently grasping the reality they endeavoured to address. The drastic British policy change of 1947, as a result of which southern Sudan was annexed to northern Sudan instead of East Africa without adequate consultation with the people concerned, constitutes the cornerstone of the genesis of the current humanitarian tragedy.

Even during the brief period of relative peace after the Addis Ababa Agreement (1972–1983), outsiders in the form of Western development agencies failed sufficiently to address the root causes of the marginalisation of southern Sudan. Equally the international community during the 1983 civil war responded superficially to the symptoms of the crisis and failed to address the root causes. Though it has been argued that humanitarian assistance is a Western enterprise, being given on Western terms, with Western motivations and involving Western money (SCF, 1998:25), there is still hope that this important enterprise will one day be transformed to contribute better to prevent and contain famines.

The experience of southern Sudan with humanitarian assistance is very recent and can be traced back to 1972 when some international development agencies started rehabilitation projects after the first civil war. Unlike the first civil war (1955–1972) when half a million persons died, partly because of the absence of humanitarian assistance, international attention was focused as early as three years after the outbreak of the second civil war in 1983.

The humanitarian assistance in southern Sudan goes back to the famine in western Sudan in 1985, which forced the government to accept the existence of famine and to allow relief agencies to respond. The pockets of famine as a result of consistent looting, devastation and raids by Arab militias on areas of northern Bahr el Ghazal were also developing in 1986 and reached unprecedented severity in 1988 when the death toll reached not less than 250,000 persons. In 1986 the first major initiative by the UN known as the Operation Rainbow, to deliver food to the needy civil population in the areas under the control of the GOS and the SPLM, was aborted by the fighting parties as they were not fully involved in the process.

The second initiative to deliver relief assistance to the needy civilian population was born out of Christian/Muslim dialogue in 1987 and failed to survive as the GOS by then dominated the entire process of dialogue, which discouraged churches from active participation. Despite the failure of these initiatives, some national initiatives by the Sudan Council of Churches and Sudan Aid managed in 1985–86 to respond in their limited capacities to the plight of people affected by war and drought.

These initiatives were later followed by international NGOs such as Norwegian People's Aid (NPA), World Vision, Oxfam (USA) and Lutheran World Federation (LWF) among others were involved in cross-border operations into the SPLM-controlled areas prior to the launching of Operation Lifeline Sudan (OLS). The long struggle by the International Committee of Red Cross (ICRC) to be permitted to assist the civil populations on both sides of the conflict finally bore fruit in 1988 when both the SPLM and the GOS gave their approval.

The 1988 famine in the Bahr el Ghazal region triggered collective efforts from the media, NGOs, western governments and UN bodies to exert intensive pressure on the GOS to allow humanitarian assistance to reach the needy population in the SPLM-controlled areas. This international pressure culminated in a national relief conference held in Khartoum in early 1989 which came up with specific recommendations pertaining to the formation of a UN/NGOs consortium. The conference came at a time when the interplay of political and military agendas was such that it was in the interests of both parties to accept humanitarian intervention by the international community.

The GOS had lost much ground to the SPLA and needed some breathing space. Also, many NGOs were already running cross-border operations into SPLM-controlled parts of the Sudan and many more were planning to become involved. Conceding and permitting these NGOs to function within the framework of OLS allowed the government to stake its claim as the legitimate authority with sovereignty. The SPLM on the other hand had captured vast territories with a large civilian population which needed humanitarian assistance: the establishment of OLS would ensure the flow of humanitarian assistance to these civilians and would also mark the official recognition of the SPLM by both the GOS and UN agencies.

OLS was officially formed in April 1989 as a tripartite agreement between the SPLM, the GOS and the UN. The UN had to mobilise humanitarian assistance to the needy population on both sides of the conflict, with commitments from the parties to the conflict to ensure full access and cooperation. OLS managed to attract considerable humanitarian assistance for the needy civilian population in war-torn Sudan and had managed to save many lives and alleviate human suffering. The framework of the OLS consortium also provided a basis for negotiating access with the parties to the conflict and provided a conducive operational atmosphere for NGOs. Despite the apparent humanitarian values associated with OLS, it faced immense difficulties including exceptionally high operational costs of airlifting relief supplies, and consistent denial of access, primarily by the GOS.

With the passage of time, OLS, which started as small relief outfit, developed into a bureaucracy, sometimes shackled by red tape, and at other times undermined by questionable conduct by some of its members of staff (Atem, 1998b:113). The huge amounts of humanitarian assistance it provided, coupled with weak local civil administration, meant that within a short period of time OLS became the *de facto* government in the SPLM-controlled areas as it assumed the government's traditional role of social services provision. This increased the importance of the role of OLS in any analysis of the effectiveness of public action in addressing the 1998 famine in Bahr el Ghazal.

### Denial of Access

One of the increasingly prevalent types of public action failure occurs when a government willingly uses famine as an important component of its counterinsurgency warfare strategy. In many complex political emergencies, governments try to exclude the possibility of relief being offered because of their political hostility towards the famine-affected population (Devereux, 1993). The consistent denial by the GOS of air access for humanitarian agencies to reach the needy population had been one of the factors that greatly limited the agencies' level of response. The GOS frequently used its veto of sovereignty (paradoxically, over areas it hardly controlled) to ban flights into the SPLM-controlled areas. OLS had remained impotent in challenging the GOS's consistent denial of access to the needy population which was apparently unilateral violation of the tripartite agreement.

The denial of access, coupled with poor road infrastructure in most parts of southern Sudan, made delivery of relief supplies to the needy population exceedingly difficult. The effects of the unilateral denial of access had been recognised by OLS as a limiting factor to its performance. In one of its consolidated appeals, the UN argued that 'the humanitarian efforts of the United Nations through Operation Lifeline Sudan (OLS) were constrained throughout 1996 by the Government of the Sudan's initiatives to control unilaterally the flow of international assistance' (UN, 1997:iii).

The GOS's practice of unilaterally controlling the flow of humanitarian assistance had not only increased the vulnerability of the needy population but had also given the government an effective tool by means of which to use humanitarian assistance for its political objectives. This made the OLS impotent to prevent the GOS from using its facilities towards its war efforts, as claimed by SPLM in 1992 when it accused the then head of OLS of allowing the government to use an aircraft painted with UN insignia to carry weapons and soldiers to the besieged town of Juba (Atem, 1998a; de Waal, 1993).

Also, the monthly requests by the OLS for the GOS to allow access to various locations in the areas under the SPLM had been used to direct humanitarian assistance on the basis not of needs identified by humanitarian agencies but of political motives – the GOS usually put a condition to OLS to deliver relief assistance to the areas under its control (HAC, 1997 and 98). It is clear from Figure 18 that there was a consistent pattern of increased denial of access by the GOS during the months of February, March and April which are important months for the delivery of agricultural inputs.

The government of Sudan used its veto of sovereignty to obstruct agricultural activities by limiting the timely delivery of agricultural inputs. It is clear also from Figure 18 that there were more incidents of access being denied during 1997 than there were in 1998. While in 1997 the increased denial of access started as early as January, reached a peak in April and started declining in May, an increased denial of access during 1998 occurred only during the months of February and March and access was relatively normal for the rest of the year.

Though it could be argued that the effects of two consecutive months of bans of flights had a multiplier effect, it can also be argued that these effects easily could have been addressed with a concerted and well-planned response as the GOS, under pressure from the international community, allowed full access to all locations in the Bahr el Ghazal region from April 1998. The argument that denial of access by the GOS was the major cause of the delayed humanitarian response is weak and a smokescreen. It clearly suggests the need to explore other factors as well. However, the denial of access to the needy civilian population in the Nuba Mountains, where more than 5,000 persons starved to death during 1998, was a clear case where denial of access by GOS was the primary cause of famine.

*Figure 18: Locations Denied Access*
*by the Government of Sudan, 1996-98*

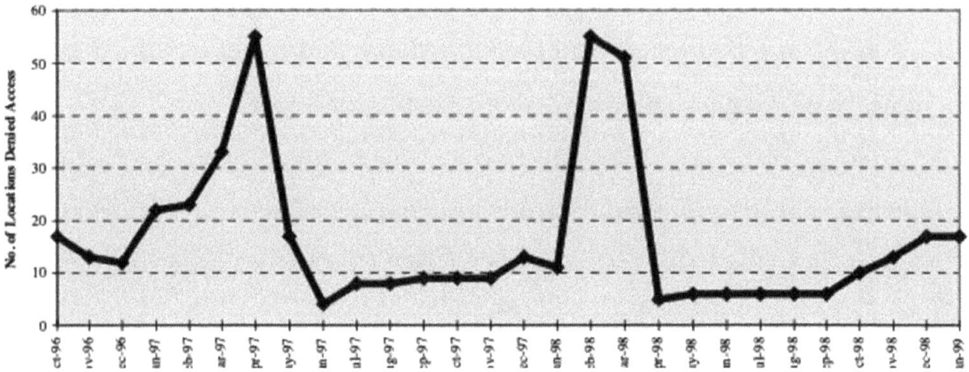


*Source: OLS (Southern Sector) and SRRA.*

### *Level of Humanitarian Intervention*

The humanitarian response was extremely relevant to the situation in Bahr el Ghazal, where market and nonmarket strategies failed to address the severe and acute food shortage of 1993–98. The need for additional resources to enable the people of Bahr el Ghazal to withstand their declining access to food was of great importance in order to smooth consumption and halt the process of downward spiral into increasing vulnerability. It has been argued that effective famine preventive public action should be early enough to save lives and livelihoods as well (Buchanan-Smith and Davies, 1995). In assessing the level of humanitarian response during 1998, the food, nonfood and feeding programmes interventions are analyzed below.

### *Relief Food Intervention*

The food security situation in Bahr el Ghazal started worsening in 1994 and reached the lowest level of the downward spiral of increasing vulnerability and subsequent famine in 1998. As shown in Figure 19, the level and pattern of relief intervention since 1993 does not reflect an early response to the gravity of the situation in Bahr el Ghazal. The relief food delivered by the WFP as the leading agency started declining, reaching its lowest level in 1996; it increased slightly during 1997. During 1996, WFP was able to deliver only 19 per cent of the food necessary to support vulnerable populations in war-affected areas in the Bahr el Ghazal region.

*Figure 19: WFP Monthly Food Deliveries to Regions of Southern Sudan, 1993-97*

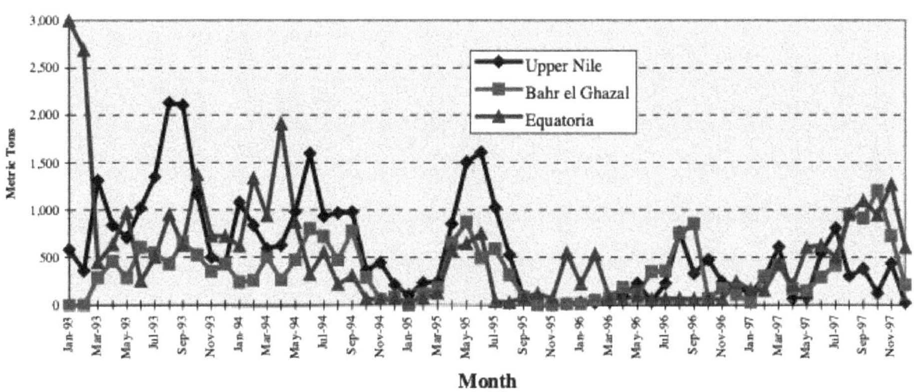


*Source: WFP/OLS (Southern Sector)*

During 1996 and 1997 actual WFP food deliveries constituted respectively only 12 per cent and 38 per cent of the OLS-measured needs. The declining trend of relief food deliveries is basically attributable to the declining resources availed to OLS/WFP – only 62 per cent (US$ 24.9 million) of the total amount pledged was actually given in 1996 and only 50 per cent (US$ 22 million) was covered during 1997 (UN, 1996, 1997). This is inconsistent with the claim made by the head of the DFID that lack of money was not the problem in the Sudan crisis (*Guardian*, 25 May 1998).

The situation in Bahr el Ghazal was further complicated by the misallocation of relief food which failed to prioritise humanitarian needs according to vulnerability. Though the declining pattern of relief food aid to southern Sudan is understandable given the decline in funding to OLS/WFP, the distribution of the relief food to the various regions of southern Sudan did not reflect the level of vulnerability. While Bahr el Ghazal region had been recognised as the most vulnerable since 1993 and is the most populated region (with approximately 2.4 million inhabitants), Figure 19 shows that Bahr el Ghazal before 1998 was generally receiving smaller relief food deliveries than other regions. Upper Nile, which was less vulnerable and less populated (approximately 1.8 million persons) than the Bahr el Ghazal region, had received disproportionately high relief food deliveries as shown in Figure 20.

*Figure 20: WFP Food Deliveries to Bahr el Ghazal and Upper Nile, 1993-97*

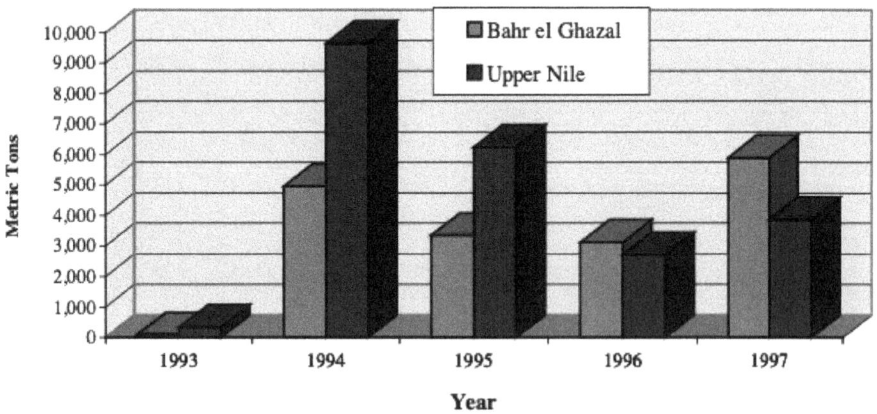


*Source: WFP/OLS (Southern Sector)*

For example, during 1994 and 1995 the relief food deliveries to Bahr el Ghazal constituted respectively about 51 per cent and 54 per cent of those of Upper Nile. The difference cannot be explained by ease of access – both Bahr el Ghazal and Upper Nile were primarily accessedby air. The apparent misallocation of relief food and the favoured position of Upper Nile began in 1991when the SPLM split and most of the Upper Nile region came under the control of GOS/SSIM and 1993 famine. The SPLM accused OLS in 1991 of meddling in internal politics.

Figure 20 suggests that despite the downward spiral of increasing vulnerability in Bahr el Ghazal, the humanitarian response failed to allocate the relief food aid effectively as an additional resource to the most-affected region. This reflects a conspicuous flaw either in the OLS assessment process or a failure in its mandate and its role of neutrally delivering humanitarian assistance to the neediest people.

### *Level of Food Relief in 1998*

During 1998 the level of WFP food relief increased drastically and improved the average household's food access, either directly through food distribution or indirectly by reducing the market prices of food staple or improving the pastoralist terms of trade. There is no doubt that the international community had managed to make adequate resources available to the WFP during 1998 which enabled it to increase remarkably its relief deliveries as shown in Figure 21.

*Figure 21: WFP Food Deliveries to Bahr el Ghazal, Southern Sudan, 1998*

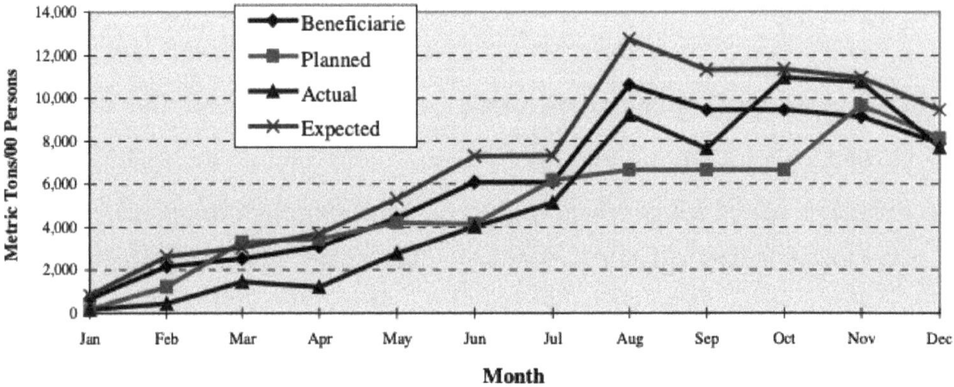


*Source: WFP/OLS (Southern Sector)*

But despite the substantial increase in relief food, the humanitarian response to the famine in Bahr el Ghazal during 1998 could be described as late and inadequate. It is clear from Figure 21 that it was only in August 1998 that actual food deliveries exceeded the planned level. The gap between planned and actual relief food deliveries to Bahr el Ghazal was exceptionally big during March and April 1998. It is interesting that the gap between actual and planned relief food deliveries remained almost the same during March, when the GOS had imposed a ban on flights to all locations in Bahr el Ghazal, and during April, when the ban was completely lifted.

This clearly shows that denial of access was not the only problem. It seems that OLS was also facing other constraints as it managed by June to receive 48 per cent of the total amount of US$ 109.4 million originally appealed for 1998, and WFP in particular received 54.2 per cent (US$ 32.2 million) of its total requirements (US$ 58.8 million). Even by June 1998, when the WFP's shortfall was only US$ 27.2

million, it appealed for additional funds of about US$ 110.2 million to cover only the period from January 1999 until the end of April 1999 when the 1998 emergency finished.

UNICEF appealed for an additional US$ 16.2 million. These appeals clearly reflected underestimation and misjudgement by OLS of the situation as a reactive planning process emerged to address the crisis. This became clear when comparing the number of beneficiaries in Bahr el Ghazal in January (68,195 persons) with that in August (1,060,947 persons) – an almost fifteenfold increase as shown in Figure 21. This indicates a serious problem in the OLS systems of assessing vulnerability in southern Sudan. The early failure to correctly assess the needy population in southern Sudan, and Bahr el Ghazal in particular, in 1998 played a great part in causing famine as it disrupted the targeting mechanism and encouraged unnecessary population movements to the food distribution centres.

When figures for the minimum daily cereal requirement of 400g per person is used to calculate the expected cereal requirements of the targeted population, the actual and planned WFP food deliveries were even further below the expected cereal requirements. This suggests that the planning of WFP food deliveries was based on a method that seriously underestimated the minimum food requirements of average households even during acute food shortage, as it implied that people would use other options for accessing food.

The inadequacy of relief food deliveries becomes apparent when we use figures for the targeted population to calculate food relief per capita as shown in Figure 22.

*Figure 22: WFP Food Per Capita in Bahr el Ghazal, Southern Sudan, 1998*

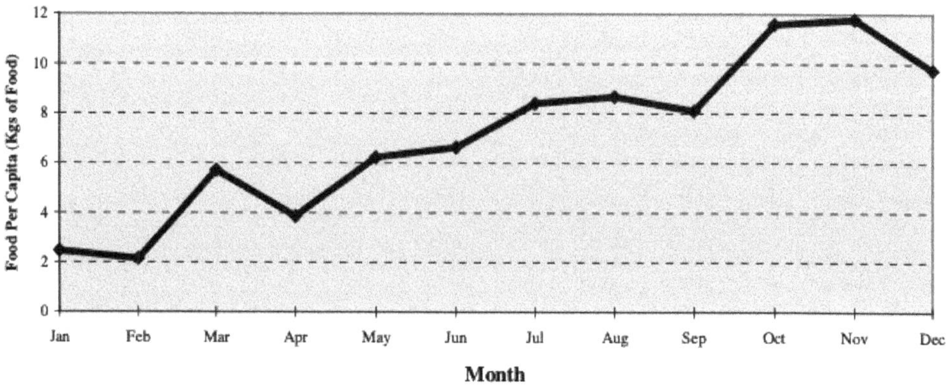


*Source: WFP/OLS (Southern Sector)*

It is clear that the monthly food relief per capita in Bahr el Ghazal was extremely low during 1998 except in the months of October and November when it nearly approached the minimum monthly cereal requirement per person (12kg, or 400g per day). The monthly food-per-capita pattern as shown in Figure 22 failed to bring an early halt to the downward spiral of increasing vulnerability. It contributed greatly to the excess mortality during the months of March to September.

***Quality of Relief Food***

The relief food intervention during the famine of 1998 was not only late and inadequate; in addition, the quality of the relief food was poor. During the first months of the famine most of the WFP food distributed was wheat flour. Local people have limited knowledge about its preparation, and its consumption resulted in increased cases of diarrhoea because of poor preparation and cooking. During the months of January to July the WFP cereal food supplied was mainly hard imported maize (corn) which requires considerable efforts to pound; as most people became very weak they resorted to boiling maize for consumption; this boiled maize became difficult to digest and also resulted in increased cases of diarrhoea and death.

The massive population movement that was basically triggered by centralised food distribution encouraged the concentration of population in food distribution centres; coupled with poor sanitation and poor access to water and health facilities, this too resulted in increased morbidity and excess death. Also, during the months of January to July there was basically no supply of pulses, edible oil and salt as the WFP was facing limited supply of these important food items. The Corn Soy Sugar Blends (CSB) general distribution was started later in July to supplement the general cereals distribution.

***Transport Costs***

The relief food deliveries to southern Sudan since the inception of OLS in 1989 had been imported despite increased food production in Western Equatoria. More than 70 per cent of all relief food deliveries had been airlifted, at an exceptionally high transport cost. It was estimated that the average cost for airlifting was about US$1,533 metric tons from Loki (northern Kenya) to southern Sudan and about US$822 metric tons for an airdrop from Loki to southern Sudan; land transport costed about US$156 metric tons from Koboko (northern Uganda) to southern Sudan (UN, 1998:34). Taking into account the cost of land transport from the Kenyan port of Mombassa to Koboko (about US$169 metric tons) and Loki (about US$116 metric tons), land transport from Mombassa to Bahr el Ghazal costed about US$325 metric tons while the land transport from Mombassa to Loki together with airlifting from Loki to Bahr el Ghazal costed about US$1,649.

Using land transport to Bahr el Ghazal, about US$1,324 could be saved on every metric ton delivered to Bahr el Ghazal. The road transport cost saving would even be higher – reaching more than US$1,493 per metric ton, if food were purchased locally in Western Equatoria. This huge difference betweenthe cost of land transport and the cost of airlifting clearly justifies new investment in road transport, including road maintenance, and the encouragement of haulage enterprise.

If OLS had started land transport as early as December 1997, and January–May 1998, more than 60 per cent of relief food would have been delivered by road and the effects of the GOS ban on flights during March and April would have been minimised. Though there are so many risks involved in land transport such as delay, damage and loss, the huge saving it makes possible could easily cover the costs associated with these risks. Other positive externalities associated with land transport include the boost it would give to trading activities between Uganda, Western Equatoria and the Bahr el Ghazal region, which would eventually help Uganda and Western Equatoria to respond to any future food shortage. Also, the indigenous entrepreneurial class would gradually emerge and develop to fill and address food needs through markets

### *Local Food Purchases*

The heavy reliance on imported relief food in southern Sudan has greatly undermined both the local communities' preference for locally produced food and important attempts to create market linkages between the relatively stable food-surplus economies in Western Equatoria and food-deficit economies in the Bahr el Ghazal region. Some NGOs such as CARE, World Vision International (WVI) and CONCERN had been purchasing limited quantities of locally produced cereals in Western Equatoria to be sold to WFP for relief intervention in Bahr el Ghazal region. These limited initiatives had indeed stimulated local production in Western Equatoria and it suggests that the aid agencies have potentials of stimulating local economies and markets even during the prolonged violent conflict.

### *The Feeding Programme*

Like relief intervention, the feeding programme during the famine in 1998 suffered from being late, poor coverage, centralised, and of low quality. All these factors contributed to excess mortality. On the basis of WFP's revised vulnerable population estimates of June 1998, the vulnerable population in Bahr el Ghazal were estimated to be around 701,000 persons; of these the population of children below five years old was estimated to be around 126,180 (about 18 per cent of the total population). Based on the weight-for- height method, the global malnutrition rate in June 1998 was about 50.9 per cent in Bahr el Ghazal (UNICEF, 1998) which put the population of malnourished children under five years old at around 64,000.

During February–June only 14,000 children (22 per cent of the total child population) were covered by the nineteen supplementary and eight therapeutic feeding centres; these centres did not have the capacity to admit all the nutritionally needy children. As a result, according to UNICEF (1998:3) the majority of malnourished children – including some severely malnourished cases – did not receive the care they needed at the feeding centres. The limited number of feeding centres coupled with their low admission capacities attracted people and encouraged unusual population movements and a high concentration of people around feeding centres. Moreover, only in June 1998, after the famine was at its peak, did OLS carry out a comprehensive nutritional survey in Bahr el Ghazal. This late assessment of the region's nutrition status delayed a timely intervention by the implementing agencies.

Because of the deteriorating situation at Ajiep in Gogrial county, by the end of August 1998 the SRRA carried out a situation assessment. The report found that the feeding programme coverage at Ajiep was extremely limited reaching about 12.5 per cent of the total number of malnourished children (SRRA, 1998:7). As a result of this low coverage the children who would normally qualify for care in a therapeutic feeding centre were admitted to supplementary feeding centres where they received the BP5 biscuits compact food.

According to the SRRA (1998:7), such biscuits compact food has a protein content that is not suitable for severely malnourished children, who in the initial phase of a therapeutic treatment regime should be receiving high- energy milk exclusively while their electrolyte and mineral imbalances are addressed. The mortality rates within the therapeutic feeding centres were as high as 50 per cent with an extremely low recovery rate of less than 50 per cent. The SRRA (1998:9) found also that the feeding programme implemented at Ajiep tended to ignore or implemented only partially the basic accepted international standards of therapeutic feeding that had been adhered to in other countries like Liberia, Somalia and Burundi with similar operational constraints to those in southern Sudan.

By the end of October 1998, the total number of children admitted to therapeutic feeding centres (TFC) and supplementary feeding centres (SFC) was about 29,000, about 45 per cent of the total malnourished children in Bahr el Ghazal as shown in Figure 23. The total population of children excluded therefore from the feeding programmes during 1998 was more than 35,000. Although how they dealt with the effects of malnutrition is unknown it is generally believed that many of them probably died.

*Figure 23: Children Covered by Feeding Programmes in Bahr el Ghazal, October 1998*

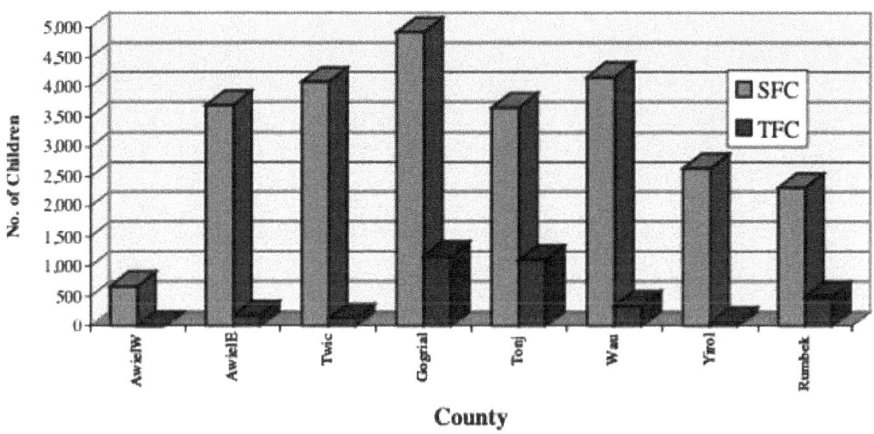


*Source: WFP/OLS Southern Sector and SRRA*

Also, despite evident increased mortality among adults during 1998, no therapeutic feeding centres were established for adults until August and September when ICRC and CONCERN successfully established feeding centres for adults; adults were a neglected group in many areas throughout the famine in Bahr el Ghazal. Also, while the priority of most feeding programmes was naturally placed on feeding, insufficient efforts were focused on the availability of clean and safe water and sanitation, particularly the latter (SRRA, 1998). Most feeding programmes in Bahr el Ghazal had no adequately functioning sanitation system, either in the therapeutic and supplementary feeding centres or in the surrounding villages. This lack of functioning sanitation system contributed greatly to increased cases of diarrhoea, diseases and morbidity which became leading causes of mortality.

The exclusion from the feeding programmes of the majority of malnourished children, the centralisation of feeding centres, poor sanitation and lack of access to safe water, the early exclusion of adults in feeding programmes and the non-adherence to minimum accepted standards all contributed with other factors to excess mortality during 1998 in Bahr el Ghazal.

### *Nonfood Intervention*

Nonfood intervention is usually neglected despite its importance during famine as attention focused primarily on food. It has been generally observed that famine is accompanied besides human suffering with massive population movements, unhealthy concentration of people in the displaced centres, loss of basic household assets and shelters, and increased cases of trauma, abandoned children and separation of families.

In Bahr el Ghazal population movements started as early in February 1998 and continued till September when there was considerable improvement in food deliveries and decentralisation of food distribution centres and feeding centres. During this period the population movement was guided by the movement of high-capacity planes like the C-130 which was dropping food; such population movement was once described by one senior SRRA staff member as C-130 invitees. During March and April people walked for two to four days to the food distribution centres, where the probability of getting food was often minimal.

In the process of this intensive movement, people became exhausted and lost almost all their basic household assets and shelters. Even when the food deliveries improved, people did not have cooking utensils and water containers, which greatly affected the preparation and cooking of food and resulted in poor hygiene and increased cases of diarrhoea. During the rainy season in June–August, most of the recorded deaths were related to exposure and diseases as displaced people had virtually no shelter, blankets or clothing. People resorted to using empty sacks from WFP food deliveries for shelter and bedding, and fire for heating. In the displaced camp at Ajiep it was only in September that the ICRC distributed blankets and plastic sheets to the displaced population.

Despite the importance of nonfood interventions as complementary to relief food intervention, the OLS airlifting of nonfood emergency supplies during 1998 was late, inadequate and of low priority, as shown in Figure 24. During the early phase (January–May) of famine and massive displacement, when nonfood emergency items could have been expected to take priority in the OLS airlift deliveries, they instead declined, reaching their lowest level in May as shown in Figure 24. The supplies of camps of the international aid agencies took priorities over most other nonfood emergencies in 1998.

*Figure 24: OLS Nonfood Airlift Deliveries by Sector to Southern Sudan, 1998*

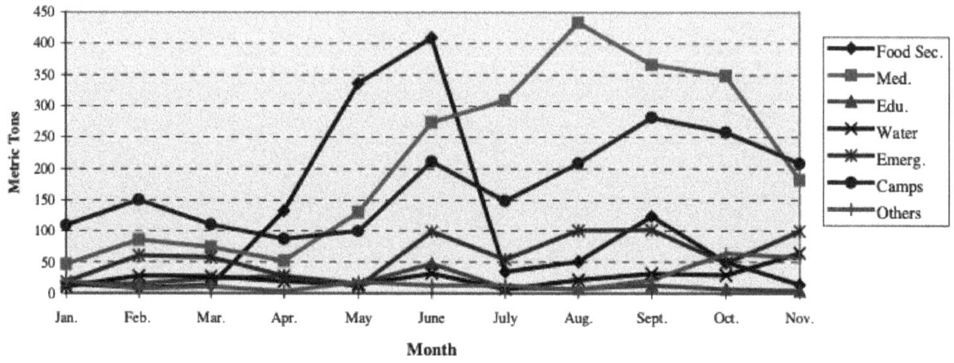


*Source: WFP/OLS Southern Sector and SRRA*

While nonfood emergency items were accorded low priority in the OLS airlift deliveries during 1998, camp supplies (mineral water, fresh food, beverages, etc.) to NGOs and UN agency expatriates and staff working in southern Sudan paradoxically remained the priority, amounting sometimes to up to 40 per cent of all airlift deliveries. Some NGOs did not use the cargo space of chartered planes efficiently as they sometimes imported trivial items from Kenya which could easily have been obtained locally in southern Sudan. For example, during the critical period of famine in 1998, one NGO from the OLS consortium chartered a caravan plane to transport imported timber from Kenya to build a bomb shelter in an area of Bahr el Ghazal which is well endowed with trees.

This high cost of maintaining the compounds of NGOs and UN agencies inside southern Sudan was related to the tendency among most NGOs to employ excessive numbers of expatriate staff to do minor duties that could easily be performed by Sudanese. SCF (1998:26) describes this phenomenon of relief workers in southern Sudan as follows: *'The first impression that OLS workers give as they get off their planes from Lokichokio is that they are rich – with their possessions and camping gear taking up most of thecargo space of the plane.'*

The humanitarian assistance in southern Sudan was delivered according to Western prescription and presented as the only solution to the problem in southern Sudan. This observation is consistent with de Waal's (1989:196) argument that nonpoor people who give aid to poor people have a marked tendency to see their aid as central to the poor people's lives. The OLS became entirely owned by Western NGOs with minimal participation from local communities.

The breaking of the vicious cycle of famine relief largely rests with generating self-employment, jobs and income for the poor from improved agricultural production, including animal husbandry at household level in southern Sudan. The delivery and distribution of agricultural inputs and veterinary drugs plays an important role in speeding the process of breaking the vicious cycle of famine relief. The delivery of agricultural inputs by NGOs and UN agencies operating in southern Sudan since the inception of OLS in 1989 could be described as late, irrelevant, inappropriate and consisting of poor-quality seeds and tools.

Though there had never been a comprehensive evaluation (a planning element that is greatly neglected and if it is carried out becomes donor-driven) of the impact of agricultural inputs, the OLS and SRRA annual needs assessments had raised concerns over timing, adequacy, quality and relevance of agricultural inputs – but with little improvement in practice. Some NGOs had been consistently and mistakenly supplying Sudan grass instead of proper seeds. The end result, with an absence of any effective system of testing the quality and relevance of seeds, has been a waste of enormous resources in terms of costs of inputs and farmers' time and labour.

This had exposed southern Sudan to the risk of becoming a dumping zone for poor-quality seeds (probably genetically modified agricultural seeds) and agricultural tools. Despite this discouraging management of agricultural inputs by NGOs and UN agencies operating in southern Sudan, some considerable and recognised efforts by some NGOs, particularly CARE International in Western Equatoria, had been successful in encouraging and promoting local seed production, which had not only satisfied local needs but supplied other regions with high-quality and appropriate local seeds.

Besides being late, irrelevant and of poor quality, the quantity of agricultural inputs delivered during 1997, a year before the famine, was extremely small and inadequate as shown in Figure 25. The total quantity of agricultural inputs airlifted and distributed in southern Sudan during 1997 by OLS agencies was only 343.2 metric tons which is less than 30 per cent of what was delivered and distributed (1,188.7 metric tons) during 1998 (limited quantities were delivered by road). It is apparent also from Figure 25 that camps supplies during 1997 were a priority for OLS airlift deliveries and constituted about 34 per cent of the cumulative nonfood airlift deliveries to southern Sudan. That is, the weight of airlift deliveries for the maintenance of NGOs and UN expatriates and staff in their compounds in southern Sudan during 1997 was more than 1.5 times that of agricultural inputs. The inadequacy of seeds distributed during 1997 coupled with other factors contributed to a considerable decline in household food availability during the last quarter of 1997 and direct food entitlement failure during the first three quarters of 1998.

*Figure 25: OLS Cumulative Airlift Deliveries of Nonfood Items to Southern Sudan, 1997*

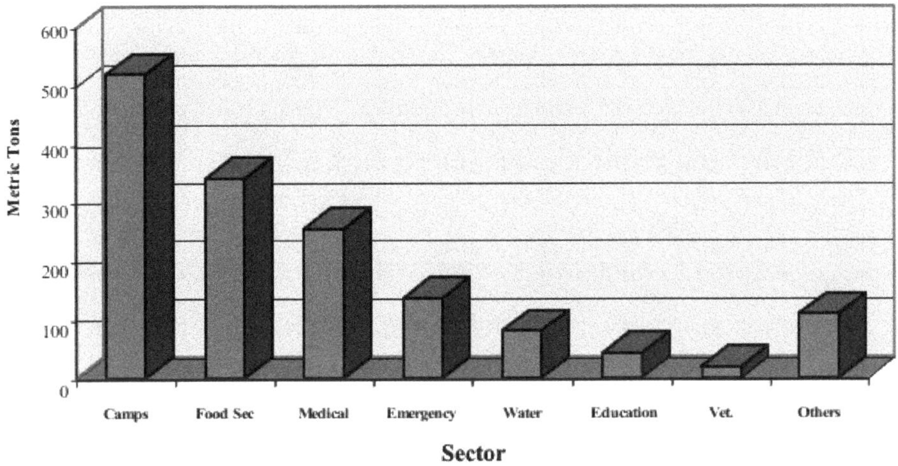


*Sources: WFP/OLS Southern Sector*

The pattern of food security deliveries during 1998, though considerably increased, was also late, inadequate and of poor quality. In terms of timing, the food security inputs, particularly seeds, should ideally be ready before the cropping season in January–March to be distributed during March and April for sowing in May particularly in the Bahr el Ghazal region. As shown in Figure 24, seeds deliveries during 1998 started in April and peaked in June. The months of May, June and July 1998 were the months when people in Bahr el Ghazal reached the lowest level in the downward spiral of vulnerability. Because food deliveries were inadequate, people were forced to consume seeds; those who endeavoured to sow the seeds were later disappointed by the poor performance of the seeds because of their poor quality.

There was a considerable increase in the quantity of seeds distributed during 1998, relative to 1997 – almost 3.4 times as much (a normal reactive pattern during crisis). Despite this substantial increase, there was nevertheless a huge seed deficit relative to the identified seed needs as shown in Figure 26. Bahr el Ghazal experienced an enormous seed deficit relative to other regions and constituted more than 40 per cent of the identified total seed needs.

*Figure 26: Cumulative Seeds Deliveries to Southern Sudan, January–June 1998*

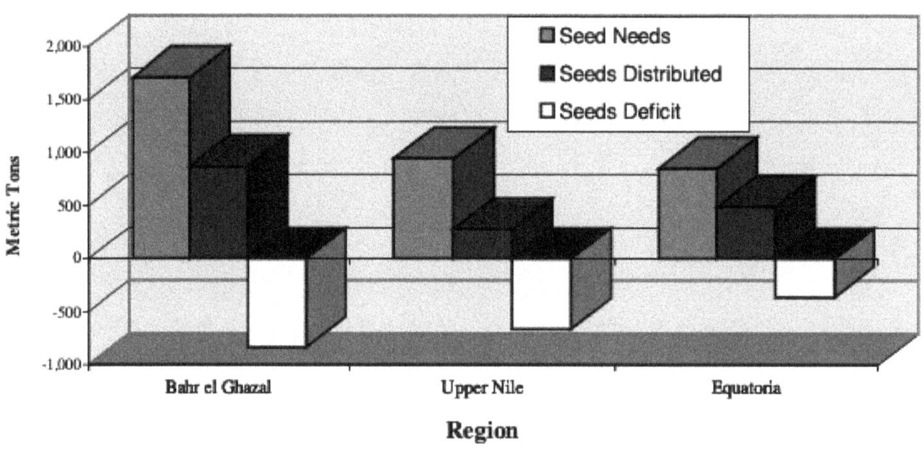


*Source: WFP/OLS Southern Sector*

In terms of access to other social services such as health, water and education, Bahr el Ghazal – particularly northern Bahr el Ghazal – had the lowest level of access relative to other regions. While in Bahr el Ghazal the proportion of people having access to health services and safe drinking water was less than 10 and 8 per cent respectively, access to these services in Equatoria was respectively about 70 and 52 per cent (SRRA, 1998:52-61).

Also, Bahr el Ghazal in terms of access to education services had the lowest population of enrolled pupils (about 4 per cent of the total population) which is almost half of that of Equatoria (8 per cent) and Upper Nile (8 per cent) (SRRA, 1998:52–61). The poor access to health, water and education services had made Bahr el Ghazal distinctively and increasingly more vulnerable than other regions of southern Sudan. It is clear from Figure 25 that the airlift deliveries to support programmes related to health, education and water were of minor importance during 1997; a similar pattern prevailed during 1998 except in relation to the health sector which experienced a substantial increase in its airlift deliveries because of the measles and polio campaigns (see Figure 24).

### *The Level of Coordination*

There is growing evidence to suggest that mortality is reduced when assistance is well coordinated. Huge humanitarian operations with significant scope, like the one in southern Sudan, in terms of numbers of people affected, area covered and the number of implementing agencies, require a well-coordinated relief effort for effectiveness, efficiency and to save lives. The need for effective coordination lies in the management of information related to needs, quality standards of programmes and the relationship withlocal authorities.

In southern Sudan there were two groups of NGOs: those within the OLS consortium and those out of OLS which operated freely without restriction by the GOS. All NGOs, particularly the international NGOs, had established their own independent forum to discuss general policy issues. UNICEF was vested with a leadership role, since the UNDP was nonoperational in the SPLM-held areas, to ensure well-coordinated and integrated operations of OLS. The SRRA as the humanitarian wing of the SPLM was mandated to coordinate all humanitarian activities in the areas under SPLM control. The coordination role of the SRRA, theoretically rather than in practice, covered all NGOs within and outside OLS and put it in a better coordinating position than UNICEF which was limited only to the NGOs within the OLS consortium.

During the 1998 famine in Bahr el Ghazal the number of NGOs operating in southern Sudan increased drastically from about 40 in 1997 to more than 60 with the majority in the OLS consortium. Neither the SRRA nor OLS succeeded during 1998 in effectively coordinating relief efforts in Bahr el Ghazal. Being under-resourced and dependent on external assistance, which drastically declined during 1998, the SRRA expected UNICEF, given its lead role in OLS and the resources available to it, to have carried out the coordination role, regulated standards and managed the crisis.

While the coordination of information related to needs and assessment will be discussed in subsequent sections, the emphasis here is on the standards and quality of relief programmes. During the early stage of the famine in Bahr el Ghazal in April–May, some new NGOs came in with resources to intervene effectively but were not given operational space as some NGOs working by then in Bahr el Ghazal overestimated their own capacity to manage the situation and denied the existence of any gaps.

This tendency among NGOs of discouraging new or expanding NGOs from entering into their operational space remained unchecked both by SRRA and by OLS and contributed greatly to delays and poor coverage of the relief intervention and subsequently excess deaths. One senior OLS staff described the behaviour of some NGOs as follows: *'These guys don't want another agency going in there. MSF (B) raises its own money, a lot of money. Funding is No. 1. When you have the money, you have the power'* (*Christian Science Monitor*, 9 October, 1998).

As discussed earlier, most of the feeding programmes implemented in Bahr el Ghazal during 1998 failed to adhere to the basic accepted international standards in feeding programmes even after the total lifting of the flights ban in April. This situation also continued without proper monitoring by SRRA and OLS. Paradoxically it was the SRRA, despite its extremely meagre resources, which managed in August 1998 to assess some feeding programmes and came out with alarming findings about the compromised nutritional state of the population in Bahr el Ghazal. This made some Sudanese think that some NGOs were deliberately prolonging the suffering of the children in the feeding centres in order to attract the media, to market their own organisations in a highly competitive voluntary sector in the Western world and justify the continuity of their programmes.

Another area of poor coordination during 1998 was the polio campaign carried out in the months of March–April, which coincided with the first phase of famine in Bahr el Ghazal. Though polio was of great concern in southern Sudan, it was not by any measures one of the most pressing priorities, which included measles and guinea worm. The polio campaign was a clear case of a Western agenda forcefully imposed as a priority in a situation where people were on the brink of imminent famine. UNICEF as a leading agency in OLS blindly embraced this campaign and this became its overriding priority instead of famine, which greatly compromised the OLS management and response to the pressing famine.

The preparation and implementation of the polio campaign diverted the attention and time of the SRRA and OLS away from the looming famine. During my monitoring follow-up of the food security situation in Bahr el Ghazal in March 1998 when only four airstrips were allowed by GOS, I personally witnessed how in Gogrial county the time of SRRA and NGO staff was overly stretched between the polio campaign on one hand and food distribution and preparation for the establishment of feeding centres on the other. At Pakor airstrip in Gogrial county, which was one of the four locations allowed access in March and attracted many people from four counties (Awiel, Twic, Abyei and Gogrial), some of those who came had walked for more than four days.

They then spent more than two days waiting for food distribution which was then suspended for extra three days for the polio campaign. During the time when food distribution was suspended because of the polio campaign, I witnessed some people fainting and more than five persons from Awiel county died while waiting for food distribution. The MSF (B) nutrition survey which was carried out by then showed a global malnutrition rate of more than 70 per cent. It was apparent in March and April 1998 that OLS and the SRRA as well were more concerned about the success of the polio campaign in meeting global targets than about averting the looming famine.

### Impacts of Food Aid

Ravallion (1996:14) shows that if income is fixed and all of it is spent on food then survival chances will be concave in the price of food, and the famine evidence from South Asia indicates that mortality is an increasing concave function of price . Food aid as an additional resource to the household's food endowment base contributes directly to consumption and indirectly through stabilisation of food staple prices, which subsequently reduces excess mortality during famine.

Some researchers have found little evidence that food aid has any impact on mortality (de Waal, 1989:208). De Waal (1989:209) argues that consumption of staple foods has little or no influence on the risk of dying during famine and the consumption of food aid will likewise not improve people's chances of surviving. This argument is surprising and rather controversial as enormous evidence from famines in pastoral economies of rural Africa, Asia and Europe shows the prices of food staples to be one of the key variables influencing mortality.

The famine experience in southern Sudan in 1998 shows that food aid had a significant positive impact on mortality as shown in Figure 27. As discussed earlier, some communities positively associated the famine in 1998 with UN intervention and named it 'the year of the UN'. It is clear from Figure 27 that when food aid deliveries started to increase substantially in June, the mortality rate started declining. The pattern of monthly food aid deliveries during 1998 as shown in Figure 27 clearly shows a positive impact on sorghum prices, particularly from June until sorghum prices stabilised in October when food aid deliveries reached their highest level.

*Figure 27: Food Aid, Mortality, Market Prices and Cattle Sales in Gogrial, Southern Sudan, 1998*

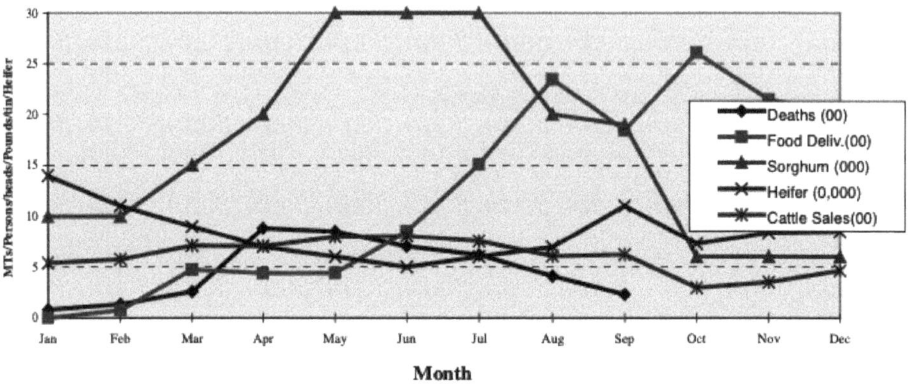


*Source: WFP/OLS/SRRA Monitoring Unit*

The stabilisation of sorghum prices through increased food aid deliveries during 1998 greatly reduced mortality to normal levels. Also apparent from Figure 27 is the positive impact food aid had on prices of heifers and the volume of cattle sales during 1998. As food aid deliveries were low from January to May 1998, heifer prices and the volume of cattle respectively declined and increased in the same period. But these trends started reversing when food aid deliveries considerably improved as from June. This clearly suggests that the early and timely deliveries of food aid during 1998 would have greatly averted famine in southern Sudan.

***Food Aid Targeting and Distribution***

The effect of food aid on mortality depends greatly on how it is distributed over time and between people (Ravallion, 1996:35). Ravallion (1996:34) argues that despite the apparent and convincing reason of increasing aggregate food availability during famine, food handouts need not be the best form of intervention to minimise mortality. Maxwell and Templer (1994) show that cash payments rather than food handouts to potential famine victims (particularly famine migrants in Western Equatoria) under competitive market conditions can provide effective mortality-minimising measures. The targeting of food aid besides its apparent role of minimising mortality also plays a critical role of linking relief to development.

Targeting of food aid implies selection of those in greater need, exclusion of others, and restriction of resources which is necessitated by reasons related to humanitarian aims (to concentrate assistance to the neediest), efficiency (to maximize the impact of scarce resources), and development (to minimise dependency and economic disincentives) (Sharp, 1998:7). Dreze and Sen (1989) identify three possible mechanisms (market, self and administrative) for targeting food aid. Sharp (1998) adds a fourth mechanism (community targeting) although it is a subcategory of administrative targeting. Sharp (1998) deliberately treats community targeting separately because of its relevance, importance and limited focus in the international literature as it seems to be almost entirely an African issue.

In community targeting, the representatives of the community or their institutions make decisions on selection which are based on a fairly subjective, complex judgement of need or local understanding of vulnerability rather than on data collection and analysis, with increasing potential risk of bias and abuse of power by decision makers (Sharp, 1998:8–9). Sharp argues that despite the apparent possible difficulties and risk, community targeting has advantages related to the avoidance of costs related to data collection, the deeper understanding of local perceptions of vulnerability, the spin-off benefits of capacity building and empowerment, and in providing relevant assistance in the context of weak administrative capacity.

Besides these advantages of community targeting, African experiences increasingly show that communities make their own (re) distribution which is reluctant to discriminate between households and tends to stretch small quantities of food aid over large numbers of people regardless of the official distribution of outside agencies (Sharp, 1998). Given the fact that redistribution after official distribution is bound to occur because of traditional customary redistribution mechanisms, Sharp (1998) argues the need to bow to the inevitable by accepting such phenomenon as a reality and to devise ways of ensuring fair and accountable decisions.

The humanitarian agencies that are involved in the distribution of relief food and nonfood items in southern Sudan used various distribution mechanisms: either a relief committee system, a system of distribution via chiefs, or a pure administrative mechanism (particularly among the organised displaced population) or a combination of both relief committee and chiefs distribution system. In the Bahr el Ghazal region only two targeting mechanisms were operational, namely relief committees in northern Bahr el Ghazal and a traditional chiefs' system of targeting in southeastern Bahr el Ghazal (Tonj, Rumbek and Yirol counties). Poor targeting of relief food during 1998 greatly contributed to the worsening famine situation in the region.

### *Relief Committees*

Following the inception of OLS in 1989, the targeting of food aid began with direct targeting by relief agencies with help from the SRRA and chiefs. Because of problems of bias and abuse of powers by chiefs, the WFP and the SRRA formed relief committees in 1994–95 for targeting food aid, particularly in northern Bahr el Ghazal. Each relief committee was to be elected by the community of a given area with gender balance and a particular emphasis on women. Each relief committee consisted of seven elected female members and six male elected members who were representatives of a given geographical location and worked closely with chiefs and the community to identify the most vulnerable within their population for food aid targeting. Theoretically it seemed that 'vulnerability' is locally defined by the community and targeting was done according to agreed community criteria.

The sequence of food aid targeting in southern Sudan started with the geographical allocation of food aid (based on number of beneficiaries for a given number of days at a set ration) on the basis of a WFP/SCF food economy assessment. Once the assessed food aid arrived at a given location, the WFP and SRRA would inform chiefs and the relief committee about the number of people to be targeted and chiefs, together with the relief committee, would then apportion (in most cases on the basis of population size rather than vulnerability) the total population to be targeted and the amount of food to the residential villages.

Once this is done, chiefs will then inform their population about the day of food distribution. It is important to note here that the entire population (particularly women) rather than the specified quota would be asked to come for food distribution. On the day of food distribution, the population (mainly women) would group according to their villages, and the relief committee would then explain to each village that the limited quantity of food was not enough for all.

Each village would then be asked to elect a trusted representative, *tieng Wai* (woman with stick), who would do the targeting on the spot. The elected woman (*tieng Wai)* would then select (in most cases not on the basis of vulnerability) the specified number of women to be targeted from the village.

The system of relief committees, though it looks democratic and gender-balanced, was a rather alien and imposed structure which only reflected the 'outsiders' perception of democracy, gender balance and vulnerability. In his response on the origin of relief committees, chief Alfred Amet in Gogrial county states the following:

> *It started when Kawaja [white person] started asking who keeps grain? … He was told women keep grain.… Kawaja then asked who keeps cattle? … He was told men keep cattle… Then Kawaja said women should be the ones to distribute and keep relief food and men with cattle … and you chiefs should keep away from food distribution … and leave it for women.… The food distribution is now confused as women start selecting their relatives.*

This view was shared by many people including women members of relief committees and SRRA staff who raised concerns about the system's effectiveness. It is clear that the *tieng Wai* has no adequate information about the situation of the entire village and probably bases her selection on extremely subjective criteria. The system also lacks continuity and follow-up as the *tieng Wai* is changed in every food distribution. The worst feature of this system is its apparent exposure of the poor *tieng Wai* to take the entire responsibility or blame for exclusion or inclusion errors of targeting which have far-reaching social costs.

The good intention of the system of empowering women turns out in practice to expose women to become socially more vulnerable, particularly in a situation of acute food shortage where everyone feels in need and vulnerable. One SRRA county secretary stated, '*we have taken off our necks the job of targeting blame to the relief committees who in turn passed it over to the poor tieng Wai.*'

During the famine in 1998, because of increasing vulnerability, the breakdown of kinship support, massive displacement, increased court cases relating to hunger and inadequate relief food deliveries, the system of using relief committees for targeting could not cope – the famine almost overwhelmed entire communities particularly in northern Bahr el Ghazal and targeting became extremely difficult. The exclusion of displaced people in particular during the targeting of relief food greatly increased death rates among the displaced population as they were not adequately represented on the relief committees.

A Dinka poet and singer called Mathuc Bol in Gogrial county composed the following hunger song lamenting the poor food aid targeting:

> *The war of armed struggle has been accomplished;*
> *Yet one war exists still … the war of a person to distribute food; A person who scoops food … where is that person?*
> *Never, never he is not yet found. If he is not found…*
> *Let me tell you to sit down and look for that person;*
> *A person who is generous and with good heart; And if he is not found on the land of the Sudan … Look for money to get him from other countries … So he can come to distribute food …*

Another problem was that the traditional authorities, particularly chiefs, subchiefs and lineage leader (*nhom gol*), felt that the relief committees had assumed their social obligations and became indifferent to the needy during famine. Some of them used the relief committees as their scapegoat not to take care of the most vulnerable members in their communities.

### *The Chiefs' System of Distribution and Targeting*

The Dinka traditional hierarchy of authority consists of the *bany dit* (executive chief), followed by *bany kor* (subchief), *nhom gol* (lineage leader) and *nhom mac thok* (leader of sublineage/headman). This hierarchy is closely linked to the tribal hierarchy which consists of tribe *(Wut),* subtribe (*Wut)* and section *(dhien/gol/lineage).* The Dinka tribal and traditional authority hierarchy is based on the cattle camp analogy as it expresses both the territorial and lineage make-up of Dinka society (SCF, 1998:5).

A dry-season cattle camp ( *Wut)* is headed by the *majok Wut* (leader of the cattle camp) and consists of many lineages in the form of a number of *gal* (plural of *gol)* headed by *gol leaders* or dung-fires around which an individual lineage tethers their cattle (SCF,1998:5). A cattle camp is usually composed of various lineages from the same Dinka permanent agricultural settlement *(baai)* who are not necessarily related. The *baai* (permanent settlement) consists of various lineages and allows intermarriage (as marriage within the lineage is not allowed in Dinka culture); the traditional authority hierarchy of executive chiefs and subchiefs which is based on *Wut* exists to crosscut the lineage structure and to ensure harmony, protection, and law and order. This hierarchy of traditional authority clearly shows the gradual transition of Dinka society from pure pastoralist to agro-pastoralist, with a pastoralist hierarchy of authority remaining the dominant feature.

The traditional hierarchy of authority which was purely based on lineage has been mixed with territorial chiefs (an alien structure imposed by the colonial regimes of the Turkish and British) which are based on *Wut* and further complicated by the SPLM administration structure which grouped people according to *payam* and *boma* (SCF, 1998). *Nuer* society, unlike Dinka, still retains a system whereby lineage corresponds with village, and where people who graze their cattle together are usually related and from a similar lineage.

The Dinka structure represents a way of trying to combine territorial loyalties as well as those of lineage and becomes difficult to administer smoothly (SCF, 1998:6). The current traditional authority hierarchy has been relatively democratised by the SPLM as chieftainship is operated in a well-developed system of local democracy and is no longer based on heredity alone. Most of the executive chiefs, subchiefs and *gol* leaders whom I interviewed unanimously confirmed that they had all been elected by the people despite a clear pattern of the presence of heredity. According to SCF (1998:7), the SPLM administration has to a certain extent encouraged a meritocratic society where even a poor man can become a chief, but in most cases chieftainship is hereditary.

The chiefs' system of relief food distribution is similar to the relief committee's system except people were grouped according to *gol* (lineage) instead of village and the *gol* leader assumes the role of *tieng Wai* (village elected representative) and targets the heads of the *thok mac* (leaders of the sublineage) rather than women heads of household.

This system also suffers similar problems to those faced by relief committees such as bias, exclusion of the displaced population, abuse of powers and corruption, particularly at the level of chiefs and subchiefs. It is complicated by the mixed systems of territorial loyalties and lineage as the relief food is first allocated according to the SPLM administrative structure of *payam* and then translated into *Wut* (chiefs and subchiefs), a traditional territorial breakdown, and then lineage breakdown.

Such a complicated process of food distribution through a system that is hardly understood by outsiders, may give rise to suspicions of subterfuge and corruption (SCF, 1998). Despite these problems associated with the chiefs system, it is closely linked with lineage structure, particularly *gol* leaders and headmen who know better than anybody the vulnerability of their people. Also, the fact that *gol* leaders and headmen have social obligations during crises to their lineage and are entirely dependent on the acceptance and political mandate of their lineage, means that they are bound to be fair and to keep high moral standards among their lineage. In emphasising the important role played by *gol* leaders in targeting food aid, Chief Ayii Madut in Gogrial stated the following:

> *The distribution started first early in 1998 with the relief committee and excess death did not stop and the situation even worsened particularly in April to June. In July people sat down to review targeting. These women [the relief committee] started selecting their own relatives and people agreed to abandon it. Earlier a chiefs system [executive chiefs and subchiefs] was tried and they were even accused of corruption and abuse of power. People agreed to come back to a chiefs system using particularly gol leaders and headmen, and with*

*displaced people to have their own representatives. This new system of distribution through lineage [dhien/gol] and in an open place [with transparency] succeeded in saving lives. The chiefs [executive and subchiefs] were told not to put their hands in the distribution and only their gol leaders and headmen will handle food distribution.*

### *Actual Distribution of Food Aid: Targeting All*

In a situation like that in 1998, when almost the entire population of the Bahr el Ghazal region was overwhelmed by famine, and almost every person became needy, it becomes morally unjustifiable to target some and exclude others during relief food distribution. The very reasons that necessitate targeting such as humanitarian priorities (to concentrate assistance on the neediest) and efficiency (to maximise the impact of scarce resources) all indicated during the 1998 famine the need to adopt blanket targeting (full coverage) with both zero exclusion (not targeting those eligible) and inclusion (targeting those who are eligible) errors, particularly in northern Bahr el Ghazal.

Despite the evident reality of widespread suffering and vulnerability, OLS insisted on targeting the limited relief quantities of food delivered to Bahr el Ghazal, which created problems with targeting whether the relief committee system or the chiefs system was used. For example, a lucky woman who happened to be targeted (on the basis of luck or favouritism) could get a 50kg bag of sorghum, while the excluded women who might be at the same level of vulnerability as the targeted woman got nothing. The targeting during the 1998 famine was not by any measure based on pure needs, and was based instead on the amount of food delivered and made available for distribution and could ideally be distributed evenly by OLS to the famine-affected population.

Concerned and mindful of the situation of their communities, the chiefs, subchiefs and *gol* leaders resorted to the establishment of a redistribution system after the OLS official distribution. During the first distribution the food was distributed according to the OLS-specified food ration and targeted according to the specified number of households to be covered. In actual fact, the first distribution was just carried out to give a positive impression that the OLS criteria of food targeting were satisfied, and those targeted during the first distribution were merely used to porter the relief food to the second redistribution site (SPLM/SRRA/OLS Task Force, 1998:15).

During the second distribution, which took place a distance from the first distribution, the food was distributed evenly to those who had been targeted in the first distribution and to those who had been excluded as well (SPLM/SRRA/OLS Task Force, 1998:16). The SPLM/SRRA/OLS Task Force (1998:17) found that the rationale for the redistribution system included the small size of the targeted population, the limited quantity of food available for targeting, the increased vulnerability in all sectors of society, the easy collection of taxes on food and an increased incidence of looting.

The system of even redistribution by the community of relief food or even the distribution of a uniform household ration, is not a phenomenon unique to the southern Sudan. It has been observed in a large number of cases in Africa (Dreze and Sen, 1989:107). Hale (1986) noted in the Red Sea Province of Sudan in 1985 that the local leaders in charge of food distribution had a very clear and accurate perception of the needs of different families, but that the allocation process made no discriminating use of this informational advantage

– and every family had to have a share (Dreze and Sen, 1989:107).

Oxfam's (1995:5) experience in East Africa also shows that *'assistance targeted to particular households or household members will often be shared beyond those individuals, given customary systems of exchanges and loans, and a certain amount of redistribution is bound to occur'*. In Ethiopia, Sharp (1997:5) also noted the community's reluctance to discriminate between households within communities, and a tendency to stretch small quantities of food aid over large numbers of people either openly or by redistribution after the official distribution.

The rationale for egalitarian African societies, and particularly Dinka, to share equally the 'foreign assistance' among their communities without discrimination is related to their perception of wealth in general and vulnerability. The Dinka communal right over property and wealth is primarily derived from their relationship to their Divinity (*yieth*), to which all wealth and property belong, and individuals are entrusted with control over wealth and property (Lienhardt, 1961:23). This mixture between individual and communal property rights among pastoralist societies is attributed by some economists to the scarcity of resources involved (Demsetz, 1967).

In the context of rural Sudan, Evans-Pritchard (1940) explicitly pointed out that it is scarcity and not sufficiency that makes people generous in a community where everyone is likely to face difficulties. While there are social classes determined by wealth, there used to be no social barriers between these classes, as the strong spirit of equality among the Dinka did not permit the rich to look down on the poor or the poor to look up to the rich (Deng, 1971). The apparent emphasis on the human element in social relations is the main feature of Dinka society that used to bridge class barriers and differentiation.

The virtues of wealth that are defined in the context of social prestige carry commensurate social responsibilities in Dinka society, as the rich are socially bound to assist the needy.

This inseparable link between wealth and social responsibilities is well reflected in the Dinka words '*adheng*' and '*ajak*', which mean 'rich' and may also be translated as 'kind', 'generous', 'gentle' or in a word 'noble' (Deng, 1971:251). Thus, calling a person 'rich' in Dinka is another way of describing what is expected of his/her relations with other people. The social relations in Dinka society; between individual and individual, and individual and community, as described by Deng (1971), are such that the individual is naturally conscious and responsive to the needs of others, and this deferential Dinka aspect of wealth paradoxically limits wealth accumulation.

Dinka consider the foreign relief assistance as additional resources to the entire community and believe that each person should have equal access to it despite the fact that they are aware of differential vulnerability. One *gol* leader told me that it is more reasonable to distribute relief food evenly – despite his well-informed perception of the needs of various families – to all households who will then decide whom to share or give to within their customary system and social safety nets. Relief assistance as a short-term measure, according to Dinka perception, should be used to support rather than supplant the traditional customary welfare system which caters for the vulnerable within their community.

SCF (1998) also argues that vulnerable individuals should remain the responsibility of their own communities, but that the international community can fulfill its mandate to target the neediest by feeding resources into the community system and understanding from a distance how this system functions in order to strengthen it rather than replace it. The perception that foreign relief assistance is the only solution to the problem of vulnerability of the recipient communities tends to 'colonise' and subsequently helps to weaken the independence and accountability of the traditional welfare system which has existed and will continue to exist to care for the vulnerable population (SCF, 1998). As rightly argued by Sharp (1998) and SCF (1998), despite difficulties associated with community targeting, it is crucial to facilitate the community systems to become more accountable, democratic and transparent.

Another community rationale for distributing relief food evenly seems to be associated with the stigma associated with foreign relief assistance as charity. In 1952, relief food was brought to Abyei for the first time and the colonial authorities at the time stressed that the food was only meant for the 'poorest of the poor' and that people eligible should be registered accordingly. Because of the stigma of poverty attached to the relief food, most eligible people preferred to starve rather than be socially humiliated.

The reluctance of people to come forward to take relief food forced chiefs to register members of their own families to get relief food as an example and to help in removing the stigma attached to it. The conduct of chiefs in Abyei helped to take away the stigma attached to relief food – it became more acceptable not by targeting but rather by sharing. Though the stigma attached by Dinka to foreign relief food in the 1950s may not exist now at the same level, the Dinka concepts of normative and aesthetic pride, honour and dignity (*dheeng* ) are still dominant and tend to attach stigma to charity in general.

According to Deng (1999:10) there is difference between *cieng* and *dheeng*: while *cieng* is a normative concept, a means which provides standards for evaluating conduct and requires people to behave in a certain way, *dheeng* is a concept of status, an end which classifies people according to a standard of conduct and labels an individual virtuous for behaving in a certain way. This point has also been emphasized by SCF (1998) which argues that it is possible to see how distributing relief food liberally and to all takes away the stigma attached to being a recipient of charity; one stage beyond this is to begin to reclassify outside assistance as a collective right – and therefore not charity at all, and in no way humiliating.

***Self-Targeting of Food Aid:***

There has been a growing policy emphasis on the need both to make relief food a developmental tool, particularly among the able-bodied people, through employment provision in public and/or community works and to restrict free food to those unable to work. This strategy of using relief food or cash to provide employment opportunities at an early stage of a subsistence crisis uses the effective targeting mechanism widely known as self-targeting. According to Maxwell (1993), 'self-targeting is an attractive alternative to administered targeting, because it reduces administrative burden, the risk of wrong judgement and the scope for corruption'.

Dreze and Sen (1989:113–14) emphasise other advantages of employment provision strategy such as avoiding the distress migration and the logistical constraint of transporting food to every village, and preservation of family ties; above all, it is an early intervention. Dreze and Sen (1989:118) also stressed that the use of self-targeting, particularly in sub-Saharan Africa has good economic and social grounds for going much further in this direction. In Ethiopia and other African countries the general free food distributions have been discouraged and replaced by 'gratuitous relief' which is free relief food provided, alongside employment generation programmes, for disaster-affected people who are unable to work (Sharp, 1998:6).

Despite such compelling argument in favour of self-targeting of food aid, the experience of OLS in relief food distribution since its inception in 1989 had been in general that of free food distribution with limited attempts in self-targeting particularly through the provision of employment in community works. Food-for-work programmes had been limited to supporting a local labour input into specific programmes related to implementing NGOs' schemes rather than community programmes as such.

OLS and other implementing agencies, including the SRRA, had been excessively and exploitatively emphasising the desirability of 'free community contribution' in the form of free community labour to support their projects even when the community faced critical food shortage. On some occasions during the famine in Bahr el Ghazal, building of some feeding centres was delayed for weeks as communities failed to provide free labour. The increasing emphasis on community participation and free labour input had failed to encourage provision of employment opportunities through employment generation programmes. This point has been emphasised by SCF (1998:17):

> *NGOs and agencies talk about 'the community' and work by the community in constructing compounds, clinics etc. What people usually do not realize is that compounds get built by an individual*

*mobilizing the multiple communities involved and obliging each community member to make their contribution.*

Besides increasing emphasis on general free food distribution and neglect of self-targeting, OLS had never thought of the possibility of providing cash instead of food for vulnerable populations, particularly in areas with relatively abundant food in local markets. During early 1997 when the SPLM captured the major garrison towns held by the GOS in Western Equatoria, many Sudanese refugees (estimated at more than 150,000 persons) in northern Uganda and Zaire decided to return to their home areas which had sufficient food in the local markets.

OLS failed to intervene immediately because of the logistical constraints of transport from Mombassa, and when food arrived it negatively affected the local markets. Such a delay in intervention and the dumping of relief food aid at extremely and unnecessarily high cost in relatively food- abundant local markets could have been simply avoided by offering cash rather than food to the returnees. During 1998, when famine migrants arrived in Western Equatoria which had abundant food in the local markets, because they were in a 'food surplus area' OLS failed to recognise their problem and also failed to make available to them either adequate food (with the exception of limited locally purchased food) or cash asthe sensible and desired intervention.

### Role of the SPLM During the 1998 Famine

The SPLM had been waging a liberation armed struggle since 1983 with the political objective of establishing a new and democratic Sudan. The SPLM was a *de facto* government in most of the liberated areas in the Sudan, with inherent obligations towards the civil society and civil population in terms of security protection, advocacy and humanitarian needs. In 1994 the SPLM convened its first national convention which was overwhelmingly attended by representatives from various communities from southern Sudan, southern Kordofan (Nuba Mountains) and southern Blue Nile and which unanimously resolved to separate civil administration from military administration and to strengthen traditional authority and civil society for effective participation, democratic accountability and good governance.

Since 1994, the SPLM had undergone drastic internal political changes which indeed aimed at enhancing the active participation of civil society and communities in political and civil administration through democratic structures. The SPLM was one of the few rebel movements that agreed unilaterally with UN agencies to abide by the *Universal Declaration of Human Rights* and *Rights of the Child*. Since 1994, the SPLM managed to project itself as a *de facto* government despite enormous difficulties in balancing the pressing priorities of armed struggle with the emerging popular need to establish democratic structures so as to ensure democratic accountability.

Such proclamations and commitments of the SPLM came to test during the 1998 famine. The SPLM came under enormous criticism for failing to act as a *de facto* government to prevent the 1998 famine in Bahr el Ghazal and other regions under its control. Some of these criticisms questioned the effectiveness of the institutions of the SPLM and its humanitarian obligations as well. Some critics accused SPLM of food diversion from the mouths of its dying and hungry people and criticised its failure to provide them with protection and security particularly from GOS counterinsurgency warfare. Some critics portrayed the SPLM and GOS as both desiring to starve the people in order to achieve their own military objectives. Others emphasised that the SPLM was obsessed with a culture of secrecy which permeated every aspect of its activities and had been exposed by the 1998 famine as damaging.

### *Alert and Advocacy*

Some critics claimed that the SPLM and its civil institutions had failed to alert the international community about the humanitarian crisis and accused them of even being indifferent to the plight of people under their care. It had been argued specifically by some critics that the SPLM showed an amazing indifference in the face of a human disaster amongst its own supporters. Malwal (1998:1) in particular argues that:

> *The institutions of southern Sudan from the SPLA and its civil administration to the Christian churches, long claiming to be the only legitimate voice of the people, were all exposed as being either inadequate or indifferent to the plight of the people under their care. These institutions should bury their heads in the shame for their roles in failing to identify and combat famine.*

While one may not utterly disagree with the above statement, it is important to qualify some of the issues raised. The SPLM/SPLA leader Dr John Garang told journalists at a press conference in Nairobi in October 1997 (earlier than anyone else) that 'acute food shortage had been caused in southern Sudan by El-Nino effect' and appealed to the international community to provide relief assistance to the vulnerable people in the affected areas (Atem, 1998a:9). Though one may disagree about his diagnosis of the cause, he was the first to forecast and alert the international community to the plight of the people in southern Sudan.

Early in 1998, he warned again of the looming humanitarian tragedy during a conference between the SPLM and churches. He was then interviewed by the BBC on the subject in May 1998. The claim that the SPLM leadership was belatedly prompted by the international community to respond to the famine in Bahr el Ghazal in which it should have taken the lead (Malwal, 1998:3), was inconsistent with the real facts. The SRRA, as the humanitarian wing of the SPLM, came out in November 1997 with a comprehensive report about the situation, the population affected and the humanitarian assistance required which was widely distributed to all NGOs, UN agencies, donors, relevant embassies, press and media and SPLM local authorities. This report was followed by another monitoring report in March 1998 and with a documented visual fact which also highlighted the looming famine and was also widely distributed to all the relevant agencies and institutions.

It is true, however, that the relevant SPLM propaganda machinery, particularly the information and humanitarian offices, did not exert adequate efforts to highlight the people's plight and to make as much noise about the famine. Also, the humanitarian agencies working in southern Sudan were perceived by the local authorities and other civil institutions as having entirely assumed the humanitarian responsibility rather than as supplementing the indigenous humanitarian responsibility. People in southern Sudan, particularly the local civil authorities, became increasingly reliant on humanitarian agencies to meet the humanitarian needs that should have been their primary responsibility. The fact that more than 100,000 persons died from preventable famine left various institutions with nothing to do except bury their heads in shame for failing to do enough.

***Role of Civil Administration***

Following the establishment of a civil administration after the SPLM national convention in 1994, it was expected that the civil administration would gradually assume its traditional role of providing basic services and attempting to create an environment conducive to the flourishing of economic activities so as to ameliorate suffering and reduce the chances of a famine occurring. Some critics argue that the talk about civil administration was empty sloganeering and that the culture of the military is still dominant. Accordingto Malwal (1998:2):

> *Following its first national convention in 1994, the SPLA talked about establishing civil administration which would organize the local population into self-reliant communities. The famine is a clear indication that the talk about civil administration was empty sloganeering. The SPLA has liberated areas and then has dealt with the local populations on a military footing. It has been a small step to move from that policy to indifference to the plight of the people.*

This statement is extremely general and would require hard facts to justify its validity. But it is a common fact that the civil administration was gradually gaining momentum despite enormous difficulties facing its growth particularly the lack of trained human resources as a result of the prolonged civil war. Simple common sense, in the context of the Sudan, suggests that lack of effective civil administration cannot be the primary cause of the 1998 famine as there were other obvious factors such as insecurity, climatic anomalies and failure of both market and non-market strategies which were exacerbated by failures of public action.

Moreover, the claim that effective civil administration was a primary factor in the cause of the famine in southern Sudan is disproved by the remarkable success in agricultural production and considerable recovery in local economies in Western Equatoria, which resulted in communities becoming not only self-reliant but produced excess food for marketing. The difference between economic recovery in Western Equatoria and famine in Bahr el Ghazal cannot be explained narrowly by difference in the type and level of civil administration; rather it suggests that factors like security played a crucial role.

A more convincing argument would have been based on an examination of what the SPLM machinery such as trade and economic planning offices at national level and local authorities at regional and county levels did to facilitate the flow of food from Western Equatoria to Bahr el Ghazal, land routes being relatively easily accessible. Malwal (1998:1) attributes the failure of the SPLM to redistribute surplus food from Western Equatoria to the famine victims in Bahr el Ghazal to 'administrative inefficiency and perhaps a lack of will'.

Certainly, although the SPLM did not have food resources itself nor direct command over the agricultural production and resources of individuals, more efforts could have been made to facilitate the flow of surplus food from Western Equatoria to famine victims in the Bahr el Ghazal region. I personally feel that at the national level, particularly the secretariats of trade and finance and economic planning, despite their meagre resources, did not exert efforts to use some of the available public funds to buy food (however little, it would be a symbol of SPLM humanitarian concern) in Western Equatoria for the famine victims in Bahr el Ghazal.

Even with meagre resources, the SPLM secretariats of trade and finance and economic planning in collaboration with local authorities at county level in Bahr el Ghazal region could have organised traders to mobilise cattle (particularly oxen) to purchase food in Western Bahr el Ghazal and could have made transport facilities available to them. In glaring contrast, one chief from Rumbek county took the initiative of mobilising more than 50 oxen and went personally to Western Equatoria to exchange them for grain from Zaire. Some traders managed to transport limited quantities of cassava and cereals from Western Equatoria to Rumbek county; such efforts would have had profound impact if traders had been facilitated with transport.

At the regional level, particularly in Western Equatoria which had excess food (cassava, maize and millet), no efforts were exerted by the local authorities and churches to mobilise locally relief food for the famine victims in Bahr el Ghazal. Even at the county level in Equatoria region there were few cases where the county local authorities took local initiatives to respond to the famine. The dominant thinking during the famine in Bahr el Ghazal predominately focusedon external assistance rather than looking at the famine as the direct responsibility of local communities and authorities.

### *Protection and Security*

One of the criticisms levelled against the SPLM was that it had not been successful in providing the civil population in Bahr el Ghazal with the necessary security and protection, particularly from GOS counterinsurgency warfare, specifically the series of attacks and raids by Arab militias. Some people believed that it was the failure of the SPLM to provide security and protection, particularly in the north of the region, that had made the civil population increasing vulnerable to recurrent famines as they could not perform their normal economic activities. Malwal (1998:1) argues that 'The SPLA's assertion that its primary concern is liberation in spite of the people must be reassessed and changed. The guerrilla army must become more responsive to the needs and the security of the civilian population than it has been in the past.'

One of the major military achievements of the SPLA during 1997 was that it managed to capture the major GOS garrisons in Bahr el Ghazal such as Yirol, Wunrok, Tonj, Warrap and Rumbek in addition to other small garrisons. The SPLM managed during 1997 to assert itself in the entire rural area of Bahr el Ghazal except some isolated GOS garrisons such as Wau, Awiel, Gogrial, Raja and Abyei. Even during 1997 and 1998 the SPLA succeeded in halting the Arab militia attacks which would have been disastrous and devastating to the entire Bahr el Ghazal region.

Most of the SPLA soldiers who were in the region in the 1990s were sons of the area who joined the SPLA primarily because of the destruction and devastation inflicted on their communities and home areas by the Arab militias. Although the SPLA had national objectives and so was reluctant to become diverted by local political grievances, it had become increasingly clear that the series of attacks and raids organised by the Arab militia were part and parcel of the orchestrated policies of the GOS. Nevertheless, the SPLA's reluctance to allow a proliferation of small firearms in the hands of the civil population to enable them to protect themselves had not been helpful in mitigating and confronting the counterinsurgency warfare in the region.

***Food Diversion***

Food diversion had been one of most critical criticisms against the SPLM during the 1998 famine, and some observers believed that this contributed greatly to the worsening famine situation as most of the food did not reach the neediest population. In mid 1998, the Catholic bishop of Rumbek diocese, Monsignor Caesar Mazzolari, accused the SPLA, without any substantial evidence, of diverting more than 65 per cent of relief food for its own use. Also, Medecins Sans Frontières (MSF) accused OLS of allowing the SPLM's humanitarian wing, the SRRA, to divert food to the SPLA. Both OLS and SPLM dismissed these accusations. Western media reported that the GOS and the SPLM had been skimming as much as 10 per cent of relief assistance for their troops.

In the light of the growing concerns about the targeting of relief food in Bahr el Ghazal, Dr. John Garan, the leader of the SPLM, established in August 1998 a task force consisting of members of the SPLM, SRRA and OLS to look into issues related to targeting, food diversion and vulnerabilities. Though the task force did not find evidence of food diversion as such, it did find a system of community voluntary contribution of rations locally known as *tayeen* (military food) for the maintenance of SPLA forces. This practice of *tayeen* began after the inception of SPLM in 1983 and is viewed, both at official and local levels, as the support deservedly due to volunteer SPLA soldiers who came from and continued to live with and protect the same community (Task Force, 1998:2).

*Tayeen* usually consisted of locally produced food staples, but at times an allowance was given for cattle, wild foods or cash contributions and was usually collected by chiefs from households with sufficient resources to afford contribution. The task force recognised, however, that the introduction of *tayeen* collection into the activity of relief food distribution had a negative effect on targeting the needy population who were normally exempted from *tayeen* contributions.

It is important to highlight the fact that the SPLA had been depending on the community long before the start of relief food distribution in its controlled areas. This clearly shows that SPLA soldiers were considered by the people as part of the local communities and had the right to be fed by the people even without coercion (SCF, 1998:7). SCF clarifies the relationship between the SPLA and community thus:

> *We are not talking of 'the military' as some institution a long way off, on a pedestal as professional army. Instead, it exists in the form of soldiers related to local people on the ground... It is therefore difficult to distinguish the contribution that goes to the military from the amount of food locals have to eat. It is clear though that the military would not be the first to starve to death.*

The policy of the SPLA of deploying its soldiers in their home areas had greatly improved its relationship with local communities as soldiers respected many of the same obligations to share as local people do. For example, the displaced people who came out from Wau town in January 1998 were greatly helped with food, shelter and even clothing by SPLA soldiers around Wau town who happened to know most ofthe displaced people. This view was also shared with by SCF (1998) which argues:

> *Soldiers behave in a less responsible way when they are away from people who they know and care about. Abuses certainly happen when soldiers represent an 'occupying army': in these situations, one could say that the army is less mindful about putting the needs of the vulnerable first, and are more likely to fill their own bellies.*

# CHAPTER SIX

## The Early Warning Systems

*"Hungry for the truth"*

*George Alagiah*

The establishment of early warning systems (EWS) in the 1980s as a result of increased numbers of recurrentfamines has improved the level of famine prediction, and to a large extent its management as well, in Africa. Despite the fact that improved famine prediction has not greatly improved famine prevention, there has been a considerable reduction in the occurrence of drought-triggered famines in Africa. The improved understanding of famine in the early 1980s as a result of the famine theories developed, particularly entitlement theory, has greatly improved the art of famine management in terms of prediction and prevention. War-triggered famines have emerged as the dominant feature in Africa and their management has remained an elusive and challenging endeavour.

### *External Livelihoods Monitoring Systems in the 1990s*

As early warning systems are becoming increasingly important in famine management, their performance is undoubtedly important in famine causation analysis. The famine experience in Bahr el Ghazal in 1998 seems to suggest that the failure of public action, particularly the relief intervention, is strongly related to the performance of the various monitoring systems in southern Sudan in the 1990s. There were in southern Sudan about five monitoring systems which were managed by external institutions, FAO, WFP/SCF, FEWS/USAID, NGOs and local institution, SRRA. The media also played a crucial role in the early warning system during the 1998 famine in Bahr el Ghazal.

### *The Food and Agriculture Organization (FAO)*

The FAO had no physical presence in southern Sudan and used to operate only from northern Sudan. It relied heavily on its Global Information and Early Warning System (GIEWS) which is food-production-oriented with minimal contact with the communities. GIEWS was established in 1975 in response to the Sahelian famines of the early 1970s and focused mainly on the monitoring of food security at national level and on assessing the yearly national food balance sheet (Buchanan-Smith and Davies, 1995). The FAO assessment in southern Sudan theoretically used to take place in September with no actual presence in southern Sudan and results were published in December.

This system was based on the assumption that local food crop production could be used as a proxy for the amount of food available to the average household. A forecasted change in crop yields or output served as an indicator of a change in vulnerability to famine

(Devereux, 1993). The FAO country representative based in northern Sudan used the 'food balance sheet' method every year to assess 'relief food requirements' on the basis of estimates of food production and subsistence consumption requirements. The information generated to assess annual food production in southern Sudan was not based at all on ground monitoring of crop performance.

Moreover, the estimate of subsistence consumption requirements was based on the population estimates provided by the GOS which was apparently intended to underestimate the civil population under the control of the SPLM. The end result was a system that was highly influenced by the agenda of GOS and that provided information that was irrelevantand in most cases with a tendency to underestimate the vulnerability of the civil population in the SPLM areas. The underestimation of humanitarian needs and vulnerable population in the areas under the control of the SPLM had become part of an integral part of the counterinsurgency warfare adopted by GOS in Bahr el Ghazal during the 1990s.

For example, while the FAO needs assessment estimated the food-insecure population during 1997 to be about 1.252 million persons in the OLS northern sector and about 1.346 million in the OLS southern sector, it oddly estimated respectively about 1.47 million persons and 995,640 persons as the vulnerable populations in the OLS northern and southern sectors during 1998 (UN, 1997 and 1998). Even during the 1998 famine, the FAO needs assessment estimated a decline in the food needs requirement in the rebel-held areas (OLS southern sector) to about 38,620 metric tons compared to its food requirement estimates in 1997 of about 46,730 metric tons.

On the other hand, the food needs requirements estimate for 1998 for the government-held areas (the OLS northern sector) increased substantially to about 43,530 compared to 31,920 metric tons for 1997. That is, the FAO needs assessment claimed that the food security situation in 1998 in southern Sudan (including the Bahr el Ghazal region) was better than in 1997 and projected a deteriorating food security situation in the areas under the GOS. This is another example where UN agencies run the risk of compromising their neutrality, becoming an element in the conflict rather than pursuing humanitarian needs. It is also a reflection of poor-quality information generated by a system which was utterly remote and distant from communities and their reality on the ground.

Despite the poor-quality information generated by the FAO annual harvest assessment, the results of its annual assessment carried credibility and come closest to the donors' notion of certainty, being particularly relied on by the United Kingdom's Department of Foreign and International Development (DFID) and the European Union (EU) which did not have their own early warning system. Buchanan-Smith and Davies (1995:38) argue that the donor agencies attach so much weight to UN assessments because they are seen to possess the international stamp of credibility, and also, they provide the single, simple and authoritative figure for country food needs which is necessary for easy decisions and to convince politicians. It is therefore not surprising that many donors were given an inaccurate FAO annual needs assessment which subsequently delayed their response.

***Food Economy Assessments (WFP/Save the Children Fund (SCF)***

The OLS southern sector usually carried out an annual needs assessment (food and nonfood) in September and results were usually out in December. The OLS assessment was usually poorly coordinated, with an apparent conflict of interest between the WFP and UNICEF. While UNICEF was usually ill-prepared for the assessment and emphasised nonfood items, the WFP had a well-established system for assessment with a distinctive emphasis on food needs. The poor coordination of assessment stemmed from overlapping and lack of clarity of the roles and responsibilities of three OLS Offices: the UNICEF Monitoring and Evaluation Office, the UNICEF Household Food Security Programme and the WFP Food Economy Analysis Unit. Generally, the OLS annual needs assessment became a bureaucratic and expensive process which generated information that was merely used for fundraising with limited relevance to effective planning within the organisation.

Unlike the UNICEF annual assessment of nonfood needs, which was a simple fundraising exercise that raised unnecessary community expectations, WFP assessments were largely based on information generated through a food economy approach. Ideally WFP needs assessment was more of one-off micro-level annual exercise than that of the FAO, focusing especially on aggregate food needs, with a view to targeting areas and groups requiring assistance (Buchanan-Smith and Davies, 1995). The food economy approach had been used by WFP with facilitation from SCF (UK) to assess food needs and to help in targeting areas and groups requiring food assistance.

The household food economy approach is a framework developed by SCF (UK) in the early 1990s for analysing household food security and how households access food (Boudreau, 1998). The main assumption of this approach rests on understanding how households gain access to food in normal years that is critical for analysing the changing access to food as a result of external livelihood shocks, particularly in a bad year (Boudreau, 1998:1). The access to food in "normal year" provides a baseline to determine key indicators for monitoring food security, and to understand the significance of changes in these indicators.

According to this approach, the household access to food comes from various sources (food economy components) and the contribution of each component depends on where and how people live (the food economy group). A food economy group is made up of people who share similar methods of accessing food and are at risk of similar shocks (drought, floods, pests and diseases). For example, in southern Sudan six food economy zones (see Map 3) have been identified: floodplains, the Nile-Sobat corridor, the ironstone plateau, the green belt, the hill and mountain zone and the arid zone).

The food analysis of each food economy zone entails looking at how each wealth group (wealth status is defined according to local perception) accesses food. The main reason for dividing the population into food economy groups and into wealth groups is to assess vulnerability and interaction across and within food economy zones and wealth groups. With baseline information and good key informants, the analysis of food economy zones and wealth groups is expected to generate the necessary information for identifying needs and targeting resources. Unlike the FAO method of producing a food balance sheet, which uses subsistence food requirements as an average minimum consumption, the food economy approach allows for other food sources besides the household's own food production in assessing the cereal requirement, which is known as the 'cereals self- sufficiency cut-off point'.

The food economy approach was effectively introduced in 1995 as food security assessment tool in southern Sudan. Since then, the food economy approach had improved the much-needed objectivity of needs assessment in OLS and had greatly encouraged for the first-time dialogue and interaction between relief workers and the communities. However, in the process of its use in southern Sudan, the food economy approach had tended to become insensitive to food vulnerability as its users had become increasingly obsessed with the current development jargon that 'Africans do not starve but they cope'.

The emphasis on coping strategies, and particularly on the expandable consumption of wild foods particularly when there is no predetermined and acceptable level of wild food consumption, makes the food economy approach increasingly insensitive to any change in vulnerability as it assumes that people will eventually cope and thus masks the gradual collapse of livelihood system. Davies (1993:61) argues that emphasis on 'coping' may blind policy makers and researchers to the need for a radical reappraisal of the requirements of people's livelihoods in marginal areas. De Waal (1989) also emphasises the need to distinguish between 'erosive' and 'non-erosive' coping so as to differentiate those strategies that erode the subsistence base of the household and compromise future livelihood security, from those which do not entail such costs.

For example, the food economy assessment estimates of the vulnerable population for 1997 and 1998in the three regions of southern Sudan show not only a considerable decline in vulnerability during 1998 relative to 1997 but also no significant difference between the Bahr el Ghazal (352,700 persons) and Upper Nile (323,500 persons) regions as shown in Figure 28.

*Figure 28: FAO/WFP/SCF Vulnerable Population estimates in southern Sudan, 1997/98*

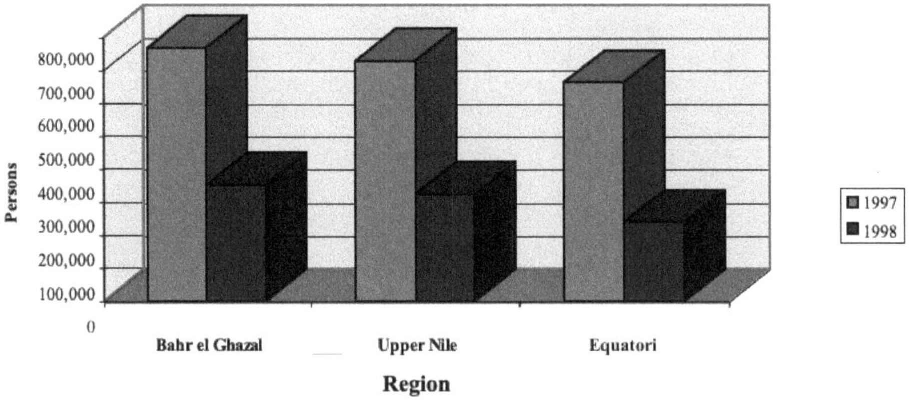


*Source: UN Consolidated Appeal for Sudan, 1997/98*

It is apparent that the food economy approach failed to predict in 1997 the deteriorating food security situation in 1998, particularly in the Bahr el Ghazal region. Unlike other regions of southern Sudan, Bahr el Ghazal had experienced a combination of adverse agro-climatic conditions, intensification of civil wars and counterinsurgency warfare. One other apparent flaw in the application of the food economy approach in the context of southern Sudan is that it failed to build up a clear food security picture from the enormous amount of information it had generated since its introduction in southern Sudan. Instead, it had become an impotent system of repetitive needs assessments. This endless cycle of assessments had resulted in a breakdown in effective communication between relief workers and communities, which resulted in the generation of irrelevant data. The high turnover of WFP field staff, coupled with 'spatial biases' (as most needs assessments take place around airstrips) and the limited time spend by relief workers with the communities during assessment, all make the food economy approach an ineffective monitoring system.

It is not surprising therefore that the WFP/SCF needs assessment in 1997 failed to differentiatebetween the increasing vulnerability in Bahr el Ghazal and the situation in the Upper Nile. Also the food economy assessments did not help in effective and objective targeting of the declining food aid to the regions of southern Sudan as Bahr el Ghazal region had been receiving lower food deliveries than other regions since 1993 (see Figure 19). This apparent masking of the deteriorating food security situation in southern Sudan, particularly in Bahr el Ghazal by the WFP/SCF greatly slowed the response of donors to the famine in 1998, and in particular the responses of the EU and DFID.

***Famine Early Warning System ( FEWS/USAID)***

The Famine Early Warning system (FEWS) project of USAID was launched in 1985 as a response to the African famines of the mid-1980s on the grounds that inadequate information had prevented the agency from managing emergency operations effectively (Buchanan-Smith and Davies, 1995). FEWS started covering southern Sudan in 1995; it uses satellite imagery extensively and relies almost entirely on secondary data which are analysed and collated into an eye-catching and concise form usable by busy officials at USAID. It was the only monitoring system in southern Sudan that regularly produced a monthly one-page update on the food security situation.

Interestingly it relied heavily on the information collected by local organisations in addition to that of international NGOs and UN agencies. Despite its low-profile focus on southern Sudan, FEWS had gradually managed to build up credibility among the agencies operating in southern Sudan and played a crucial role in pooling various data together into a simple and usable form for major donors. During 1997 FEWS managed on the basis of information generated by the local monitoring system, SRRA Monitoring Unit, to give an early warning of the likelihood of a deteriorating food security situation during 1998 in southern Sudan and the Bahr el Ghazal region in particular. Its information was widely used in Washington, occasionally even in Congress and by the Select Committee on Hunger (Buchanan-Smith and Davies, 1995), and during 1998 FEWS managed to trigger an earlier response by USAID to the famine than that of the EU.

### *Other External Monitoring Systems*

The international NGOs operating in southern Sudan played a significant role in providing food security information to their donors, particularly in the complex political emergency of the Sudan where development programmes had been cut by donors. This had helped in forging close donor–NGOs relations. The EU, for example, depended on information supplied by the main European- based NGOs; and DFID (formerly the ODA) had developed a close relationship with British NGOs (Buchanan-Smith and Davies, 1995). This type of relationship between donors and NGOs helps greatly to establish links between headquarters-based bureaucrats and conditions on the ground as NGOs had the benefit of being able to talk from direct field experience (Buchanan-Smith and Davies, 1995:39).

This new relationship between donors and NGOs had encouraged most NGOs to establish their own information systems to improve their understanding of local conditions. Buchanan-Smith and Davies argue that NGOs have considerable lobbying power and have usually developed links with politicians and with the media. For example, British NGOs managed in 1990 to persuade the ODA through their lobbying pressure to respond to the food crisis in the Sudan (Buchanan-Smith and Davies, 1995:39).

In southern Sudan most international NGOs established their own monitoring and information systems in their respective areas of operations. Before the famine in 1998, Oxfam, MSF (Belgium) and SCF were among the few international NGOs operating in the Bahr el Ghazal region. While Oxfam operated in Rumbek county where it established a livelihood monitoring system, SCF operated in northern Bahr el Ghazal, particularly in Gogrial, Wau and Awiel counties, and monitored generally the food security situation. MSF (B) like SCF (UK) operated in Gogrial, Wau and Awiel counties and established a health information system.

The World Vision International (WVI) had an integrated programme in Tonj county and before the 1998 famine it started a limited relief intervention in the southern part of Gogrial county. Of all the international NGOs operating in southern Sudan, SCF (UK) was particularly well-positioned with an integrated programme in northern Bahr el Ghazal and with a well-established presence among the communities even during the difficult times of intensified counterinsurgency warfare.

Although the field staff of Oxfam and SCF started towards the end of 1997 to alert their offices in Loki and Nairobi to the imminent famine in the Bahr el Ghazal region, their offices in Nairobi seemed to have failed or been reluctant to pass on the message to their headquarters in the UK. This point was emphasised by Alagiah (1998), who argues that even among the agencies that were most skeptical about announcing a national appeal there were some aid workers who believed their bosses were wrong and who complained that they were not being heard. Interestingly it was WVI, with limited presence in northern Bahr el Ghazal, which came out in March 1998 to alert the international community about the famine.

This breakdown in the flow of information from the field to the NGOs' headquarters in the UK created a lukewarm and skeptical response on the part of some British agencies to proposals for national appeal for the Sudan and affected the British government position, and particularly that of DFID. SCF (UK), Oxfam and MSF, which were among the few agencies operating in Bahr el Ghazal, decided that the crisis in the Sudan did not warrant a national appeal when it was first mooted on 27 April, 1998. The following extract from an article in *The Times* shows that SCF, despite its field reports and its food economy monitoring system with WFP, did not at that stage see the situation in Bahr el Ghazal as a famine. Rather, it saw the situation as one of a normal transitory food insecurity:

> *Save the Children … estimates that three months' supply of food for Bahr el Ghazal and other affected areas is available in Kenya and parts of the north … But unless the airlift can be trebled and access guaranteed both for food, and for the tools and seed which must reach people before the planting season ends in four weeks, there could be famine in 1999. (The Times, 30 April 1998)*

Based on information provided by the UK-Based NGOs, Clare Short (the then head of the DFID) argued in early May 1998 that famine victims in southern Sudan needed peace not charity (*Sunday Telegraph*, 5 May 1998). A month later she attacked as unnecessary the national appeal for the Sudan as she believed that lack of money was not the problem (*Guardian*, 4 June 1998). The position of the DFID and the stand of some British NGOs towards the crisis in southern Sudan in 1998 were more or less similar. Given the fact that the DFID had no field presence in southern Sudan, it was presumably supplied with information by some British NGOs, most likely SCF or Oxfam either directly or indirectly. On the other hand, the nonoperational charity agencies such as Christian Aid and CAFOD which relied largely on the information supplied by their local partners, the SRRA Monitoring Unit, supported the national appeal and opted to launch their own independent appeal.

The apparent disadvantage of donors relying on information supplied by international NGOs is the high risk associated with misjudgment of the overall situation as NGOs usually operate in small areas and their information tends to be very fragmentary (Buchanan-Smith and Davies, 1995). Cutler (1993) argues that NGOs can suffer from 'tunnel vision' which can in turn distort the donor agency's perspective. There is also growing concern that the voluntary sector which was once expected to be the desired alternative to the bureaucracy of the public sector is gradually becoming a facet or extension of public sector. Alagiah (1998) argues that:

> *Once, these agencies were a seedbed for alternative thought, organizations where many different views were not simply tolerated but*

> *encouraged. They were the kind of places to go to when you needed to know where the government of the day was going wrong. They took risks, they campaigned. That may be changing. Today some of these agencies may be in danger of becoming hierarchical and careerist.*

There is no doubt that the famine in Bahr el Ghazal which claimed more than 70,000 lives in 1998 was an example of how a monitoring and information system that is a distant of the communities and not cross-checked with other systems can easilymask a humanitarian crisis with far-reaching consequences.

***Local Monitoring System: The SRRA Monitoring System***

In 1995, the SRRA established a community-based monitoring system to monitor the food security and livelihood security of the civil population in the areas under the control of the SPLM. With initial support from Christian Aid, USAID and later Norwegian People's Aid (NPA) and UNICEF, the SRRA Monitoring Unit managed to train about seventeen county monitoring officers – who were selected from within their own communities – in data collection methods, participatory rural appraisal, early warning systems, food security and the food economy approach.

This locally based monitoring system used to collect at a community level a wide range of regular data related to agro-climatic conditions, socio-economic conditions, market conditions and prices, population movements and shocks related to insecurity. It had also a continuous presence among the communities in all parts of southern Sudan, particularly in the areas under control of the SPLM. Besides the traditional methods of monitoring, this system also used local knowledge for predicting crisis, agro-climatic conditions, the outbreak of diseases and pests. It produces an annual needs assessment and periodic special monitoring reports.

In November 1997, The SRRA Monitoring Unit came up with its annual food security assessment report. This was based on a vulnerability analysis related to food availability and food accessibility. The report was widely distributed to all agencies operating in southern Sudan, and to donors, relevant embassies, media and the SPLM authorities. Its performance in predicting the food security situation in 1998 was relatively better than other information and monitoring systems as shown in Figure 29.

*Figure 29: Food needs estimates and actual WFP food delivered to southern Sudan, 1998*

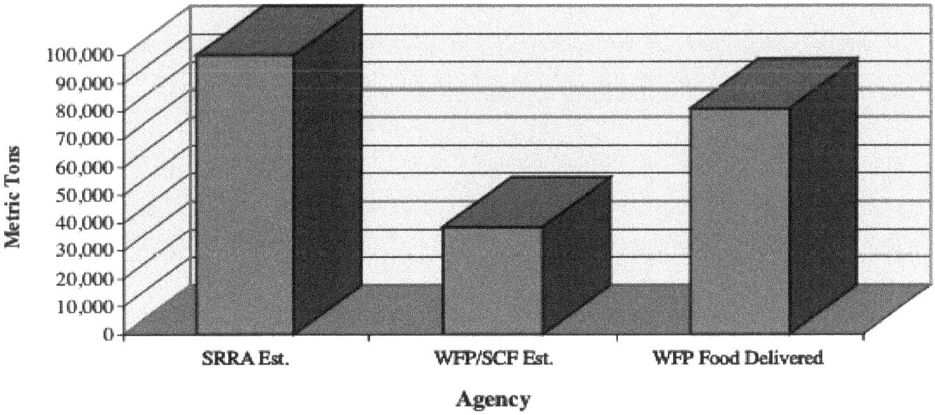


*Source: UN Appeal and SRRA*

While the SRRA estimated food deficits of about 80,000–120,000 metric tons (Bahr el Ghazal, 40,000 metric tons) during 1998, the WFP/SCF/FAO needs assessment estimated about 38,000 metric tons (Bahr el Ghazal, 17,500 metric tons) as the food required from outside for the vulnerable population in southern Sudan, and WFP actually delivered during 1998 about 80,000 (Bahr el Ghazal, 61,000 Mts.) metric tons of food. While the WFP/SCF/FAO annual needs assessment estimated the vulnerable population who would require food assistance in Southern Sudan during 1998 to be 995,640 (Bahr el Ghazal about 352,700), the SRRA food security assessment suggested a figure of about 2.37 million persons (Bahr el Ghazal about 1.12 million persons) (SRRA, 1997).

Despite its relatively better performance in predicting famine in 1998 than other systems, the information provided by the SRRA food security assessment was not taken seriously by the donors and implementing agencies operating in southern Sudan because of lack of trust. This lack of trust does not necessarily reflect the poor performance of national early warning systems but it is more related to the use of knowledge in a self-interested way. Buchanan-Smith and Davies (1995:23) argue that *'when it is Northerners who are using knowledge about Southern beneficiaries to inform public action (such as levels of food relief), the relationship is essentially hierarchical – Northern assumptions, values and analyses predominate'*. The relatively good performance of the SRRA Monitoring Unit clearly suggests that the indigenous and locally based monitoring system, particularly in a conflict situation, is more effective and efficient than 'outsiders' informationsystems.

### *The Role of Media in the 1998 Famine:*

Though the media, particularly the Western media, are not a source of famine early warnings, they have a significant influence on the intensity of advocacy for a relief response. The international relief response to the Ethiopian famine of 1984–85 was mainly triggered by the Western media, not by any conventional early warning system (Buchanan-Smith and Davies, 1995). Despite the fact that pre-famine situations are not sufficiently dramatic to make news, it is increasingly important that information generated by early warning systems should be shared with media as this helps to ensure speedy response by creating public pressure on donors government to cut through their usual bureaucratic procedures. Mooney (1987:182) argues that much damage may also be done to relief efforts if the media is confronted by a babble of views and opinions, lacking coordination, cohesion and, ultimately, the appropriate authority and knowledge.

Particularly in UK, the humanitarian response to the 1998 famine in Bahr el Ghazal was largely influenced by Western media coverage when opinion was divided among the charity agencies about the severity of the humanitarian crisis in southern Sudan. It is clear from Figure 30 that the British press coverage of Sudan peaked in May and resulted in the announcement on 21 May of a national appeal for the famine victims by all British aid agencies including those NGOs that downplayed the severity of food insecurity in 1998. Surprisingly, the British press coverage in the early months of 1998 was less than in 1997, but it started increasing in April when the famine situation worsened.

This late press coverage in UK was greatly related to the way some British aid agencies perceived and handled the early stages of famine.

When a national appeal for the famine in Sudan was first opposed on 27 April by some British agencies which had field presences in southern Sudan, this prompted the British press and media to verify for themselves whether a humanitarian crisis existed. The British media rather than the British-based NGOs operating in southern Sudan were responsible for triggering the British humanitarian response to the famine in southern Sudan in addition to some nonoperational charities such as Christian Aid.

*Figure 30: Selected coverage of Sudan in the British Press, 1997-98*

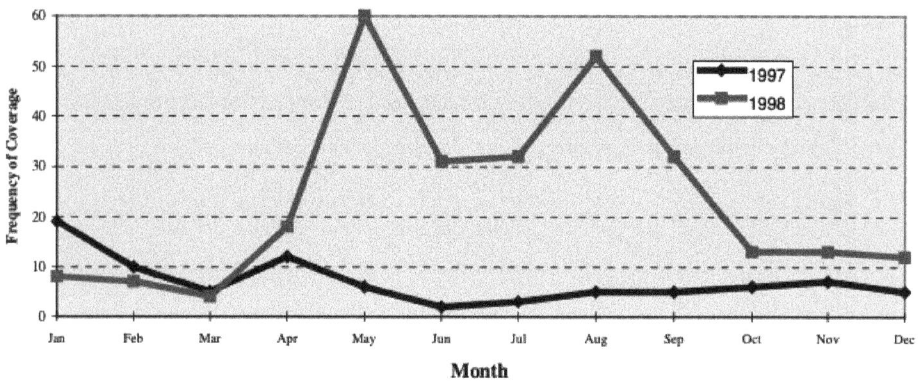


*Source: Christian Aid*

During the 1998 famine, the Western media found that the humanitarian agencies had poorly coordinated and divided opinions about the nature and extent of the crisis; these divisions existed within and across agencies and caused bitter rivalry and political infighting between and within the charities (Alagiah, 1998). Instead of developing a coordinated and common understanding of the crisis in southern Sudan to be shared with the press, OLS and some of its agencies took rather restrictive measures designed to manage the press. Alagiah describes the deliberations of some OLS meetings about the press as similar to that of a cabinet meeting of the Sudanese government which takes press freedom ever so seriously.

# CHAPTER SEVEN

# Conclusions and Policy Implications

### *General Conclusions*

There is a clear recognition by policy makers and researchers that policy reform and an appropriate policy environment are at the heart of the development process with research and information playing a critical role in the policy cycle process. There is a growing concern, however, over the role of information and the extent to which policy impacts can be traced to research. The dominant thinking seems to suggest a linear relationship, with information generated by research being viewed as a rational input into the process and immune from any failure. Despite increased recognition of the need for a more interactive relationship between information generated by research and its stakeholders, some still believe that policy-related research tends to be more of a 'one-off event' than a process of dialogue.

For information generated by research to have a tangible impact on policy, it must address real-life problems and its findings must be easily accessible to all its stakeholders. In order for research both to effectively explain people's behaviour and suggest practical intervention, it must be subject to the disciplines not only of scholarship but of the real-life concerns of its stakeholders to whom researchers are accountable.

Despite the considerable growth in the 1980s of famine theories and research related to famine management, the experience of the 1998 famine in the Sudan suggests that the art of famine management has not adequately improved. This study suggests that the research both failed to address the real-life problems and subsequently failed to change the art of famine management. It also suggests that the implementing agencies are caught up in a culture of change resistant to the new ideas generated by various research.

### *War Famines*

The deaths of more than 70,000 persons in 1998 in the Bahr el Ghazal region of the Sudan were the result of a combination of factors related not only to increased historical political vulnerability as a result of prolonged conflict and political marginalisation but also to primary shocks during 1997, particularly an intensification of counterinsurgency warfare, and conventional war between the SPLM and the GOS, and the El-Nino phenomenon, which all resulted in a failure in direct food entitlement and was further exacerbated by failures in exchange entitlement and public action. The study suggests that the so-called 'war famine' cannot be explained by war alone as other factors such as climate change and anomalies, exchange entitlement and public action are equally important in famine causation analysis.

### *Communal Law and Order in Midst of Violent Conflict*

The dominant thinking among many researchers that conflict is an endogenous factor in famine analysis and that the communities in violent conflict resort to violence as means of accessing assets, food and power fails to grasp the real-life facts. The increasing emphasis on violent conflict has concealed the pattern of normal livelihood of the communities in prolonged conflict. This study shows that during the 1998 famine the communities in Bahr el Ghazal retained a relatively stable law and order among themselves; people died peacefully from starvation around local markets that had grain while the legal apparatus and traditional norms managed to uphold entitlements and guard ownership rights.

During the 1998 famine the traditional legal system set up'hunger courts' to resolve cases related to claims and transfers to famine victims. The traditional norms and practices in Dinka society allow a famine victim rightfully to claim any available resources for his or her survival with the understanding that they will be payed back in normal times. This finding suggests a need to isolate prolonged conflict as an external shock to the communities and their normal pattern of law and order. Most researches seem to confuse these two aspects and tend to see conflict and violence as endemic among the communities in conflict. The study finds that the external shocks related to counterinsurgency warfare and war between SPLA and GOS did not trigger absence of law and order among the communities of the Bahr el Ghazal region, and nor did famine itself.

### *Functioning Markets During Violent Conflict*

The assumption that violent conflict and war limit the normal functioning of markets and makes it extremely difficult to analyse economically famine in the framework of the entitlement approach is also challenged by the finding of this study. The study shows that the markets not only functioned in the Bahr el Ghazal region and played an important role during famine, but also became forums for lower-level conflict management and interaction of communities from areas under the control of the opposing parties.

Paradoxically, local markets had encouraged both fighting parties – the SPLA and the GOS – to allow free trade and relatively free movements across the areas under their control. The behaviour of market prices of both cereals and livestock in Bahr el Ghazal clearly indicates that the failure of exchange entitlement was one of the causes of famine in the region. The study shows that the entitlement approach can be extended to a prolonged conflict situation to analyse the causation of famine.

### *Poverty, Famine and Violent Conflict*

The study suggests that the poorest group died most during the famine and that those who managed to survive are relatively well-off in terms of cattle ownership and social relationships. This suggests that even in the egalitarian society of the Dinka which has been exposed to a prolonged history of vulnerability and erosion of the asset endowment base, a positive relationship between poverty and famine still exists. However, more in-depth livelihood analysis shows that the non-poor households were more susceptible to counterinsurgency warfare in the 1990s in Bahr el Ghazal and became not necessary less vulnerable than poor households (Deng, 2010b). This finding is consistent with de Waal's (1989) findings in Darfur in western Sudan. It is important to highlight that although the cause of the civil conflict in Bahr el Ghazal and vulnerability of the Dinka was their abundant natural resources and livestock, the causation of the famine in 1998 was largely related to limited access to food, which was only partially a result of the violent conflict.

### *Relevancy of Food Aid*

The study shows that food aid as an addition to the household's food endowment base contributed positively during the 1998 famine towards reducing excess mortality, both directly through consumption and indirectly through stabilisation of food staple prices. This observation is consistent with that of Ravallion (1996) who argues that if income is fixed and all of it is spent on food then survival chances will be concave in the price of food and mortality will be an increasing concave function of price. By contrast, some researchers (de Waal, (1989) surprisingly have found little evidence that food aid has any impact on mortality and maintain that the risk of dying will not improve with the consumption of food aid. Besides limited food access, the study also found that the population in Bahr el Ghazal had in the 1990s the lowest level of access to health, education and clean water of any region of southern Sudan. The way that food and nonfood aid were managed during 1998 in terms of timing, quality, quantity and targeting greatly helped to increase excess mortality.

### *Measuring and Monitoring Food Security*

Like other findings on the performance of national early warning systems, the study suggests that the national and community-based early warning system – run by a local and national institution – performs far better during violent conflict than other systems which are 'on–off' monitoring systems. The SRRA Monitoring Unit performed distinctively better than other systems not only by predicting the magnitude and level of famine but also by identifying the administrative areas most likely to be affected for easy targeting. Also, the indicators used in monitoring food security were more comprehensive and complementary in locally based early warning systems than other systems. In measuring household food security, the SRRA Monitoring Unit used the salient features and indicators provided by different approaches to provide not only aggregate food requirements not only at national level but also at subnational and community levels. This observation is not surprising as the local and indigenous monitoring system is within the communities and cannot be discontinued by violent conflict like other systems.

There is no doubt the multidimensional nature of food security makes its measurement very elusive and difficult, but it requires clarity and understanding not only the dimensions to be measured but also the choice of indicators to be used. Some of these dimensions and indicators include the Coping Strategies Index (CSI) used by the Integrated Food Security Phase Classification's (IPC's) Acute Food Insecurity Reference Table for Household Group Classification, Food Consumption Score (FCS), Household Dietary Diversity Score (HDDS), and Household Hunger Scale (HHS) as proxy measures of household food consumption (Vaitla et al, 2017). Investigating the effectiveness of these indicators for measuring food security in both humanitarian and development contexts, Vaitla et al (2017:193) found the measurement of food security could be improved when these indicators are used in complementarity manner.

Although the complementary use of these indicators could improve the measurement of food security, the community and locally based regular monitoring of these indicators could make a major difference as shown in the case of the SRRA Monitoring Unit. If these indicators are one-off and distant monitored as was in the case of southern Sudan, such indicators are likely to misclassify the households and produce food security estimates that might not reflect the reality on the ground.

### *Famines and Mass Starvations as Crime Against Humanity*

The 1998 famine clearly shows a clear failure of public action not only from the SPLM as local authorities, but also from the aid agencies that were operating in Bahr el Ghazal region. The death of more than 70,000 innocent lives from a famine that could have been easily averted makes a compelling case for making the local authorities and aid agencies accountable for such serious crime. As famines and mass starvations are becoming increasingly man-made, there is a growing call for criminalization of famines and mass starvation as crime against humanity (Edkins, 2006). Such a call came into fruition in 2005 when the United Nations Security Council passed 1593 Resolution to recognize the appalling situation in Darfur region of the Sudan as a crime against humanity and referred it to the Prosecutor of the International Criminal Court (ICC) in The Hague (United Nations, 2005). This resolution was unprecedented and significant in incriminating and bringing to justice anyone responsible for the humanitarian crisis described as a famine in Darfur.

### *Policy Implications*

Since shocks related to counterinsurgency warfare and the war between SPLM and the GOS contributed substantially to the famine in 1998, the principal policy implication of this study is that international donors should go beyond addressing the symptoms and effects of violent conflict to its root causes. As already noted, it is apparent also from this study how the traditional structures have played an important role in maintaining lawand order during the famine and have also supported the famine victims by means of the traditional legal systems. This clearly suggests that the implementing agencies and donor community should extend their programmes to include support to these traditional institutions and safety nets systems that are directly responsible for taking care oftheir vulnerable groups.

There has been considerable interest in applying the concept of the 'relief–development continuum' in complex political emergencies as it has been assumed that as aid can be used to reduce vulnerability to natural hazards, so it might be used to reduce vulnerability to hazard of violent conflict. Some researchers argue that violent conflicts and the humanitarian crises they generate are not temporary interruptions in a linear process and that it may be anti-humanitarian to use relief aid for 'developmental' purposes. Some donors argue that as violent conflict is the dominant mechanism used to access assets and power in the Sudan it becomes inappropriate to pursue developmental strategies in southern Sudan.

This study clearly shows, as discussed earlier, that even during famine the traditional institutions managed to uphold entitlements and guard ownership rights. USAID in particular had taken the initiative of starting a small programme of rehabilitation within the conflict zones through Sudan Transitional Assistance for Rehabilitation (STAR). On the other hand, the EU and its member states were caught up in a cautious policy of 'wait and see' and limited their assistance to emergency relief. One clear policy implication is that where in a situation of prolonged civil war the traditional institutions and the rebel movements have relatively developed mechanisms for the protection of entitlements and ownership rights, rehabilitation programmes are possible, even during violent conflict.

The role of markets during violent conflict situations has hitherto been ignored, but this study shows clearly that markets are important institutions not only for making essential goods available but also act as forums for initiating lower-level conflict management and interaction. This implies that there is a need to move beyond relief and to encourage activities that promote local markets and small businesses which will gradually develop entrepreneurial capacities to respond to food shortages.

As food aid was so relevant in a situation like Bahr el Ghazal, it is important that relief food should be made developmental by encouraging programmes related to community public works through self-targeting schemes; it is also important to move gradually away from free handouts which should be limited to the neediest. Targeting of relief food should be done through recognised community institutions which have direct responsibilities to their vulnerable groups, whilst the role of implementing agencies should be limited to facilitation and promotion of democratic decision processes and transparency. Relief food can also be effectively used to encourage restocking of the poor households that have lost their cattle during counterinsurgency warfare.

The performance of various early warning systems clearly suggests that there is a need to invest more in local, indigenous and community-based early warning systems in a prolonged conflict situation. There is enormous and rich local knowledge which can easily be made use of by early warning systems that are based within the communities rather than 'on-off' systems. The dominant thinking that early warning systems should be run by international agencies because of their credibility is inappropriate in prolonged conflict situations, which necessitates development and improvement of the credibility of locally based early warning systems.

As famine persists because of political choices and it strikes when accountability fails in autocratic and authoritarian political environment, there is a need to define famines and mass starvations within the tools of international criminal law; namely genocide, crimes against humanity and war crimes. There is option of including famine or starvation in the definition of residual category of the Rome Statute of the International Criminal Court (ICC, 2002) as other inhumane acts in the crimes against humanity. In the case of Africa, there is an opportunity in Article 4(h) of the African Union Constitutive Act (AU, 2000) of including starvation or famine as one of the grave circumstances such as war crimes, genocide and crimes against humanity that warrant African Union to intervene in member state.

Although famines and starvation could be defined as crime against humanity, there is difficulty in enforcing them as such crimes occur in non-international armed conflict and authoritarian environment that are outside the jurisdiction of International Criminal Court. There is also the difficulty to prove or gather evidence and it may be politically contested with backlash in setting precedent. In championing the agenda of ending famine, the Tufts University adopted a manifesto with a goal to render mass starvation as political scandal and so morally toxic and it is universally publicly vilified (Tufts University, 2018). If such a manifesto could be adopted by the United Nations Security Council and the African Union Peace and Security Council, then famines and mass starvations are likely to be averted in the future and if they occur, the authorities involved will be accountable and brought to justice.

# REFERENCES

Adams, A., 1993, 'Food Insecurity in Mali: Exploring the Role of Moral Economy', *IDS Bulletin* 24(4).

African Union, 2000. The Constitutive Act of the African Union. Addis Ababa: African Union.

Alagiah, G., 1998, 'Hungry for Truth', *Guardian*, 25 May 1998.

Alier, A., 1990, *Southern Sudan: Too Many Agreements Dishonoured*, Exeter: Ithaca Press.

Atem, Y., 1998a, 'Famine in Bahr el Ghazal', *Horn of Africa Vision*, 4(1).

Atem, Y., 1998b, 'The Story of OLS: An Interpretation of a Mission', *Horn of Africa Vision*, 4(1).

Boudreau, T., 2006, "The Food Economy Approach: a framework for understanding rural livelihoods". *Relief and Rehabilitation Network (RRN) Paper* 26. London: Overseas Development Institute (*ODI*).

Buchanan-Smith, M. and Davies, S., 1995, *Famine Early Warning and Response: The Missing Link*, London: Intermediate Technology Publications.

Bush, R., 1985, 'Briefings: "Drought and Famines"', *Review of African Political Economy*, 33.

Bush, R., 1987, 'Explaining African's Famine', *Social Studies Review*, 2.

Chambers, R., 1983, *Rural Development: Putting the Last First*, London: Longman.

Collins, R., 1971, *Land Beyond the Rivers: The Southern Sudan, 1889–1918*, New Haven and London: Yale University Press.

Currey, B., 1978, 'The Famine Syndrome: Its Definition for Relief and Rehabilitation in Bangladesh', *Ecology of Food and Nutrition*, 7.

Cutler, P., 1984, 'Famine Forecasting; Prices and Peasant Behaviour in Northern Ethiopia', *Disasters*, 8(1).

Cutler, P., 1986, 'The Response to Drought of Beja Famine Refugees in Sudan', *Disasters*, 19.

Cutler, P., 1993, 'Responses to Famine: Why They Are Allowed to Happen', in J. O. Field (ed.), *The Challenge of Famine: Recent Experiences, Lessons Learned*, Hartford, CT: Kumarian Press.

Davies, S., 1993, 'Are Coping Strategies a Cop Out?', *IDS Bulletin* 24(4).

De Waal, A., 1989, *Famine That Kills: Darfur, Sudan, 1984–1985*, Oxford: Oxford University Press.

De Waal, A., 1993, 'War and Famine in Africa', *IDS Bulletin*, 24(4).

De Waal, A., 2018. *Mass Starvation: The History and Future of Famine*. Cambridge: Polity Press.

Demeny, P., 1968, 'The Demography of Sudan: An Analysis of the 1955/6 Census', in W. Brass (ed.), *The Demography of Tropical Africa*, Princeton: Princeton University Press.

Demsetz, H., 1967, 'Toward a Theory of Property Rights', *American Economic Review* 57: 347-53.

Deng, F., 1972, *The Dinka of the Sudan*, New York: Holt, Rinehart and Winston.

Deng, F., 1973, *Dynamics of Identification: A Basis for National Integration in the Sudan*, Khartoum University Press.

Deng, F., 1978, *Africans of Two Worlds: The Dinka in Afro-Arab Sudan*, New Haven and London: Yale University Press.

Deng, F., 1986, *The Man Called Deng Majok: A Biography of Power, Polygamy and Change*, New Haven and London: Yale University Press.

Deng, F., 1998, 'Dinka Moral Values and Human Rights Principles', *Sudan Democratic Gazette*, IX, No. 100.

Deng, F., 1999, 'Dinka Perspective', *Sudan Democratic Gazette*, Vol. X, No. 106.

Deng, L., 2013, "Changing Livelihoods in South Sudan", *ODI Humanitarian Practice Network Issue No. 57.*

Deng, L., 2010b, "Livelihood Diversification and Civil War: The Case of Dinka Communities in the Sudan's Civil War", *Journal of Eastern African Studies Vol 4 (3), pp. 381-399.*

Deng, L., 2010a, "Social Capital and Civil War: The Case of Dinka Communities in the Sudan's Civil War", *Journal of African Affairs 109 (435) pp. 231-250.*

Deng, L., 2008, "Are Non-poor always less vulnerable? The Case of Households exposed to protracted civil war in Southern Sudan", *Journal of Disasters 32 (3).*

Deng, L., 2007, "Increased Rural Vulnerability in the Era of Globalization: Conflict and Famine in Sudan in the 1990s", in Devereux, S., 2007 (eds.), "*The New Famines: Why famines persist in an era of globalization*", London: Routledge Inc.

Devereux, S., 1993, *Theories of Famine*, New York: Harvester Wheatsheaf.

Devereux, S., 2006, *The Famines: Why Famines Persist in an Era of Globalization?* Abingdon: Routledge.

Dirks, R., 1980, 'Social Responses during Severe Food Shortages and Famine', *Current Anthropology*, 21(1).

Dreze, J. and Sen, A., 1989, *Hunger and Public Action*, Oxford: Clarendon Press.

Dyson, T., 1993, 'Demographic Responses to Famines in South Asia', *IDS Bulletin*, 24(4).

Edkins, J., 2002. "Mass Starvation and the Limitations of Famine Theorising". *IDS Bulletin* Vol 33(4): 12-18.

Ellis, F., 2000, *Rural Livelihoods and Diversity in Developing Countries*, Oxford: Oxford University Press.

Evans-Pritchard, E., 1951, *Kinship and Marriage Among the Nuer*, Oxford: Clarendon Press.

Evans-Pritchard, E., 1951. T*he Nuer: A Description of the Modes of Livelihood and Political Institutions of a Nilotic People*. Oxford: Clarendon Press.

FEWS/USAID, 1997, 'Special Report', Washington: FEWS/USAID.

Gray, J., 1961, *A History of the Southern Sudan, 1839–1889*, London: Oxford University Press.

Hale, S., 1986, 'The Oxfam Food Targeting and Monitoring Programme in the Red Sea Province, Sudan',mimeo, Oxfam, Oxford.

Hendrickson, D, Mearns, R, and Armon, j, 1996, "Livestock Raiding Among the Pastoral Turkana of Kenya: Redistribution, Predation and the Links to Famine", *IDS Bulletin* 27(3):17-30.

Henderson, K., 1939, 'A Note on the Migration of the Messiria Tribe into South West Kordofan', *SudanNotes and Records*, 32.

Holt, P., 1958, *The Mahdist State in the Sudan, 1881–1898: A Study of Its Origins, Development and Overthrow*,Oxford: Oxford University Press.

Holt, P., and Daly, M., 1988, *A History of the Sudan: From the Coming of Islam to the Present Day*, London and New York: Longman.

HAC (Humanitarian Aid Commission), 1997 and 1998, *Monthly Flights Clearance*, Khartoum: Ministry ofSocial Planning.

Hufstader, C., 2020. "What is famine and how can we stop it?". OXFAM, May 14.

Hutchinson, S., 1996. *Nuer Dilemmas: Coping with Money, War and the State*. California: University of California Press.

ICC, 2002. Rome Statute of the International Criminal Court. The Hauge: International Criminal Court (ICC)>

IDS Bulletin, 2002. "The New Famines". *IDS Bulletin* Vol 33(4).

Johnson, D., 1989, 'Political Ecology in the Upper Nile', *Journal of African History*, 30(3).

Karam, K., 1980, 'Dispute Settlement Among Pastoral Nomads in the Sudan', Master's thesis, University of Birmingham.

Keen, D., 1994, *The Benefits of Famine: A Political Economy of Famine and Relief in South Western Sudan, 1983–1989* , New Jersey: Princeton University Press.

Kuol, L., 2021 (eds). *Confronting Civil War in Africa: Vulnerability and Resilience in South Sudan and Sudan*. Africa World Books Pty Ltd.

Kuol, L., 2014, "Confronting Civil War: The Level of Resilience in Abyei Area During Sudan's Civil War in the 1990s", *Journal of Civil Wars*. Volume 16(4). pp 468-487.

Kuol, L., 2017, "Dinka youth in civil war: between cattle, community and government" in Report titled "*Informal Armies: Community defence groups in South Sudan's civil war*". London: Saferworld.

Laya, D., 1975, 'Interviews with Farmers and Livestock Owners in the Sahel', *African Environment*, 1.

Lienhardt, G., 1961, *Divinity and Experience: The Religion of the Dinka*, Oxford: Clarendon Press.

Mahmud, U.A. and Baldo, S.A., 1987, *Al Daien Massacre: Slavery in the Sudan*, Khartoum: Human RightsViolations in the Sudan.

Makec, J., 1986, *The Customary Law of the Dinka: A Comparative Analysis of an African Legal System* , London: Afroworld.

Malwal, B., 1998, 'Burying Our Heads in Our Own Shame in the Preventable Famine', *Sudan Democratic Gazette*, IX (97).

Mawson, A., 1990, 'Murahaleen Raids on the Dinka, 1985–89', *Disasters*, 15(2).

Maxwell, S., 1993, 'Can a Cloudless Sky have a Silver Lining? The Scope for an Employment-based Safety- net in Ethiopia', *WFP Food-for-Development Discussion Paper*, No. 1, Addis Ababa: World Food Programme.

Maxwell, S. and Templer, G., 1994, 'The Monetization of Project and Emergency Food Aid: Project-level Efficiency First!', *Food Policy*, 19(1).

Mesfin, W., 1986, *Rural Vulnerability to Famine in Ethiopia, 1958–1977*, London: Intermediate Technology Publications.

Mooney, T., 1987, 'Coordination of International Relief Efforts', *Disasters*, 11(3).

Oxfam, 1995, 'Community Managed Distribution: Oxfam's (UK/I) Experience from East Africa', mimeo. Oxford: OXFAM.

Platteau, J., 1991, 'Traditional Systems of Social Security and Hunger Insurance: Past Achievements and Modern Challenges', in E. Ahmaed, J. Dreze, and A. Sen, (eds), *Social Security in Developing Countries*, Oxford: CLarendon Press.

Rangasami, A., 1985, 'Failure of Exchange Entitlements Theory of Famine: A Response', *Economic and Political Weekly*, 20.

Ravallion, M., 1987, *Markets and Famines*, Oxford: Clarendon Press.

Ravallion, M., 1996, 'Famines and Economics', *World Bank Policy Research Working Paper*, No. 1693, New York: World Bank.

Ravallion, M., 1992. "On "Hunger and Public Action": A Review Article on the Book by Jean Dreze and Amartya Sen". *The World Bank Research Observer.* Vol 7(1): 1-16.

Ryle, J., 1989, 'Displaced Southern Sudanese in Northern Sudan with Special Reference to Southern Darfur and Kordofan', mimeo, SCF (UK).

Saeed, A., 1982, 'The State and Socioeconomic Transformation in the Sudan: The Case of Social Conflict in Southwest Kordofan', PhD thesis, University of Connecticut.

Sanderson, L., and Sanderson, N., 1981, *Education, Religion and Politics in Southern Sudan, 1899–1964* , London: Ithaca Press and Khartoum: Khartoum University Press.

SCF (Save the Children Fund) (UK), 1998, *The Southern Sudan Vulnerability Study*, Nairobi: SCF (UK) South Sudan Programme.

Schweinfurth, G., 1873, *The Heart of Africa.* Vol. 2. London: Sampson Low, Marston, Low and Searle.

Scott, J., 1976, *The Moral Economy of the Peasant*, New Haven: Yale University Press.

Seaman, J., 1993, 'Famine Mortality in Africa', *CDS Bulletin*, 24(4).

Seaman, J. and Holt, J., 1980, 'Markets and Famines in the Third World', *Disasters*, 4.

Sen, A., 1981. *Poverty and Famines: An Essay on Entitlement and Deprivation*, Oxford: Clarendon Press.

Sharp, K., 1997, 'Targeting Food Aid in Ethiopia', mimeo, SCF (UK), Addis Ababa.

Sharp, K., 1998, 'Between Relief and Development: Targeting Food Aid for Disaster Prevention in Ethiopia', *Relief and Rehabilitation Network (RR1) Paper*, No. 27, Overseas Development Institute.

Shoham, J., 1987, 'Does Nutritional Surveillance have a Role to Play in Early Warning of Food Crises and in the Management of Relief Operations?', *Disasters*, 11.

Spaulding, J., 1982, 'Slavery, Land Tenure and Social Class in the Northern Turkish Sudan', *International Journal of African Historical Studies*, 15(1).

SPLM/SRRA/OLS Task Force, 1998, 'Targeting and Vulnerabilities', Nairobi: OLS and SRRA.

SRRA, 1997, 'Southern Sudan Annual Needs Assessment', Nairobi: Sudan Relief and Rehabilitation Association (SRRA).

SSCSE, 2006. Southern Sudan Livelihood Profiles: A Guide for Humanitarian and Development Planning. Juba: Southern Sudan Centre for Statistics and Evaluation (SSCSE).

SRRA, 1998, *Annual Assessment Report*. Nairobi: Sudan Relief and Rehabilitation Association.

Swift, J., 1989, 'Why are Rural People Vulnerable to Famine?', *IDS Bulletin*, 20(2).

Swift, J., 1993, 'Understanding and Preventing Famine and Famine Mortality', *IDS Bulletin*, 24(4).

Torry, W., 1987, 'Evolution of Food Rationing Systems with Reference to African Group Farms in the Context of Drought', in M. Glanz, (ed.), *Drought and Hunger in Africa: Denying Famine a Future,* Cambridge: Cambridge University Press.

Tufts University, 2018. Join members of Tufts University Faculty: sign the statement on ending famine. Boston: Tufts University.

Vaitla, B., Coates, J., Glaeser, L., Hillbruner, Biswal, P., and Maxwell, D., 2017. "The measurement of household food security: Correlation and latent variable analysis of alternative indicators in a large multi-country dataset". *Food Policy* 68: 193-205.

UN (United Nations), 1997, 'Consolidated Appeal for Sudan', New York and Geneva: Department of Humanitarian Affairs (DHA).

UN (United Nations), 1998, 'Consolidated Inter-Agency Appeal for Sudan', New York and Geneva: Department of Humanitarian Affairs (DHA).

UNICEF/OLS, 1998, *Nutrition Assessment in Southern Sudan , May/June 1998*, Nairobi: UNICEF/OLS.

Watts, M.J., 1984, 'The Demise of the Moral Economy: Food and Famine in a Sudano-Sahelian Region in Historical Perspective', in E. Scott (ed.), 1984, *Life Before the Drought.*

Young, H., and Jaspars, S., 1995, 'Nutritional Assessments, Food Security and Famine', *Disasters*, 19(1).

# INDEX

## About The Author

Luka Biong Deng Kuol, PhD, is the Dean of Academic Affairs at the Africa Center for Strategic Studies at National Defense University in Washington, USA. In addition, he is the faculty lead of three academic programs: National Security Strategy Development and Implementation in Africa, Managing Security Resources in Africa, and Emerging Security Sector Leaders in Africa. His work focuses on national security strategy, security sector budgets, social contracts, food security, vulnerability and resilience, and the security-development-governance nexus.

Dr. Kuol is also a Global Fellow at the Peace Research Institute Oslo (PRIO), a Fellow at the Rift Valley Institute, and an Associate Professor of Economics (on leave) at the University of Juba in South Sudan. He also sits on the editorial board of the Disasters Journal, published by the Overseas Development Institute. Prior to joining the Africa Center, Dr. Kuol served as director of the Center for Peace and Development Studies at the University of Juba in South Sudan. He was also on the teaching staff of the Faculty of Economics and Rural Development at the University of Gezira in Sudan.

He was a resident fellow at Harvard Kennedy School and a Visiting Fellow at the Institute of Development Studies in the United Kingdom. He served as Minister of Presidential Affairs for the Government of Southern Sudan and as National Minister of Cabinet Affairs for the Republic of Sudan. He has also worked as a senior economist for the World Bank in Southern Sudan. He was the founder of the New Sudan Center for Statistics and Evaluation that became the South Sudan Bureau of Statistics.

He has published scholarly articles in a wide array of prestigious international journals and contributed with many peer-reviewed chapters in various books. He is a co-editor of a book entitled "The Struggle for South Sudan: Challenges of Security and State Formation" and co-editor of a book entitled "Abyei: Between Two Sudans". He is also the author of "Confronting Civil War in Africa."

He received his BSc (Honors) from the Faculty of Economics and Social Studies at the University of Khartoum, Sudan, an M.A. (Distinction) in Economics, an M.B.A. (Distinction) from the Catholic University of Leuven, Belgium, and a Ph.D. from the Institute of Development Studies (IDS) at the University of Sussex in the United Kingdom.

Email: luka.kuol.civ@ndu.edu and lukabiongdeng@gmail.com

www.ingramcontent.com/pod-product-compliance
Ingram Content Group UK Ltd.
Pitfield, Milton Keynes, MK11 3LW, UK
UKHW060116010826
14089UKWH00003B/24

9 780645 210514